A LETTER
FROM FRANK

A LETTER FROM FRANK

An Unlikely
Second World War Friendship

Stephen J. Colombo

DUNDURN
TORONTO

Copy Editor: Allister Thompson
Design: Jesse Hooper
Printer: Webcom

Library and Archives Canada Cataloguing in Publication

Colombo, S. J. (Stephen John)
    A letter from Frank : an unlikely Second World War friendship/ Stephen J. Colombo.

Issued also in electronic formats.
ISBN 978-1-55488-968-6

    1. Colombo, Russ, 1916-1986. 2. Sikora, Frank, 1924-. 3. World War, 1939-1945--Personal narratives, Canadian. 4. World War, 1939-1945--Personal narratives, German. 5. Soldiers--Germany--Correspondence. 6. World War, 1939-1945--Veterans--Canada--Biography. 7. World War, 1939-1945--Veterans--Germany--Biography. 8. Veterans--Canada--Biography. I. Title.

D811.C65 2011   940.54'8171   C2011-902593-0

1   2   3   4   5   15   14   13   12   11

We acknowledge the support of the **Canada Council for the Arts** and the **Ontario Arts Council** for our publishing program. We also acknowledge the financial support of the **Government of Canada** through the **Canada Book Fund** and **Livres Canada Books**, and the **Government of Ontario** through the **Ontario Book Publishing Tax Credit** and the **Ontario Media Development Corporation**.

Front cover image: Russ (top row, first from left) and his officer cadet graduating platoon outside the Royal Memorial Chapel, Sandhurst Military Academy, February, 1944.
Front cover portraits: left, Frank Sikora; right, Russ Colombo

Printed and bound in Canada.
www.dundurn.com

Dundurn	Gazelle Book Services Limited	Dundurn
3 Church Street, Suite 500	White Cross Mills	2250 Military Road
Toronto, Ontario, Canada	High Town, Lancaster, England	Tonawanda, NY
M5E 1M2	LA1 4XS	U.S.A. 14150

*This book is dedicated to Russ Colombo and Frank Sikora,
and to ordinary people able to find the decent thing
to do in impossible circumstances.*

CONTENTS

INTRODUCTION

Imagine what I felt, sorting through a cardboard box filled with dusty family photographs, discovering a letter to my father from a German paratrooper. Signed only "Frank," it thanked my father in Canada for his help at the end of World War II.

My father died in 1986, and twenty years later I found the letter. I was consumed with curiosity about the mysterious German correspondent: Who was Frank? How had he met my father? What had my father done for him? And most important: Was Frank alive? I felt compelled to enter this gateway into the past.

This book documents my journey to discover the story behind the letter from Frank. It tells the stories of two lives briefly interwoven but forever linked. The first is about my father, Russ Colombo, who grew up in a small town in Ontario during the Depression, joined the Canadian army in 1940, and served as a tank commander in northwest Europe during World War II with one of Canada's most prestigious army divisions.

I also tell Frank's story. With little more than a first name, sixty years after he wrote that letter, I did find him, alive and living in Germany. In our first phone conversation Frank described how on the final day of the war, my father and he fought for opposing armies. His voice breaking with emotion, he explained the circumstances under which the next day my father accepted his unit's surrender.

A year after our first conversation, Frank and I met in Berlin, where I learned more about his life as a German in Czechoslovakia growing up under the Nazis. His story provided me with insight I rarely had of what it was like to be German in Europe between the First and Second World Wars and to fight against the Allies. Frank also explained how my father's actions and friendship helped him take his first step in coming to terms with being German after the war, culminating in his work in Israel with the German diplomatic service.

Russ and Frank's stories come from an important time in each country's history. Such stories are fast disappearing from living memory and theirs might have been lost forever if not for the letter from Frank. To understand these men I needed more than just an account of the battles they fought in. I also wanted to know what it was like growing up when they did and in the places they came from.

The men and women who took part in World War II overcame challenges few today can imagine. By piecing together my father's life, I hoped to learn what it was like to be part of his generation, and how it differed from mine. What was it like living through the Great Depression? Could I have handled the extreme physical and mental challenges and the dangers of being a soldier in World War II? And would I have been able to accept the friendship of a man who, only hours before, I had been trying to kill and who had been trying to kill me?

In the end, this became my story too: my search for Frank, the piecing together of events from my father's life, my search to understand what it meant to be a Canadian in those extraordinary times, and its significance for Canadians today.

ONE

"Sweet"
Ein Kleiner Junge

A lone Sherman tank stood silently in the sun. The tall man in its turret, field glasses to his eyes, scanned the countryside, searching and listening. "Kill the engines," Russ ordered the driver. He strained to hear. Far in the distance came the clatter and pop of weapons firing from the direction of Falaise. He ignored them, seeking the groan of a tank motor or the crack of its cannon. There was nothing.

He stared into the shade of a nearby grove of trees. The breeze brought the pungency of the decaying leaves blanketing the forest floor. The smell was sweet compared to the foul odours below; the unwashed bodies and hundreds of cigarettes smoked in that small space. For a week they had not more than an hour or two sleep each night as they hunted German soldiers escaping from the terror around Falaise. Now they hunted two of their own tanks. In the warm sun Russ relaxed, and with the scent of the forest in his nostrils, his eyes slid closed. That moment he dreamed he was a boy in the forest near his home.

———◆———

Russ's feet sounded like a drum on the path as he ran through the sun-flecked forest. From behind he heard the excited yells of boys chasing him. Volunteering to be their quarry, he'd run ahead while the pack shouted as they counted down. They yelled the final number, announcing the beginning of the chase from the base of an old rough-barked maple tree in an opening in the forest. If caught before making it back to the tree, the penalty was to be dragged to the river and thrown in.

Hearing their calls, a shiver ran down Russ's spine. He imagined his pursuers not as sons of respectable families, but as German soldiers from the Great War chasing him behind enemy lines, branches in their hands serving as rifles tipped with razor-sharp bayonets. The boys' voices grew louder as they spread out along the paths running like veins through the forest. Owl hoots and wolf howls were their signals to one another. Evading capture, Russ finally emerged into the clearing where the large maple stood. But just as he felt triumph surge through him, shouts came from behind.

"There he is!" they called, the thrill of capture and punishment in their minds. Other boys appeared, all of them sprinting to catch Russ before he reached the tree.

With a lunge, his hand touched the trunk, just as several pursuers dragged him to the ground. Rising to his feet, one of the boys, bigger than all the others, boldly claimed Russ was caught before touching the tree. The other boys gathered like a jury to listen to the learned arguments of these forest attorneys. Other than Russ, no one was sure what had actually happened, but the thought of throwing someone in the river appealed to them, and Russ knew he was losing the argument. Staring at the bigger boy, Russ said he'd reached the tree safely, and if they insisted on throwing him in the river, he would not go in alone. Everyone knew a challenge had been issued. This might be more interesting. All eyes turned to the bigger boy.

Before he could reply, to the disappointment of all, the high-pitched blast of a factory whistle sounded in the distance. No one waited to hear the bigger boy's response as they rose as one to walk towards town. The whistle, heard throughout Owen Sound, signalled the end of their fathers' workday.

The boys emerged from the forest along the western side of town. In the distance a large grain elevator stood on the edge of the harbour. The town was the fulcrum between eastern Canada's cities and western Canada's farms. The elevators were filled with wheat from the Prairies, brought by lake-going steamers from the western end of Lake Superior across the great inland lakes to Owen Sound. There it waited to be loaded onto rail cars for the final leg to eastern cities.

Owen Sound was once a small village of fisherman and farmers. But the coming of the railhead created a boom, and it grew wild, like many frontier towns. Strangers and saloons came looking to make cash quickly. Other industries followed; small factories, sawmills, and boat builders. The town was brought under control by those who built churches, elected a mayor, and supported a local constabulary. Among those men who wrestled Owen Sound into order was William Kennedy, who by the 1920s built his father's business into a thriving metal foundry. It was Kennedy's whistle the boys heard. As ten-year-old Russ walked towards home, his father Charles emerged from inside Kennedy's walls, soot on his clothes and pipe clenched between his teeth.

———◆———

Russ jerked awake from that blessed moment of unwanted sleep. Any slight distraction could all too easily get him and his crew killed. It was the throaty engine rumble and creaking tracks of an approaching tank that had woken him. In that disoriented instant he couldn't tell from which direction the tank came. "Start the engines!" he bellowed below, cursing his moment of weakness. How long had he been out? As his heart raced, his mind cleared and he remembered they hadn't seen a German Panzer in days, other than burned out hulks littering the countryside around Falaise. The tall outline of a Sherman tank churned into view, a cloud of dust billowing behind it. Relief turned to hope, and then to disappointment when Russ saw it was not one of the missing tanks, but one nicknamed Margorie. Standing in its turret was his friend, Jim Derij ("pronounced Derry," as Jim tired of telling those who butchered his name).

Russ and Jim were assigned to the same unit a few months before D-Day, both newly qualified as lieutenants, each given four tanks as their first command. Together they guarded the Fourth Canadian Armoured Division's headquarters — General George Kitching and his mobile communications centre. Besides being the most junior lieutenants in the divisional headquarters, they were also its only combat officers. And they were about the only two officers at headquarters not calling themselves British by descent. That may have had something to do with the bond they formed.

Jim directed his driver to bring Margorie alongside Russ's vehicle. The lieutenants climbed down in the narrow space between the tanks, exposing themselves as little as possible, aware of the risk of German snipers. Talking tiredly, they found neither had encountered any sign of the missing tanks. Eighty tons of steel and ten men had simply vanished into the French countryside.

———◆———

Owen Sound had a quiet caste system neatly segregating its society. There were those who were British and those who were not. Those it favoured seldom disregarded that system. The British — English, Anglo-Irish, or Scots — occupied the top rungs. Everyone else came below that. Near the lower end were those from southern Europe. This was the society Charles Colombo entered when he arrived in Owen Sound in 1905. It was a far cry from Baden, the largely German town he'd grown up in. Hearing German spoken on the streets of Baden and nearby Kitchener was common. But speaking German on the streets of Owen Sound would have been frowned on by some.

In Owen Sound, Charles's last name identified him as a foreigner. Few knew the ethnicity of his name. Charles learned soon after arriving in Owen Sound to expect a cold response at best when he told someone his father spoke only Italian and his mother only German. It was hard to say which people considered less desirable: German, still stigmatized by the Great War, or Italian, a people viewed as unwanted and undesirable. Though Charles was born in Canada, being maligned for one's "foreign" nationality was common-place in Victorian towns. Despite the stigma attached to his name, Charles was made foreman of a crew of men with names like McDearmid, Sutton, and King. Their resentment was hardly surprising.

If Charles had wavered in the face of social standards, his son Russ would never have been born. Owen Sound's respectable society would never have approved of Charles, the Italian boarding house resident, romancing his landlord's visiting niece. But this is what happened when Blanche Cheney, a young American, visited her aunt in Owen Sound.

When Blanche returned to Genoa, Ohio, after her visit, she broke the news to her parents. She hoped they would respect her wish to marry Charles and move to Canada. She also had to break the news to the minister she was engaged to. Her parents reluctantly gave their blessing, allowing Blanche to marry the enigmatic Charles that summer. It was not often an Italian Catholic such as Charles married an English Protestant.

Together they prospered in Owen Sound, raising three boys in their sprawling house. They grew peonies and roses in their garden, and gathered

Charles and Blanche with Russ (lower left), Verdun, and Jack in 1916 in front of their home on 492–14th Street West, Owen Sound.

eggs from the coop Charles built in the backyard. Russ was the third of their three boys, born on Valentine's Day, 1916. Blanche nicknamed him "Sweet." He had two older brothers. The first was born a year after Charles and Blanche married. The second arrived on Christmas Eve, 1914. When his second son was born, Charles patriotically flew a Canadian flag on his front porch and named the boy Verdun, after the French city that had stood almost alone against the Germans. At the time, the outlook for the Allies was terrible, and each day's newspaper headlines were viewed with foreboding.

Charles did not join either of the volunteer regiments Owen Sound sent to join the Canadian Expeditionary Force. Men in war industries were told anyone could learn to carry a rifle, but they were needed to keep production moving at Kennedy's, an important manufacturer of propellers for navy ships and shell casings for the army.

Kennedy's boomed from war contracts during the Great War and continued to boom in the 1920s. Charles and Blanche and their small family likewise flourished. Their automobile was made possible by the thirty dollars a week Charles made for the fifty-five hours he worked. Each workday began at seven a.m. with a blast of Kennedy's whistle and ended with another ten hours later. Kennedy's was the hub of their lives.

The large machinery at Kennedy's fascinated ten-year-old Russ. His father showed him how the wooden forms were like hollow eggs when packed with a shell made of wet sand and clay. Mold-making was an art complicated by the shrinkage of the metal as it cooled, requiring forms to be larger than the final size of the cast object. On the Sunday afternoon of his visit the large metal bucket hung on a hoist from the ceiling was still warm to touch. When the sand in a form dried, the bucket was manoeuvred overhead for pouring. If the sand mold was not dry enough, his father explained, there would be an explosion of high-pressure steam, and molten metal would fly into the air like an exploding volcano.

Charles watched Russ run to the far end of the foundry, where a massive bronze propeller stood. Russ ran his hand along the swan-like curve of the giant propeller's edge. It had come out of a gigantic wooden form and was destined for a Great Lakes freighter being built in Collingwood. Before the form was cracked open, a crowd of factory workers gathered. A major flaw was costly, requiring the casting to be started over. Charles, accompanied by Mr. Kennedy, closely examined the expensive casting. The suspense lasted close to thirty minutes, and in the end Mr. Kennedy shook Charles's hand. The final step was cleaning the layer of sand adhering to the casting's surface. A high-pressure air hose blew the sand off the metal, filling the foundry with a fine dust.

———————◆———————

Russ coughed as dirt thrown in the air by Jim's tank settled in his throat. As the two lieutenants discussed where to take their search, a jeep came bouncing towards them. Russ recognized Major Campbell in the passenger's seat, one hand steadying himself on the jeep's dash while holding his helmet on with the other. Russ involuntarily looked at his uniform to see if anything was out of place.

When Major Clarence Campbell had taken command of the Headquarters Squadron, only weeks before D-Day, word quickly spread that he was the same Campbell who was a referee in the National Hockey League. His troops became familiar with the fiery temper he sometimes displayed as a referee. Opinions on Campbell were split between the career soldiers and some of the volunteers. Most career soldiers, like Jim, found Campbell tough but fair. But to some, like Russ, volunteers for the Canadian army who for four years had trained interminably while often living in miserable conditions, Campbell's criticisms for minor lapses were harder to accept. Now that the Division was in Normandy, to the men, stressed by near constant combat and lack of sleep, an eruption of his temper was the last thing they needed.

Since reaching Normandy in late July 1944, the Fourth Division's armoured regiments had been badly mauled by the Germans. Within the first week of arriving, their deadly 88-mm guns destroyed many Canadian tanks. As the division's tank regiments were decimated, Russ and Jim increasingly found their tanks dispensed to the hottest parts of the battlefield. But the missing Headquarters tanks had vanished during what should have been a simple reconnaissance mission. Since then, the Major had pushed Jim and Russ to locate them, as if he held them responsible. It was another case of the Major causing Russ's anger to roil just below the surface.

———————◆———————

Russ's fist slammed into the other boy's cheek, snapping his head backward. At six feet, sixteen-year-old Russ was as tall as the nineteen-year-old. The older boy stumbled backwards and fell. Russ rained punches on him, his blue eyes cold as steel.

"I give up!" the boy said, blood running from his nose and an eye beginning to swell shut. Russ stopped punching and stood up.

Shortly before, the older boy had seen Russ making a beeline across the road towards him. Russ had already started a fight with two of the older boy's friends. Both older boys were left bruised and bloodied. The first had not remembered why Russ was angry with him. The second boy knew why, and though at first he'd held his own, Russ's willingness to be hit if it meant he could hurt someone more proved too much. Now Russ was on to the third and last.

The older boy retreated into a nearby park, apologizing as Russ swiftly covered the last few feet. Russ swung without hesitating, hitting the older boy squarely on the face. It was too late to apologize.

The older boy lay on the ground as Russ walked to a nearby drinking fountain. He took a long drink then wiped his mouth on his sleeve. He held his fist under the stream and washed blood from it. Taking a final look at the vanquished boy, he pushed his wavy brown hair out of his eyes and walked away without saying a word. Now they were even.

Three years earlier at this same drinking fountain, they'd caught Russ in the park. The three sixteen-year-olds thought it fun to push the thirteen-year-old around, laughing as he fought to get away. Dragging Russ to the fountain, they sprayed him with cold water, soaking his hair and clothes, and finally they spat on him, the yellow spittle stinking of chewing tobacco. They shouldn't have laughed when Russ swore he would get even.

———◆———

Major Clarence Campbell returned the salutes of his two lieutenants, joining them between the tanks. They reviewed where the missing tanks were last seen, what direction they were travelling in, and what areas had been searched.

The tanks had disappeared after escorting General Kitching to meet the Division's senior officers at a small quarry near the village of Noney-en-Auge.[1] Even though the tank regiments had swept the area the evening before, Kitching had taken the Headquarter Squadron's tanks for his protection. He was asked if the tanks could reconnoitre an area for a nearby British artillery unit. He let them go, one his command tank with its radio serving as a mobile command post. The cannon was a wooden replica, allowing room for the radio equipment the General needed to communicate across the battlefield. When the meeting ended, the tanks still had not returned. With no radio message from the command tank, Campbell, Colombo, and Derij knew the missing troopers were likely dead or had taken been prisoner.

———◆———

A small group of men stood at the entrance to Kennedy's foundry and stared at a handwritten sign on the door. It contained only two words in large block letters: "No Jobs." It was there to stop the steady stream of men looking for work. What a change 1933 was compared to the boom years of the 1920s. Desperate men would do anything for a few hours of work and to get a foot in the door. "Need another man today?" they'd ask. "Sweep the floor for you? Can I run a letter across town?"

Since the start of the 1930s, orders had slowed to a crawl. The foundry was now surviving from month to month. Some of the men were showing signs of stress, the result of constant worry about their jobs. A few became reclusive and sullen, others were overly friendly and talkative. One imagined plots by coworkers to take his job or by management to lay him off. Charles knew his job was secure as long as orders trickled in.

The first incident happened so innocently, it passed Charles unnoticed. As the end of the workday approached, he prepared to run the gauntlet of those waiting outside. He stepped outside the foundry door at the end of his shift, lit his pipe, clamped it between his teeth, and began briskly walking home. This day, though, he found himself short of breath. He stopped walking but for just a moment felt he could not get enough air. He put the episode down to his age, though he was not yet fifty.

In coming weeks his shortness of breath grew worse. The idea emerged that his age was not the problem. When he could no longer ignore it, he visited his doctor, and when X-rays were taken and the diagnosis made, it wasn't a complete surprise. Silicosis, the disease dreaded by miners, was not uncommon among men who worked in foundries. Charles had seen the effects in others. He even knew the cause was years of breathing silica dust. For decades, sand from the castings had settled in his lungs, silently inflaming the tender tissues. Its effects remained hidden until the damage became critical. It was so bad, his scarred lungs made it impossible to take in enough oxygen. The feeling was like being tortured by slow suffocation. His doctor described how the lack of oxygen was causing the blood vessels to constrict, and the resulting high blood pressure was straining his heart. The doctor was blunt — this would lead to a heart attack. The only question was when.

Charles grew thin, and soon his clothes hung on him like a scarecrow. His eyes sank into his gaunt face, and all but a few strands of his once wavy black hair disappeared. But a son can be the last person to see his father's mortality, and Russ denied the reality of his father's decline.

The scales finally fell from Russ's eyes one day when he walked with his father to Kennedy's. Charles halted at the corner, grasping Russ's arm. "We have to stop." As he stood there, waiting for the breathlessness to pass, it grew worse.

Putting his hand on his son's shoulder for support, Charles said, "We have to go home. If I cross the road, I'm sure I'll die." The words were like a knife sliding between Russ's ribs. After slowly making their way home, Russ helped his father onto the couch. He finally realized how ill his father was, seeing him gasp for air like a fish out of water, mouth agape and eyes silently pleading. Later, when he was alone, Russ cried quietly for his father and for himself.

Since his diagnosis, Charles planned for a future he knew he would not be part of. He brought Jack home from Niagara Falls, hiring him at Kennedy's. Verdun had completed high school and was working. Charles told Russ he must quit high school and find a job. He was sixteen. Each paycheque the three boys earned was given to their father.

But in 1932, jobs were scarce and Russ was fortunate to find even manual labour, or pick and shovel work as he called it. One job was as a lumberjack, cutting trees for a local sawmill. The dense beech and maple wood was hard enough in summer, but in winter, the frozen wood turned hard as steel. Even on the coldest days, standing thigh deep in wet snow, Russ was soaked with sweat from pulling the bowsaw or chopping wood with his axe. His arms and shoulders grew, and inches of muscle were added to his lean six-foot frame.

Saturday morning of August 4, 1934, was cool, and Charles looked forward to a shift that lasted only until noon. Charles and Jack began work promptly at seven. Although foreman, Charles enjoyed working with the sand, clay, and water, bringing it to the proper consistency for the forms. As he mixed the sand and water, he felt the familiar shortness of breath, and a throbbing in his left arm. He ignored both, as he always did. But this time it grew worse. He fell to his knees and was unconscious before his head reached the foundry floor. He died there on the cold floor at Kennedy's.

Charles died during the depths of the Depression. Soon after, Verdun departed for the United States. Jack kept his job at Kennedy's, and Russ, then eighteen, worked at any job he could find, usually hard physical work. Although close to one in five in Owen Sound were on public relief, they earned enough to avoid it. Despite the Depression, the death of his father, and the departure of Verdun, Russ's life slowly regained a sense of normalcy.

———————◆———————

Russ directed his tank's driver onto a narrow lane leading into a large patch of forest. The lane was well-hidden by a fold in the perimeter of the trees, which had gone unnoticed when they passed this way the day before. Only by chance did Russ notice the lane leading into the forest this day. The Sherman moved forward slowly. From his position in the turret, Russ was first to see the missing tanks. Ordering his driver to stop, he surveyed the scene. There was no movement or sound.

"I'm going to have a look," Russ told his crew. He climbed out, taking his pistol from its holster. Walking towards the two tanks, he felt exposed. They were lined up on the narrow path, some forty yards from where Russ had stopped his own tank. Reaching the first of the tanks, he climbed up onto its deck. It was the General's command tank, its wooden cannon easily identifiable. Peering through the open hatch, Russ saw the radio torn to pieces — and none of the crew.

Jumping down, he walked to the other tank. He saw a hole on the hull where a shell had exploded. He climbed up and peering inside smelled the sulphurous odour of the explosion. He imagined the panic when the tank was rocked by the explosion, filling the turret with smoke. They were fortunate the explosion had not ignited the ammunition. He understood the indecision the crew must have felt, knowing if they bailed out they would likely be shot down, but waiting inside they might be hit at any second by another shell.

Climbing down, Russ examined the three-inch hole in the hull. He traced a path away from the tank, in the direction of some bushes lining the laneway. Walking behind the bushes, he found a discarded Panzerfaust launch tube, a hand-held anti-tank weapon.

Russ pieced together what must have happened. The tanks were ambushed by a band of Germans attempting to escape the area. The joining of the Canadian and American armies near Falaise had completed the encirclement of the German Seventh Army. The Germans were desperate to escape north of the Seine, fighting through the thin cordon of Canadian troops spread out across the countryside. Despite closing the Falaise pocket, it was a leaky trap, and small groups of Germans continued to filter through the Canadian lines. The Germans hid during the day and moved at night. When the Canadian tanks entered the forest, they'd unknowingly disturbed a hornet's nest.

The concealed Germans would have heard the approaching tanks, but seeing no infantry, they would have known it was safe to let them approach. When the trap was sprung, the lead tank was fired on from close range with the Panzerfaust. With the first tank disabled, the Canadian troopers would have pulled their hatches closed, making themselves virtually blind. Then the Germans could easily approach. They must have climbed onto the tanks and told the trapped Canadians to give themselves up or face the consequences.

The Germans had done their best to disable the captured tanks. They destroyed the breech of the tank's cannon and shot up the command tank's radio equipment. The only reason they hadn't siphoned off gasoline and poured it inside the crew compartment to set the tanks alight was the attention the smoke and explosions would have brought.

There was no sign of the ten men who had been in the tanks. The troopers must have been taken prisoner, but by no means were they safe. Forced to accompany their German captors, the Canadians would be subject to attack from their own troops. But with the Germans desperate to flee north, dragging prisoners along would be difficult and a threat to the their escape. It was also no secret that members of the 12th SS Division had executed Canadian prisoners at nearby Ardenne Abbey. Remnants of that infamous division continued to be the nemesis of Canadian troops in the fighting around Falaise.

Russ returned to Headquarters and reported the discovery. Several days later one of the captured troopers turned up. He was a British artillery officer who confirmed what Russ had pieced together. He also told how he had escaped and reported the troopers were all alive and without serious injury. They were taken north by their German captors and were surely on their way to Germany and a POW camp.

———◆———

During the 1930s, economic hardship forced thousands of Canadian teenagers to grow up quickly, taking on the responsibilities of adults. In 1938, Russ was twenty-two and the Depression was all he had known as an adult. He already had spent six years supporting his mother by working demanding jobs for low wages. It was pick-and-shovel work and bush jobs, with no end in sight. But it was hard to ignore concerns about a looming war in Europe, trumpeted in newspaper headlines and on radio. The world was split in two camps, the democracies led by Great Britain, the United States, and France, and the dictatorships of Fascist Germany, Italy, and Spain, and Communist Soviet Union.

Every day newspapers reported the threat posed by Germany to democratic nations. The focus shifted from trouble spot to trouble spot in Europe, fanned by the threat of Nazi aggression, from the Ruhr to Austria, the

Sudetenland, Danzig, and Czechoslovakia. Since taking absolute power, the Nazis had shown their willingness to treat their own citizens with violence. Canadians already were reading about concentration camps, where brutal treatment was the norm.

While other nations stepped up the production of armaments, Canadian politicians said they would support Britain in the event of war, but did little to increase the size of the armed forces or to equip them. When 1938 came to a close, Canadians had a sense of foreboding that war was inevitable. If war came, it would require young men like Russ to put their lives on hold and shoulder even greater responsibilities than they had faced during almost a decade of the Depression.

TWO

Fremd im eigenen Land
A Stranger in His Own Land

Frank's pulse raced with the roar of the engine. He was the lone passenger on the small Junkers W34, skittering across the runway in northern Finland as the pilot swung the tail around, coming to a stop facing down the long asphalt strip. The pilot pushed the speed control lever forward, causing the small craft to shake in anticipation. Suddenly, it jumped forward as he let go of the brakes, and Frank grabbed the edge of his seat, his hands slippery with sweat. The accelerating aircraft bounced along the runway, and as the nose lifted, the pilot pulled back on the control column.

The pilot turned to look at the blond paratrooper, whose face was pressed against the window as the plane rose into the air. He looked barely more than sixteen, like a boy dressed in a soldier's uniform, though his identity card said he was twenty. The pilot chuckled, remembering when he had checked the young man's orders against his identity card. Both said he was Franz Sikora, but when the pilot called the boy Franz, he was told, with a hint of defiance, that despite what his papers said he was Frank. Franz was his father's name.

———◆———

The weather in Freistadt,[1] Czechoslovakia, was cold and rainy and, as always in such weather, Franz Sikora's legs ached. He limped slightly, walking slowly to the court office. His head also ached from the celebration of the previous evening. His friends had joined him, raising glass after glass to celebrate the birth of Franz's first child, a son. The men he celebrated with, all in their early thirties, were veterans of the Great War, members of the same regiment from their town. The regiment was raised in 1914 in the Teschen region, part of Austria-Hungary. Glasses were raised to toast Franz's son and his wife Josefina. Though his drinking this night was an exception for Franz, the celebration continued late into the evening. As usual when the old comrades met, the conversation turned to the former commander of their regiment, to friends who had not returned from the war, and to those like Franz who had been badly wounded.

When his friends asked what the boy would be named, Franz paused for a second then told them his son would also be named Franz. The friends stood up, held their glasses before them, and in unison said, "To Franz." They refilled their glasses but then sat silently. They thought of happier times for Germans like themselves.

Franz looked in the mirror at his legs as he dressed for work the next morning. They were thin and very white, like two fragile sticks. He ran his hands over the pockmarked skin, puckered and purple where the machine gun bullets had struck him as he had gone over the top of the trench in an attack on Allied lines. Finished dressing, he put his son's birth registration in the breast pocket of his jacket. As he walked the narrow cobbled street to the court building where he worked, he felt nervously for the papers, anticipating the reaction of the Czech official when he saw the name printed on the forms.

Naming first-born sons after the emperor was a tradition all Germans in Teschen had once followed. But in 1924, when Franz's son was born, Austria-Hungary no longer existed. Teschen had been made part of a new country, Czechoslovakia, ruled by the Czechs from Prague. And the emperor was long dead. Franz-Josef died in 1916, when the Great War still had years to run. It was just as well he had died when he did, Franz thought, since it would have tormented the great old man to see the country he'd ruled for more than fifty years split up. Naming his son Franz was a tribute to a time when Austria-Hungary still existed and Teschen was ruled by Germans, as the Czech in charge of the court office would be well aware.

Franz's family was German not because they lived in the country of that name. They were German by heritage, descendants of the migration in which, centuries earlier, their forbears moved east across central Europe. Just as there were large differences among people in different regions within the borders of Germany itself, Germans living in Teschen had their own distinctive culture. The region, with its unique dialect and traditions, had a reputation for peaceful coexistence, with Germans, Poles, Jews, Czechs, and Slovaks living in reasonable harmony. That changed after the Great War.

———————◆———————

The pilot pushed the control column forward, causing the plane to plunge earthward. He turned to see his passenger's reaction. He was not disappointed as he saw Frank's eyes the size of saucers and his arm braced against the fuselage.

When readying the plane for takeoff, the pilot had asked Frank how long he had been a paratrooper. Frank had volunteered for the Luftwaffe when he was seventeen and was starting his third year as a Fallschirmjäger. He told the pilot he too had wanted to fly but had been turned down by the doctors. He was excited to finally have the chance to go up in an airplane. The pilot remarked at the irony of a member of the Luftwaffe never having flown, and decided to give the young man a first flight he would never forget.

As the plane hurtled earthwards, it gathered speed, the air roaring over the wings causing everything to vibrate uncontrollably. Watching the earth, Frank saw a farmhouse rapidly growing in size. Just as he was sure they would crash, he felt a tremendous pressure on his body, like a giant hand pushing him down into his seat. As the pilot pulled the plane out of its steep dive, Frank felt he could breathe again. But the relief was short-lived. The plane turned on its right side, wings perpendicular to the ground, pressing Frank against the fuselage. From the cockpit came the sound of laughter.

———————◆———————

Franz was furious with the Czech in charge of the court office. The man had examined the birth registration form, written a short note in the margin, and filed the document away. The man had not had the decency to say anything; he'd acted as though the name Franz meant nothing. It was an insult to the old emperor's memory.

Franz had to let all the arguments he had prepared slowly dissipate without being spoken. His longing for the old days was painful. The Sikoras had once been among the town's large landowners, part of the local ruling elite. The Sikora farms had produced food for market and provided employment for others. Their horses were so prized that the best were sold to the Habsburg monarchy.

But after the Great War, the Sikora farms had been taken from them by the new Czech government. Like other large landowners, most of them German, their family farms were split into small parcels and given to landless Czech peasant farmers. With the loss of their land followed the loss of the status and prestige it had brought them. The payment Franz and Josephina received was a fraction of what the land was worth. Franz had nothing against the Czech peasant farmers, but he believed the Czech government and the Allied powers lacked sympathy for Germans. During the chaos enveloping Central Europe after the Great War, three million Germans from Austria-Hungary and Germany became minorities in lands annexed and awarded to Czechoslovakia, Poland, or France. The Allied powers decided to slice off parts of Germany and to dismember Austria-Hungary. The new Czechoslovakia contained regions with large German minorities.

The changes in Teschen affected Germans more than any other ethnic group. In the time of the emperor, the Habsburg policies supported cultural and linguistic diversity and a degree of cultural autonomy. An uneasy peace reigned in the country. For the most part, the Germans of Teschen were landowners and took care of the government and administration, while the Czechs were active in business. The Poles mostly owned smaller farms and the Slovaks were often labourers and peasant farmers, many tending to pastures in the nearby Beskydy Mountains. In this rich cultural mosaic, a Jewish population also co-existed, its membership in the community and religious rights respected. Small communities of Romani wandered the countryside in their horse-drawn wagons, itinerant labourers who came seeking work. The different ethnic communities in Teschen continued living tolerantly after the Great War. But the loss of prestige among the Germans following the creation of Czechoslovakia had at a deeper level upset this peaceful co-existence among the region's social classes and ethnic groups. Freistadt was on the surface still a quiet town, but the German population struggled to adapt to the new reality, a struggle the Sikoras exemplified. In this town of about five thousand people, predominantly German, many had difficulty accepting the loss of wealth and social position.

The town square in Friestadt (now part of the city of Karviná, Czech Republic).
Reproduced with the permission of photographer Lumír Částka (www.loomeer.cz).

Frank was oblivious of the upheaval his family was going through. His boyhood was an idyllic time. With other boys from different ethnic groups, he played in Freistadt's cobblestone roads, running down the narrow streets lined with medieval buildings, many of them more than seven hundred years old. In the town's Central Square stood a tall clock tower, a reminder of a time centuries earlier when it was a bulwark against invaders. Farmers from the surrounding countryside came to Freistadt's market to sell homemade cheese, curds, eggs, and poultry. In summer, the farmers brought berries to market and in the fall wild mushrooms, picked by women from the forests carpeting the Beskydy Mountains. Poachers from nearby Poland arrived in Freistadt to sell rabbits and venison from the forests to the north.

The rolling countryside surrounding Freistadt was made up of fertile farms and forests. The lush forests were playgrounds for children of all backgrounds. Frank attended a German school, and his fellow students included the Jewish children of Freistadt. Life was not a Garden of Eden, but it certainly seemed it to Frank.

The cold mountain streams cascading through the forest were full of fish. Trout and crayfish brought high prices in the market. But the rivers were protected from fishing, preventing city boys from fishing outside of town without a licence. Luckily for Frank, the local game warden was a family friend who finally relented and issued him a fishing licence. It was a prize to have one, although it only permitted Frank to catch minnows and chub. His fishing equipment was a simple hazel branch, a few metres² of ordinary string, and a hook. His fishing license didn't even allow him to use worms as bait. Frank spent most spare time in the forests, walking to favourite fishing spots with his homemade rod over his shoulder. He would return hours later, usually without any fish, but having spent time in nature doing what he most enjoyed.

While Freistadt seemed a near-perfect setting to grow up in, his parents came to realize there was little future for them there. With their lands gone and the small remuneration they'd received used up, the small family struggled. The court office was small and his father's paycheque never seemed adequate. Franz found himself passed over for advancement in favour of Czechs who came from elsewhere. With the family grown to include a daughter, Eva, Frank's parents decided to move to the larger city of Ostrau, a few dozen kilometres west.

Their parents told Frank, who was eleven, and Eva, seven, that life would be better in Ostrau. Franz would stand a better chance of obtaining a promotion. To children, moving to a new city meant making new friends, and on arriving Frank immediately noticed a glaring difference. In Freistadt, everyone mixed together, regardless of their background. In Ostrau, German and Czech children tended to keep to their own groups, each having their own schools, praying in their own churches, and frequenting shops run by their own people.

Ostrau's court office, where Franz worked, used German or Czech, depending on the language of the legal participants, as was the case in Freistadt. This was emblematic of the thorny issue the Czechs faced, between granting more autonomy to Germans or trying to draw them into an active role in Czechoslovakia's government. Allowing greater freedom in the country's German regions, the Czechs worried, might eventually move Germans there to seek union with Germany.

In the early 1930s, many German Czechs were thrilled when a party came to power in Germany whose policies included the return of territory taken away after the Great War. The National Socialists took power in the German Reichstag through political opportunism, violence, and duplicity. By 1932, their leader had become the chancellor of Germany. He was an Austrian who had fought in the Great War and who, until the mid-1920s, had been a minor right-wing political figure. His name was Adolf Hitler.

While jailed in the 1920s, Hitler wrote a book describing his views on the causes of Germany's problems. He used a visible minority as the principle scapegoat for the loss of the Great War and the country's economic problems. The book was *Mein Kampf*, and the group he targeted was the Jews.

By March 1933, Hitler had consolidated political power in Germany, eliminated his major adversaries, and declared himself Führer. Nazi slogans proclaimed, "Hitler is Germany, Germany is Hitler." By July, the Nazi party became the only political body allowed by law, and Hitler took absolute power.

Frank was not yet a teenager in 1935, when his family arrived in Ostrau. In Czechoslovakia, he was not exposed to the Nazi propaganda taught to schoolchildren in Germany. But adult Germans in Czechoslovakia were well aware of the Nazis and their doctrines. There was even a branch of the party in German sections of Czechoslovakia. Despite Nazi violence against their adversaries, and their persecution of Jews and Communists, for some their support of autonomy for Sudeten Germans made them an appealing political option.

As the 1930s went on, the German government flouted clause after clause of the Treaty of Versailles, which had set restrictions on defeated Germany after the Great War. In 1935, the government implemented conscription into the armed forces. In 1936, the demilitarized Rhineland was occupied by

German troops, and in March, 1938, they unified Germany and Austria in the "Anschluss," or "joining up." The Anschluss was part political union, part incorporation, and entirely forbidden by the Treaty of Versailles. However, the Allied powers' response was nothing more than disapproving public statements. German newspapers described cheering crowds greeting troops entering Austria. In Vienna, a quarter of a million Austrians gathered to hear Hitler speak from Emperor Franz-Josef's Imperial Palace. Meanwhile, Jews, Communists, and Socialists were fleeing the country to escape persecution and imprisonment.

The Anschluss was watched enthusiastically by Sudeten Germans intent on gaining autonomy from the Czechs. Before the end of March, Hitler met the leader of the Sudeten German Party, Konrad Heinlein. Shortly after, Heinlein demanded the Czechs allow complete autonomy of the Sudetenland, and Hitler declared the urgent need to solve the "Czechoslovak problem." Through the summer of 1938, tensions ran high, with the threat of war looming.

Some Czechs reacted to the threat of war from Germany by harassing Germans in Ostrau. Fourteen-year-old Frank heard about and witnessed the harassment. The names and addresses of leaders of the German community were collected by Czech authorities. Some Germans were forced from their houses and segregated in tenements. Czech police receiving calls for help from someone speaking German or with a German accent sometimes ignored the call. Army barricades were erected across streets, the men manning them asking those attempting to pass to use the Czech language, since most Germans could not pronounce certain Czech words without an accent. Frank's parents were concerned for the family's safety and looked for a way to keep Frank and Eva safe.

———————◆———————

The plane twisted like a corkscrew as it slowly spiralled and plunged once again towards the ground. Straightening out at treetop level, it shot over a farmer's field. Cows began running at the plane's loud, sudden appearance. It dipped, passing just over their heads. In the cockpit, the pilot whooped like a cowboy at a rodeo, shouting back to Frank that the farmer would be surprised when his cows gave him sour milk the next day.

At the southern coast of Finland, he brought the plane to a normal cruising altitude and settled in for strictly routine flying. After landing at an airfield in northern Germany, the pilot disembarked and waited for Frank.

When the boy emerged a moment later, the pilot asked his young passenger if he was still sorry he hadn't been able to become a pilot.

Frank answered, "Of course, more than ever."

The pilot smiled and vigorously shook the younger man's hand. But when Frank grimaced, the pilot noticed the wound ribbon on Frank's uniform.

The pilot apologized, telling Frank he hadn't known he was injured, and hoped the in-air antics hadn't hurt him. Frank replied that he shouldn't worry. He wouldn't have missed flying for anything, though it did feel good to be standing on solid ground.

———◆———

Many Sudeten Germans felt Germany's newfound strength was a great thing. Finally, they hoped, some of the wrongs done to them by the Allies after the Great War would be righted and their lot would improve. In September, 1938, Hitler issued the Czech government a series of ultimatums. First he threatened war unless Sudeten Germans were given autonomy. When this was agreed to, Hitler demanded the Sudetenland be put under German control. This too was granted. Finally, he threatened to invade unless German troops were allowed there. At the brink of war, the leaders of Britain and France met face-to-face with Hitler in Munich. In the end, Germany's occupation of the Sudetenland was accepted, exchanged for a promise of peace. The outcome of the Munich meetings was presented as a fait accompli to Czechoslovakia. Most Sudeten Germans were glad to no longer be part of Czechoslovakia. But not all in the Sudetenland felt that way. For Jews and Communists, the Nazi takeover was cause for fear, and many fled in response, as had been happening in Germany and Austria almost from the moment the Nazis took power.

On the first day of the occupation, Frank and his friends rode their bikes, looking for German soldiers. They found them just outside of town, on the other side of the Oder River. They waved to the German tanks across the river, and the soldiers waved back. That night at dinner Frank talked excitedly to his family about the soldiers and tanks.

Frank's parents were shocked to hear that the Germans had stopped short of Ostrau, and only then did they discover, to their horror, that the border Germany had negotiated did not include them. They were more concerned than ever that the Czechs would turn against Germans remaining in their territory. As if on cue, Franz was threatened with the loss of his job unless he moved Frank from his German primary school to a Czech one. It was only Frank's mother's refusal that stopped it. He wrote the Gymnasium entrance examination, which he passed allowing him to enter the German equivalent of high school.

There was scarcely a pause in the fast-moving events involving Germans in Europe. In Paris, two months after the occupation of the Sudetenland, a young Pole shot and killed a German diplomat in the German embassy. The assassin was distraught at the inhumane treatment of his family and other Polish Jews. His parents were expelled from Germany, where they had moved to work, but Poland refused to take them back. With neither country willing to take them, the refugees were trapped in a no-man's land between the border posts. The diplomat's death in Paris was followed by two nights of violence against Jews across Germany, Austria, and the Sudetenland, which became known as Kristallnacht. German newspapers reported it as a popular response to the murder of the German diplomat.[3] In the violence, Jewish businesses were vandalized and synagogues destroyed. Thousands of Jews, even though they were the victims, were arrested and sent to concentration camps. The violence extended into some parts of Czechoslovakia where large numbers of Germans lived.

Fearing a backlash against Germans in Czechoslovakia for the loss of the Sudetenland, Frank's parents decided their only recourse was to leave the country. They would move yet further west, into the area under German control. Their focus settled on the city of Leitmeritz, where Frank's father interviewed for a job as court clerk. Returning from the interview, he told his family it would be perfect, a warm climate, fruit trees lining the river running through the city, and a high school for Frank. A mile south of the city sat the garrison town of Theresienstadt, used in 1939 as an army base for several thousand soldiers.[4] They would be safe from the violence that threatened Germans in Czechoslovakia.

The Sikoras' relocation passed without fanfare. Frank and his sister said goodbye to their friends while their parents loaded their possessions. Frank felt no sadness at leaving Czechoslovakia. Instead, he was excited by the adventure of moving to a new city. His parents were relieved. Living in an area under German control, uncertain days would at last be behind them. Their relief was to be short-lived. Before the year was over, Hitler would push Europe into a new world war, and their son would be drawn into it.

The train for Leitmeritz left Czechoslovakia for the Sudetenland without having to pass through a border crossing. There were no Czech border guards restricting what they could take with them, and no German guards to inspect their papers. Their personal documents were the most important things they had brought with them. Those papers would be needed to prove they were pure Germans, their blood not mixed with that of Poles, Slovaks, and especially to the German authorities, not Jews. As Frank sat with his sister Eva and his parents on the train, he had no idea how worried his father was that someone might look closely into the family's past.

THREE

Hometown Heroes
Helden der eigenen Stadt

In the early Sunday morning hours, people in Owen Sound emerged in ones and twos from house after house. They walked almost trancelike along the tree-lined streets, drawn towards the downtown. It had been a hot night, the kind where you lay awake in bed, the sheets sticking to your sweat-soaked back. But many found sleep elusive, not because of the heat, but because of worry. A war ultimatum had been issued. British Prime Minister Neville Chamberlain warned Hitler to withdraw German forces from Poland, or Great Britain would declare war. Canadians were told by Canada's Prime Minister Mackenzie King that they would join Britain in such a war.

By dawn a small crowd stood outside the office of Owen Sound's *Sun Times* newspaper. Seeing movement through the plate glass window, the crowd pushed forward. Inside, a group of newspaper workers read from a sheet of teletype. When they were done, a clerk approached the storefront and placed the teletype in the window. It was six a.m.[1]

"What does it say?" someone near the back of the crowd yelled.

A man at the window quickly read the bulletin and called out, "It's war!"

Another man began reading the message aloud. "In a radio broadcast made today," he told the hushed crowd, "Prime Minister Chamberlain announced that this morning the British Ambassador in Berlin handed the German government a final note, stating that unless we heard from them by eleven o'clock that they were prepared at once to withdraw their troops from Poland, a state of war would exist between us. I have to tell you that no such undertaking has been received and that consequently this country is at war with Germany."

The news spread quickly through the city. There was a sense something awful was coming that would test the country's courage and resolve. In churches across Owen Sound that Sunday, September 3, 1939, ministers led their parishioners in prayer, asking for "God's protection and support in the coming war." When Blanche walked home from church, she thought nervously about the war and her sons. Jack, twenty-nine, was working full-time

at Kennedy's. She was certain Kennedy's would be an important war manufacturer, as it had been when Charles worked there during the Great War.
Jack, she felt, would follow in his father's footsteps and contribute to the war
effort where he was. Verdun had been in Philadelphia for five years, and
had recently married. Verdun would not return to Canada, but even had he
wanted to enlist, his bouts of severe asthma would have prevented it.

She felt less sure about Russ. He was twenty-four with a rebellious streak
and had never found steady work, taking labourer's jobs seldom lasting more
than a few months. He was also her only son born in Canada. Now, more than
ever, she regretted not travelling back to her parents' home in Ohio for his
birth. If he was American, he might be less likely to join the Canadian army.

While Blanche and other Canadian mothers worried their sons would
enlist, Canadian politicians were worrying like adolescents on the verge of
leaving home — wanting to show their independence but craving parental
approval at the same time. Or so it seemed when Canada's prime minister
thought he would make a point by waiting seven days after Great Britain's
declaration of war before convening a special session of Parliament to declare
Canada was at war with Germany. It was only a slight change from 1914, when
Canada was committed to the Great War not by its own parliament, but by
Britain's declaration of war. Canada's official announcement in 1939 was made
in a short news bulletin read over CBC radio, but everyone knew it was a
formality. And like many adolescents leaving home, Canada overestimated its
readiness, since her permanent armed forces were woefully small and poorly
equipped.

Some blamed Chamberlain for the war almost as much as they did
Hitler. They felt that war might have been avoided if he had taken a hard
stand earlier. Since 1936, Hitler had aggressively ignored the Treaty of
Versailles. He had moved the German army into the Rhineland, rearmed
Germany, and in the space of six months in 1938 had annexed Austria and
taken the Sudetenland. In March, 1939, Germany had threatened to invade
what remained of Czechoslovakia (to protect Germans living there, Hitler
had claimed). In a misguided attempt to negotiate, the Czech president
travelled to Berlin in search of a compromise.

Instead of negotiations, he was threatened with invasion. Prague would
be destroyed by bombing if Germany was "forced" to take military action,
and the Czech president would be responsible for the deaths of thousands
of his countrymen. Without Britain and France to defend them, the Czechs
had no hope of changing the outcome militarily. The elderly president chose
to save his people from attack by agreeing with Hitler's demand to create a

German "protectorate" over what remained of Czechoslovakia. On March 15, 1939, the German army entered Czechoslovakia, and the country ceased to exist. The past year's attempts at negotiated settlements with Germany by Britain and France were now seen as a wasted appeasement of an aggressive dictator. The invasion of Poland was the line they had drawn in the sand, and Hitler had crossed it.

The war came almost a decade into the Great Depression. Many Canadian men had seen little steady work through the 1930s, and to some, the war provided cause for optimism. Enlistment at least offered a steady paycheque, and for those opting for overseas service, an opportunity to see the world. Most also believed enlistment would protect Canadian values and way of life from fascism. However, at the outbreak of war, the Canadian army consisted of only 3,000 full-time soldiers.[2] Years of cutbacks to military budgets had left the armed forces short even of boots, socks, and blankets, and weapons were scarcer yet, causing enlistment to be phased in slowly.[3] Owen Sound's local regiment, the Grey and Simcoe Foresters, was among those forced to wait to begin recruitment.

With war trumpeted in daily newspaper headlines across Canada in the summer of 1939, Russ found part-time work with the Canadian National Railway doing summer maintenance on the rail lines. When he could, he also played for the city's new senior lacrosse team. He'd been invited to try-out by his childhood friend, Jack MacLeod. The team sweater he gave Russ had "Georgians" (for nearby Georgian Bay) emblazoned across the chest. The team manager was Jack's father, Jim, and it was he that had introduced many Owen Sound boys to the sport, bringing lacrosse sticks home from a work trip and selling them to neighbourhood boys for fifty cents. Russ was one of those who had shown up with the money and, along with other boys, spent hours throwing a ball high in the air and jostling one another to catch it before it fell to earth. As skills improved, impromptu games took place.

The 1939 season was the Georgians' first, and at the end it was considered successful. They'd finished behind only the strong Orangeville team. Russ was a dependable defenseman, and Jim MacLeod asked him to return the following year. Players drifted apart, and the lacrosse sweater Jack had loaned Russ was packed away for the winter.

His summer job on the railway ended not long after the declaration of war. Needing work for the winter, Russ decided to head to northern Ontario. In past winters he had worked for an Owen Sound sawmill owned by the American timber baron J.J. McFadden. But it had closed, and two of its managers had moved to work at McFadden's new lumber mill in Blind

River. As many as five lumber camps were needed to feed logs to the Blind River sawmill, and experienced men were sought. When word went out in Owen Sound that McFadden needed men up north, Russ applied and was told to report.

When Russ reached Blind River, he arranged for most of his forty-five dollar monthly paycheque to be sent to Blanche. From the $1.50 per day he earned, McFadden deducted the cost of food and purchases from the camp's company store. Russ was driven north from Blind River to a camp deep in the northern wilderness.

He entered a spartan existence. The men were housed in large log bunk-houses. Beds were constructed from rough-sawn lumber, each man taking straw from the barn where the horses were kept and piling it on planks inside the wooden bed frame. There was no running water for washing, only metal bowls that could be filled with water heated on the wood stove. Food was the same every day: bread, beans, and fatback. Fatback was nothing more than pork fat. If lucky, you found a thin seam of meat running through it. With the bunkhouse closed up in winter, lit by oily kerosene lamps, no showers for the men, and a steady diet of beans, the air inside smelled like spoiled cheese.

Work began in the dark hours before sunrise, the temperature during winter often -30 degrees Fahrenheit or colder. After breakfast, the men piled onto a horse-drawn logging sleigh, coats buttoned with collars raised, scarves

Russ, most likely at a McFadden lumber camp near Owen Sound.

wrapped around their faces, and hats pulled down over their ears. To stay warm, Russ pulled on as many layers of clothing as he could, including the Georgians lacrosse sweater.

The ride to the work site could be wild on the ice roads, kept slippery by water sprinkled from large horse-drawn tanks. Younger boys, nicknamed "chickadees," walked the roads, scraping horse droppings from the ice so sleigh runners would skate smoothly along the ice roads. Traversing hills could be treacherous. With a full load, the horses took running starts to pull loads up the sides of slippery hills. Reaching the crest, the sleigh would perch for an instant before suddenly starting downwards. Sand, hay, or brush placed on the lee side of hills was meant to slow the descent, but if there was not enough sand or the hill was steep, the sleigh would hurtle downhill with the men hanging on white-knuckled, the horses galloping for their lives to avoid being crushed.

The men were lucky if there were packed trails from the road where they unloaded to their allotted sections of land. If not, they might have to wade through waist-deep snow. The lumberjacks worked near enough to one another to hear the sounds of saws and axes and the crash of trees hitting the ground. It provided each man a measure of his progress to hear those working nearby.

Most of the rough-barked white pine trees were two to three feet in diameter, a few monsters as much as four feet across. After a tree was felled and cut into lengths, horses pulled the logs through the snow to the roadside. The logs were loaded on sleighs and hauled to frozen lakes and rivers, where they waited to be floated to the sawmill after the ice broke up in the spring.

Russ listened as each tree was felled, the cracking and popping of the hinge of wood breaking at the base of the stem sounding like gunshots, branches snapping as each falling giant gained speed and brushed against neighbouring trees. Finally there came the thunderous "Whoompf!" as the tree hit the ground with explosive force.

It was dangerous job. Frostbite was an ever-present risk, and cuts from the sharp axes were commonplace. But the falling trees themselves presented the greatest danger. They weighed many tons and stood up to a hundred feet tall. The men were forced to stay on the narrow paths of trodden snow or be trapped in the deep snow as the hulks hurtled to the ground. Magnifying the danger was the fact the nearest doctor was in Blind River and medical help in the camp was practically nonexistent.

While everyone knew the work was dangerous, it was still jarring when one of the men was seriously injured. Russ could hear nearby men chopping and sawing at trees. He listened as another lumberjack's tree began falling. But the snapping and scraping sounds of the falling tree stopped prematurely, leaving an eerie hush in the bush, except for the sound of a man cursing. Perhaps the other lumberjack was careless and left too much wood in the hinge, or perhaps he was nervous when the tree looked like it might fall and hadn't gone deep enough with his backcut. Regardless of the cause, the tree was hung up, leaning, threatening to fall.

The leaning tree placed tremendous pressure on the remaining wood in the hinge, with thousands of pounds of force pushing on it. The man waited for it to fall, willed it to do so, but it would not break on its own. He would have to release it by cutting into the hinge. It was a dangerous operation, since the weight of the tree leaning on the hinge made it unstable and unpredictable. Russ listened and waited, the sweat leaving a cold trail down his back.

Cursing, the lumberjack approached the tree. Suddenly the hinge cracked, and in one massive release of energy, it snapped free at its base. The butt of the tree kicked back with abrupt explosive force, hitting the man squarely in the chest. It lifted him off his feet, tossing him onto the snow, where he lay limply.

Not able to see the other lumberjack, Russ called out. When no answer came, Russ dropped his axe and ran back up the trail, winding his way through the trees. He found the man lying in the snow, conscious but moaning and unable to move. Other lumberjacks came running through the undergrowth.

The injured man's screams echoed among the trees as he was carried to the road, his cracked and broken ribs grating together. One of the lumber-jacks ran for a sleigh to take him to camp. But since the only help was in Blind River, all they could do was give him rum from the camp stores to help numb the pain for the long ride to town. As the sleigh carried him away, his cries grew faint. No one asked his fate, and no one coming from town brought news. Perhaps it was out of superstition or to avoid showing weakness.

Harvesting and hauling logs continued through the long winter. The melting of the ice roads and spring ice break-up on the rivers and lakes signalled the end of the cutting season and the start of the river drive. The camp foreman asked Russ to stay for the coming river drive. Russ agreed. The extra weeks of work would be easier than the bush work, he thought, and at three dollars a day, the pay was double what he'd earned as a lumber-jack. The idea of easy work did not last long.

In the turbulent water, clearing logjams amid the floating river ice, often soaked to the waist in icy water, was far more dangerous than bush work. There was no training for Russ, who simply walked out on the wet, rolling, icy logs, spiked boots providing traction, manhandling the logs to break up jams using only a peevie, a wooden pole with a steel hook and a hinged jaw on the end.

The work required strength to move the logs and agility to balance on their slippery surfaces as they bobbed and rolled. Falling would send a man into the freezing water with tons of floating logs.

Russ was working with several other drivers to free a jam, when one of the men lost his balance and fell among the logs into the near freezing river, dropping his peevie. Russ and other men raced across the logs to help.

"Leave that man — save the peevie!" yelled the foreman, seeing what was happening.

The man was trapped in the water among the floating logs, unable to pull himself out. With his head just at the surface of the water, he was in danger of being crushed between the massive trees or drowning if he ducked his head and the solid mass of logs closed above him. Ignoring the yelling foreman, Russ helped pull the soaking man out of the water. As the foreman cursed them in the foulest language, one of the river drivers threw the peevie he had rescued from the water at the foreman's feet. Turning his back, the driver went back out onto the logs to resume work. Russ quit the river drive that day in disgust.

Emerging from the bush, he was glad to be heading home. It had been a long winter, with scant news of the outside world reaching camp in the half year he had been there. From infrequent newspapers he knew little had happened in the war, neither side mounting a strong offensive. It seemed as though the dire expectations might have been wrong.

Arriving in Owen Sound in April, Russ was rehired to do summer maintenance on the rail lines for the Canadian National Railway. One person glad to see him was Jack MacLeod. Jack immediately approached him to invite him to the lacrosse team's coming practice. Later, when Russ arrived at the arena wearing an old practice sweater, Jack came to talk to him.

"Where's my lacrosse sweater?" Jack asked, surprised Russ was not wearing the team jersey.

Russ hesitated, surprised by Jack's question. "Your sweater? But you gave it to me. I wore it all winter up north. By spring, it was full of holes and falling apart, so I burned it in the fire."

Jack could not believe what Russ had said. When Jack's father, Jim, heard what had happened, he told Russ he would have to replace the sweater. Russ felt this was unfair. The team charged admission to games, Russ played for free, and he refused to buy another sweater.

When the team was selected and Russ was chosen to it, he continued wearing his old practice sweater to their games. He was the only player without a team sweater bearing the Georgians name. Had Jim MacLeod selected the team, the dispute over the sweater might have caused Russ to be excluded. However, the players were selected by the Georgians' new player-coach, Gerry Johnson. Gerry had been recruited by Jim and came from Hamilton with his wife Marge and their three young children. They had arrived before April to meet the league's requirement allowing only town residents to play. In return for playing lacrosse, Gerry was provided a house to live in, a job, and was named team captain. Local players, like Jack and Russ, played only for pride.

When the season began, Gerry and Russ were often playing partners on Owen Sound's defence. Gerry found the younger man dependable and tough, and liked his quiet confidence and subtle sense of humour. Another player, Perry Wilson from Fergus, Ontario, was a slick forward with a good scoring touch. Russ, Gerry, and Perry soon became inseparable. The Georgians entered the season as one of the favourites, their chief rival the team from Orangeville.

Owen Sound was proud of its sports teams, a feeling surpassed only by the community's feelings for its army regiment, the Grey and Simcoe Foresters. With a war underway, even a "phoney war," as newspapers had dubbed it, the city's expectations of the Foresters were high. The town was home to two Great War Victoria Cross recipients, the highest military award conferred by Great Britain. One was Billy Bishop, the British Empire's top flying ace and by far Canada's best-known veteran. Owen Sound's other Victoria Cross had been awarded to Private Tommy Holmes. Holmes was the youngest Canadian to earn the award, given for his bravery at Passchendaele in 1917. Described as frail and delicate, he appeared an unlikely hero. Two Victoria Crosses in a city of eight thousand was almost unheard of, and it created an air of expectation of great things to come from the young men of Owen Sound.

Many of Owen Sound's men over the age of forty were veterans of the battles of Vimy Ridge and Passchendaele. They had a keen interest in the new war in Europe and strongly felt that Owen Sound's young men should enlist, as so many in the city had in 1914. However, when Russ returned from northern Ontario in the spring of 1940, the Foresters still had not opened their ranks for enlistment. Russ knew some local men had travelled elsewhere to join up, but many preferred to wait for the Foresters to put out their call for recruits.

Several hundred local men had been training with the militia for months. They marched two nights a week in civilian clothes through the city, led by the drum and bugle band. But the drills lacked a sense of urgency. That changed dramatically on May 10, 1940, when the German army released its Blitzkrieg on the Western Front.

The lightning attack, spearheaded by German armoured forces, smashed the relative quiet and blew massive holes in the static front. German tanks rapidly pushed through weak points in the Allied lines, threatening to encircle bypassed French and British positions. The speed of the German advance and the collapse that followed was so fast and complete, it was barely more than two weeks from its start until the British desperately evacuated their armies across the English Channel from the Belgian port of Dunkirk. By June 14, Paris was occupied, and the world waited for what seemed the inevitable invasion of Britain. It seemed incomprehensible to Canadians that the British and French armies could be so incapable of stopping the Germans.

In that depressing time, when the French capitulated and it seemed Britain might soon follow, there was a feeling that if Britain were conquered, Canada's future would be in question. This was not a vague threat. In 1938, the Canadian government and the Canadian military's joint staff committee considered it possible that in the event of war with Germany that Toronto, Ottawa, and Montreal would be bombed, and coastal cities like Halifax, St. John's, New Brunswick, and Quebec City shelled by naval bombardment by the heavy guns of the German navy.[4]

Following Dunkirk, Britain was pushed back to the defence of the island homeland. The badly mauled British army would need years to replace the masses of artillery, tanks, and transport left in France and Belgium. In the air over Britain, Hermann Göring's Luftwaffe fought to destroy the Royal Air Force, the final step before a cross-channel invasion could take place. In preparation for such an attack, the Germans were gathering ships and barges on the coast to ferry troops, tanks, and guns across the English Channel.

———————◆———————

The first Canadian troops arrived in Britain too late to join the battle against the Germans. Though untested in battle, these Canadians carried the hard-earned reputation of their fathers from the Great War as exceptionally tough fighters. More importantly, the Canadians brought with them troop transportation and artillery, and for that they were given responsibility for being a mobile first line of defence in southern England. When the Germans attacked, the Canadians would respond to German paratroop landings inland, and when that threat was dealt with, would rush to the English coast to push back anticipated landings.[5]

Canada's military command knew their troops would suffer heavy casualties if forced to fight in coming months. There could be no retreat for the Canadians in the event of an invasion, and the reality was, in 1940, Canadian troops in England were just a smattering of permanent force and militia troops, leading mostly civilian volunteers with only a few months of training. They would likely have been annihilated.[6]

In those weeks when the shadow of invasion darkened the British Isles and Canada, the call finally came for more volunteers for overseas service. When things appeared their worst in 1940, there was no shortage of Canadians impatient to enlist.

In early June, the Foresters finally were allowed to call for volunteers. When the volunteer militia gathered for drill practice that week, commanding officer Colonel Tom Rutherford announced they were being disbanded so enlistment for overseas service in the regiment could begin. Those from the militia who qualified, he told them, would get the first chance to sign up, but those under eighteen would have to drop out until old enough. Speculation quickly spread through Owen Sound about which of the young men would show up at the recruiting office.

Early on June 18, Russ and Perry walked to the militia barracks on 14th Street West, barely a five-minute walk from Russ's house, and joined the line of men waiting to enlist.

Owen Sound was small enough that Russ knew every man his own age by name. Those in line he didn't know were men from nearby farms and towns such as Wiarton, Meaford, and Chatsworth. There were some locals in line he may have been surprised to see, smaller men and some who were mild-mannered.

Perhaps he was also surprised at who had not shown up. Where were some of the men with a reputation for toughness? Some of the city's athletes? With Canada and Britain at risk and relying on Canadian volunteers to step forward, it crossed his mind that he may have underestimated some and over-estimated others. Finally Russ and Perry reached the front. They sat beside one another, each with one of the Foresters' permanent force NCOs, who oversaw their filling out the enlistment form. In a few minutes they were done and were told anti-climactically they would be contacted shortly.

The following Wednesday, Russ and Perry reported back to the barracks. The list of men who had signed papers had been winnowed down, and it was time for those selected by the Regiment's officers to go through a medical inspection. Russ and Perry were told to strip to their underwear. They stood in their boxer shorts with the other enlistees, waiting to be examined by a doctor.

It was a straightforward eye-ear-nose physical exam, testing of reflexes, and listening to heart and lungs. Russ and Perry passed the Medical Board and were sent to the hospital for a chest X-ray. Once it was confirmed there were no signs of lung disease, their enlistment was finally official. Returning to the barracks with the results of their X-rays, the army's rough reward was an inoculation against typhoid, a thick needle punched under the skin on the chest.

Not everyone who tried signing on was accepted. More than a third of those enlisting in Owen Sound were turned down: In the first week, one hundred eighty men signed up and sixty-nine were rejected. Some were turned down for medical reasons, others were eventually excluded because the officers did not want them in the regiment.[7] It was normal to think the biggest and most brawling local men would be most sought after. But this was not the case with the Foresters. Potential troublemakers were well-known and moved out. Whether such decisions made sense to the community, or even followed military protocol, didn't matter to Colonel Rutherford. He had seen first-hand during the Great War that discipline and a sense of devotion to comrades were more important than mere physical strength. If an example was needed, he could point to Tommy Holmes, one of the youngest, smallest, and bravest men from Owen Sound to fight in the Great War. The officers also knew that if those they turned down were serious, they could enlist elsewhere. The officers kept only those they considered the best of Owen Sound's young men.

There was a third group of men in town. These were single men who were physically capable and of the right age, but who chose not to enlist. It is hard now to say whether pressure was placed on such men to enlist, but it would not be surprising. There would be instances in Canada of men not in uniform being openly called "yellow" or "chicken." Sometimes such disdain was aimed at men who had tried to enlist but were medically unfit. Harassment became severe enough that an "Applicant for Enlistment" badge would be issued in 1941, given to those who had volunteered but been judged not fit. They were told to wear the badge on their lapels to avoid embarrassing public encounters.

After passing his medical, Russ quit his job with the CNR and went under pay with the army. He and Perry received uniforms they were to wear at all times when in public. They were among the three hundred and fifty men from Owen Sound accepted by the Foresters Active Force, volunteers to travel overseas. It had taken only a few weeks to fill the Foresters Active Force Company. There was also enlistment in a Foresters' Home Force, mainly filled by older men who joined with the promise that they would not be sent outside North America.

At seven a.m. daily, they reported to the barracks in uniform for training. In large measure, this consisted of hours spent on the parade square. Being a rifle battalion, the Foresters were taught the quick march: one hundred forty paces per minute — each pace about thirty inches long, with arms swinging to the height of the breast pocket. As the recruits learned to perform simple march steps in unison, increasingly intricate drills were introduced.

"Squad, move to the right in threes, right — turn, by the left, quick — march!" echoed across the parade square outside the Owen Sound barracks. This was not the movie portrayal of an army drill, where profanity and sarcasm were hurled at left-footed recruits by drill instructors. Instead, there was a professional and sharply given series of instructions. After initial curiosity and some amusement at the exaggerated drill movements, many recruits probably wondered why the army kept them practicing drills when soldiers were supposed to be taught to fight. There was no doubt the army took drill very seriously. Even if it had been explained that drill was a way of instilling discipline, pride, and the cohesion needed for success in battle, to the young men the repeated practice of the same routine over many hours was almost certainly a disappointment. What seemed needless attention to detail on the parade square was seen by their officers and non-coms as instilling qualities

Russ photographed beside his home in Owen Sound shortly after enlisting with the Grey and Simcoe Foresters.

needed to endure the stress of war. In the army's view, the skill with which a unit drilled was a direct indication of the skill of the troops and their officers.[8]

The Foresters lacked room to house all the new troops, so men from town stayed at home overnight, while recruits from the surrounding towns and countryside stayed in the barracks. Owen Sound now had a military feel to it, as the more than five hundred men in the overseas and home service units were required to wear their uniforms at all times. The feeling that Canada was at war was unmistakeable.

———◆———

Russ and Perry arrived at the arena for the Georgians' next home game following a full day of training. For the first time they arrived in their army uniforms. It gave a different feeling to the dressing room. Since the Foresters began recruiting, local men on the team now fell into two categories: those who had enlisted and those who had not. When Russ and Perry took to the floor and looked into the stands, there too they saw men in uniform peppered among the spectators. There was a filter now separating them from those not in uniform. The Georgians easily defeated the visiting Burlington club. Perry was quick on his feet, darting tirelessly through the opposition defence, while Russ was reliable stopping opponents who ventured toward Owen Sound's goal. Their team had so far only been beaten twice this season, both times by Orangeville, the league leaders. After the game, Perry, Gerry, Jack MacLeod, and several other Georgians players dropped by the Colombo house. They sipped rye whiskey on the front porch. Their voices and laughter grew louder as they relaxed. Before long Blanche came outside, and they fell silent.

"Oh, Sweet," she said to Russ, "could you and your friends be a little quieter. I'm afraid you are going to disturb the neighbours." Addressing the others she said, "It's so nice to see you boys. I don't know why Russel never brings his friends home." Russ turned his eyes towards the ceiling as she went back inside.[9]

The silence was palpable as Russ's friends and teammates looked at each other.

"Sweet?" one of the players was barely able to get out before breaking into hysterical laughter.

"Sweet!" the others took up the refrain. "Sweet!" they repeated over and over, howling with laughter. Twenty-four-year-old Russ wondered what his mother could have been thinking. Inside, Blanche heard the laughter and was glad that Russ was having such a good time with his friends.

———————◆———————

The following Saturday, at seven a.m. sharp, the Active Force Foresters from Owen Sound arrived at the barracks with an army knapsack holding personal belongings. They boarded twenty trucks and travelled in convoy to Camp Borden, escorted from Collingwood by two Royal Canadian Air Force planes.

Camp Borden was the country's major army base and home to Canada's largest military airfield. Driving into the camp that Saturday afternoon, the Foresters entered a small military city, with dozens of huts and barracks, fifteen thousand soldiers, and fields filled with hundreds of tents. Feelings among the arriving recruits were mixed. Some felt they were at the start of an adventure, others wondered what they had gotten themselves into, and some were already homesick. As the trucks stopped, and the men jumped out, the Foresters saw a small village of tents erected by their advance party. Arranged with precision in rows and columns, the tents were allocated to the four companies comprising the Foresters: Company A from Owen Sound; B Company from Barrie; C from North Bay, Kirkland Lake, and Timmins; and D Company from Sault Ste. Marie and Sudbury.

The men were taken to the camp storehouse where they were issued a blanket and a straw-filled mattress called a pallaise. Soon after, the Foresters' mess tents were opened and the men received their first army meal.

That evening there was time for reflection, and it began sinking in that they had committed themselves to a way of life ending most personal freedoms. Some were undoubtedly having second thoughts, but those were by and large kept to themselves. Despite orders to the contrary, liquor bottles appeared from soldier's knapsacks, and as the evening wore on it helped turn the mood more cheerful. A recruit was hoisted onto the roof of one of the latrines by his mates and began singing. Foresters strolled over for the impromptu concert, a crowd forming and joining in the songs. It helped relieve some of the melancholy, and the officers, sitting in their mess, took it as a good sign as the men strolled back to their tents singing "Pack Up Your Troubles."[10]

The next day Russ woke at six a.m. to the harsh blaring of a trumpet playing reveille. A sergeant yelled they had an hour to wash, shave, eat, and then assemble for an address by the colonel. The thousand men rushed about and assembled at the appointed time in their platoons on the crowded parade ground. They were inspected by their officers, and then Colonel Rutherford took his place in front of them. He told his second-in-command to have the men stand easy. The thousand men spread their legs shoulder width and relaxed, their arms at their sides, eyes focused straight ahead.

The address lasted more than an hour in the hot Sunday morning sun. Rutherford spoke of his expectations for them, and what their expectations should be of one another. He told them of the need for "comradeship, cooperation, cleanliness, and good conduct." Rutherford had been a lieutenant with one of Owen Sound's regiments in the Great War, and he told them of the camaraderie shared by the men he'd served with. He described the training they would undergo, from map reading to marksmanship. He would stand by them as their commanding officer, just as he expected each of them to stand by him and their fellows in representing the regiment.

The next weeks were filled with activities intended to turn the civilian recruits into soldiers. The days were spent with marching drills, rifle practice, and skewering with bayonets straw dummies strung from wooden gibbets.[11] After four weeks, the men seemed transformed. Their faces were tanned from the outdoor exercise, and they were already well-schooled in military discipline. However, the novelty of camp life had worn off.

By the middle of July, after a month sleeping in tents, the Foresters moved into newly constructed huts. Bugle reveille at six a.m. was followed by a rush to be one of those fortunate to shower before the supply of hot water was exhausted. The men shaved shoulder to shoulder at long galvanized tubs, hot and cold taps spaced every few feet. They arrived to stand in line for breakfast with their metal dishes. Each man had to eat and put his part of the hut in order before the bugler's call-to-parade at eight a.m. Blankets, pallaise, extra uniforms, personal belongings, and dishes had to be arranged in neat rows along the centre of each hut. After daily inspection, the officer in charge awarded a flag for the most orderly hut. That flag was displayed for long periods on the hut belonging to Owen Sound Company's segregated platoon of Native American soldiers, volunteers from the Cape Croker Reserve north of town.

Every morning except Sunday, the men assembled in the parade ground for inspection, followed by callisthenics until nine. Most days they marched in the parade ground from nine until noon. Training resumed after lunch, sometimes at the rifle range. At other times it might be a lesson in semaphore or a route march through the countryside.

In the few hours of free time in the evenings, many went to one of Borden's regimental canteens. Located near the Foresters' section of the camp, the Salvation Army hut was a popular place to write letters home, sit and talk, watch movies, or listen to a visiting band. By ten, everyone was back in their hut for lights out at 10:15. But often lights out was short-lived, as moments after the orderly officer made his rounds, the bulbs strung the length of the hut were switched back on to resume poker games.

———————◆———————

Russ found the physical challenges of life at Camp Borden easy compared to the tough winter at McFadden's camp. But the mental challenges of the army were different than those in civilian life. After eight years of manual labour jobs, Russ must have grown used to taking direction from those who might be more experienced but lacking his bright mind. To not suffer fools in civilian life was possible if you were prepared to walk away from a boss who proved intolerable. But a lowly army private displaying that attitude almost certainly found himself in trouble.

Compounding Russ's rebellious attitude towards mindless authority was the fact that he was sensitive about not having completed high school. With a sharp mind, he could derive pleasure from demonstrating that education and rank didn't necessarily translate into superior intellect. He may already have adopted the fractured Latin phrase he espoused in later years: "*Illigitimus non carborundem est.*" For those not familiar with the saying, he would translate it: "Don't let the bastards grind you down."

Even in a regiment as forgiving as the Foresters, where building esprit de corps was considered more important than crisply saluting every passing officer, Russ likely found use for his Latin maxim. He was, after all, not part of the permanent army, and must have at times found the army's insistence on arcane military protocol akin to water torture. It was hard for most recruits, much less one who was sharp-minded and of a rebellious spirit, to see how the manner a blanket was folded, or the very precise arrangement of personal items in a footlocker, was going to help win the war.

———————◆———————

Alcohol was not allowed in the barracks, but it was practically impossible to prevent it. On a few occasions Russ consumed more than someone should who had to rise early the next morning. Once, after he fell into an alcohol-aided sleep, someone put a chocolate bar down the back of his shorts. The next morning, Russ realized there was a sticky mess. His reaction to what he thought had happened more than satisfied the perpetrators.

On another occasion, he woke with a pounding hangover. Staggering out of bed after the six a.m. reveille, he pulled on his uniform and stumbled onto the parade square. He groaned inwardly when the Sergeant told them to report back with packs and rifle. They were going on a ten-mile run.

With packs on their back and rifles in their hands, Russ's platoon left the parade ground at a slow run. His legs felt like lead weights were attached to them and the pack jarred with each step. Soon others began passing him, then he was running by himself. He continued, his head feeling like it would explode. With his eyes fixed on the ground Russ became aware that someone had dropped back. Glancing up, he saw Perry.

"How are you feeling, Russ?" he asked.

"Words won't do it justice," Russ said.

"We'll go together," said Perry. Russ grunted in reply as the pair ran, the platoon pulling further ahead of them. As they slowly trod on, it seemed as though Russ might make it. But both knew what lay ahead. Rising before them in the distance was a steep hill. Reaching the bottom of it, Russ stopped.

"I'll never do it," he said, leaning forward and gasping for breath. He dropped his pack and rifle and fell to his knees.

"Wait here," said Perry. He picked up Russ's pack. Carrying both packs and two rifles, he proceeded up the hill. Within a few minutes he was back.

"Climb on my back," he said.

"What? You're crazy! Leave me here to die."

"C'mon, you sunovabitch. If you don't finish this run, you'll never get your pass for this weekend. We have a lacrosse game we promised to play, and you are going to be there."

Russ looked up at his friend, standing over him with his hand extended. Grabbing onto it, he pulled himself upward. As he did, Perry went down on one knee and pulled Russ over his shoulders, wrapping his arm around Russ's leg and balancing his friend's weight across his shoulders. Grunting, Perry stood up and began climbing the hill. Step over step he carried Russ forward. When he reached the top, the two men collapsed in the grass. Perry started laughing, and soon the two of them were lying on their backs, howling like schoolboys.

After a few minutes, they climbed to their feet and put their packs on. When they reached the parade ground, the rest of the column had long since arrived and been dismissed. They went to find the Sergeant, who briefly studied them, saying nothing to the troopers before dismissing them.

———◆———

Relief from army discipline, close living quarters, and mediocre food came every other weekend when passes were issued. Most of the thousands of soldiers and airmen boarded trains for Toronto, where hostels were cheap and entertainment plentiful. Many of Owen Sound's Foresters headed home. Russ and Perry used their weekend passes to join the Georgians wherever they were playing.

Sometimes, someone from the team would come by with a car to pick them up. At others they drove to the game in the Colonel's personal car, which he loaned them. Perhaps the Colonel felt it would boost morale to have two of the Owen Sound Company playing for the hometown Georgians.

The lacrosse season had been exciting. After falling behind Orangeville early in the year, they had clawed their way back, finishing tied in points. In a two-game series to choose an overall winner, Owen Sound won both games, entering the playoffs as regular season champion. The Georgians won their first-round playoff, progressing to the final against Orangeville. The Georgians won the first game of the series in Owen Sound, but Orangeville struck back to take game two at home. They exchanged wins at home in the next two games, setting up a fifth and deciding game in Owen Sound. Perry and Russ were in Owen Sound to take part in the league final on September 5. Two thousand fans packed the arena, and they tensely watched the close contest. They were able to relax and enjoy the game in the second period, when with Perry up front and Russ and Jack MacLeod on defence, Owen Sound scored nine unanswered goals to burst the game open. Despite missing their star player, Gerry Johnson, who was injured, the Georgians went on to an overwhelming 32–13 win and the series victory. They would next enter the provincial playdowns.

In a team picture taken on the floor of the arena after the final game, Russ wears the practice sweater he'd used all season, the rest of the team in striped team jerseys bearing the Georgians name. Wives and girlfriends waited outside the arena for the Georgians to shower and dress. Gradually the players came out, each wearing a new team jacket. When Gerry, Perry, and Russ emerged, Russ and Perry in their army uniforms, carrying team jackets, Gerry without one. Gerry's wife Marge knew from the looks on their faces something was wrong. Later that evening Gerry explained.

After winning the championship, Jim MacLeod had entered the dressing room carrying a large box. He called for the players to be quiet and gave a short speech, thanking them for their hard work and for such a fine season. Then he opened the box and from it took a Georgians team jacket. The players saw the team name embroidered on a crest. The jackets were a token of gratitude from team management, he explained.

Jim threw the jacket he was holding to the nearest player. Reaching into the box he took out another jacket, throwing it to the next man. Jim threw a jacket to each man in turn as Russ waited his turn. Perry, sitting to Russ's right, caught his. But as Russ readied himself to catch the next jacket, it was not thrown to him. It went to the man on his left. The players fell silent as everyone looked at Jim and then at Russ.

Gerry watched as Jim continued tossing the jackets to the remaining players; he knew about the disagreement over the sweater. Finally Jim reached the last player on his right. It was Gerry. The room was silent as Jim kicked the now empty box into the centre of the room. Saying nothing, Gerry walked across the room and handed his jacket to Russ.[12]

The Georgians' opponent in the provincial semi-finals was the team from Brooklin, a town near Oshawa. Russ and Perry continued appearing at the Georgians games, made possible by Colonel Rutherford approving their leave from Camp Borden. Owen Sound beat Brooklin in three straight games. It qualified them to play for the provincial Senior B Lacrosse Championship against Sarnia. Everyone expected the series to be their toughest challenge.

The Owen Sound Georgians lacrosse team, on winning the Ontario Senior B Championship in 1940. Back row, left to right: Roy "Sally" Tyler (trainer), Andy Blair, executive members Bill Gilligan, Charlie Gagan, Charlie Peacock, Ted Manners, and Harry Ashcroft, Jack MacLeod, and manager Jim MacLeod. Middle row, left to right: Bun White, Ken MacLeod, Russ Colombo, John McConachie, Harvey LeBarr, Orville McDonald. Front row, left to right: John Standeaven, Fred Smith, Gerry Johnson, Chuck Harden, Jack Fletcher, mascot Bud Rush, Tommy Burlington, Hiram Dean, Perry Wilson, Maurice Cassidy.
(Photo courtesy of the Owen Sound Sports Hall of Fame)

———————◆———————

After nearly three months at Camp Borden, the regiment's officers decided to take the Foresters on the road. It would allow the regiment to practice moving across country and give the men a few days break from camp life, showing off their training in their hometowns. The Foresters marched through Barrie, Orillia, Midland, and Collingwood that first day. In each town, a thousand soldiers jumped from the trucks and marched down the town's main street, greeted by cheering crowds at each stop.

While the Foresters spent the night in tents in Collingwood, Russ and Perry left to play lacrosse in Owen Sound that evening. The Georgians easily won the opening game in the best of three series, beating Sarnia 24–5. The crowd in the arena, packed to standing room capacity, cheered their team as the time clock ticked off the seconds.

The next morning, the regiment paraded at the Indian Reservation at Chippewa Hill. Foresters from Owen Sound were excited at their chance to parade in front of friends and family. They had come a long way from the group who had left town a few months earlier. Their arrival was also anticipated by the people of Owen Sound. For the first time the town was going to see its sons parade in uniform. Anyone with a Canadian Red Ensign, Canada's national flag, had it hanging in front of their home, businesses decorated their stores and put out their flags, and children were let out of school to attend the parade. The city and local businesses took a full page in the local newspaper to welcome the Foresters, with the message:

> Now, after nearly three months of strenuous training at Camp Borden, the Battalion is coming back to visit. Owen Sound, the home of many of the Grey-Simcoe officers and men is mighty proud of this Regiment and we know every man will live up to the splendid traditions and achievements of the famous 147th and 248th Regiment in the last war. Thrilling with pride Owen Sound extends a royal welcome and wishes every one of these men the Best of Luck and God's Blessings when they go forth to battle a ruthless foe threatening our Homes and Civil Rights.

The Foresters arrived in Owen Sound early in the afternoon. Russ and Perry were waiting when they arrived. When the regiment began to march, it was led by Colonel Rutherford, followed by the drum and bugle band,

and then the troops, who marched in their platoons, each man with a rifle on his shoulder. People stood three and four deep along the main street, applauding, waving and calling greetings to soldiers they knew. Young boys on bikes made an impromptu addition, riding back and forth along the column of soldiers. Children waved small Canadian flags and cheered the soldiers parading past. It was a stirring sight, the Regiment stretching for blocks, marching three abreast, each with one arm swinging to breast pocket height, the other holding the butt of his rifle, a thousand boots striking the pavement in unison sounding like drums.

Marching with his platoon, Russ heard his name called several times as the parade wended through town. Then he heard his mother's voice calling. From the corner of his eye, he saw her and his brother Jack. It was hard to say who was prouder, the people of Owen Sound whose young men had been transformed into soldiers, or the men marching proudly in front of family and neighbours.

As the regiment reached the end of the parade route, it continued marching south to Harrison Park. Waiting trucks took the soldiers to the barracks on 14th Street West, where the men fanned out towards their homes or downtown.

Russ and Perry walked together, greeted by friends and acquaintances. Perry, who was from Fergus, was invited to stay with Russ. During dinner they told stories of life at Camp Borden. Later, the two soldiers slipped out of the house and made their way to Gerry and Marge Johnson's home, stopping to buy a bottle of whiskey. Although Prohibition had ended in Ontario more than a decade before, a city plebiscite had kept Owen Sound a dry town. Nevertheless, Russ and Perry had no problem buying liquor, since bootleggers' houses were well-known throughout town.

It was early in the morning when they returned home. Russ hoped his brother's snoring would cover the creaking wooden stairs. Perry proceeded to the bedroom on the third floor. Russ went to his room on the second floor and was asleep almost before his head touched the pillow.

His eyes flew open after what seemed an instant. Light streamed through the window and Russ reached for his watch. It was seven thirty, and he knew the Foresters had boarded their trucks at seven and left town. He and Perry were instead headed to the next game in the series that evening in Sarnia as the Foresters continued their tour to other towns in the district.

Sarnia took the early lead before Russ replied with the Georgians' opening goal, halfway through the first period.

"Russ Colombo and Johnny Standeavan started the ball rolling in the first period, when trailing 2–0, the two players combined on a lovely passing attack to sink the first Owen Sound goal," the Sun-Times reported.

When the Georgians finally took the lead, Sarnia all but collapsed. The Georgians won 15–9.

"One of the Owen Sound players who couldn't be stopped last evening was Perry Wilson," said the paper. "… Wilson picked up a pair last night, but he went like a million dollars all through the game. Jack MacLeod with a pair of goals and a like number of assists turned in a good game for the winners … (and) coach Gerry Johnson formed the backbone of the club's powerful … defence."

It was Owen Sound's first Ontario Lacrosse championship in thirty years, and the players were greeted as returning heroes.

———————◆———————

Thanksgiving weekend was a three-day leave for most of Camp Borden. Like many Foresters from Owen Sound, Russ made his way home, joined by Perry. But instead of returning Monday night when his leave was over, Russ and Perry showed up at Gerry's house. They were staying a few more days. As their absence stretched to Wednesday, the provosts began searching for them, phoning Blanche, asking if she knew where Russ was. He was constantly on the lookout for provosts. When Russ appeared at Gerry's house, he asked if the provosts had come looking for him there. It was cloak-and-dagger in Owen Sound.

When Russ woke Sunday morning, he was five days late returning from leave. He relished the luxury of relaxing a moment longer without a bugler's reveille shattering the peace. When he came out of this room, he called to Perry, who was already coming downstairs. The smell of breakfast had woken them. As they sat down at the kitchen table, Blanche asked how long they were staying. Russ told her they were heading to Camp Borden later that day. He didn't tell her they had been AWOL since Monday.

Later that day they decided to go downtown, wearing their uniforms as military protocol required. They split up, agreeing to meet for coffee in an hour.

However, Russ and Perry were not the only Foresters in Owen Sound. Russ was just across the 10th Street Bridge when he heard someone shout, "There's one of 'em!"

Russ heard the sound of army boots striking the pavement. Looking behind, he saw two provosts running towards him. He instinctively began running and people stopped to watch the humorous sight of three soldiers in a footrace through downtown. Someone called out encouragement to Russ, while others laughed.

Russ raced towards a phone booth. Close behind came the provosts, and Russ barely closed the phone booth door before they arrived. Inside, he put his legs up, holding the door closed with his feet, his back braced against the phone booth wall. One of the provosts put his shoulder to the door to force his way in, while the other yelled at Russ to come out. Russ's legs barely budged. Coolly, he reached into his pocket and pulled out a handful of coins, from which he took a nickel. Lifting the receiver while the provosts continued hammering at the door, Russ reached behind his head, inserted the coin and dialled.

The phone rang. "This is Russ," he said to his mother.

"Sweet … what is that noise?" she asked.

"It's a couple of friends from the army," he said. "It looks like I'm going back to Camp sooner than I'd thought." Russ tried to talk calmly.

"When will you be leaving?"

"I doubt I'll be able to get back to the house. So I'll say goodbye now." He hung up and lowered his legs. The provosts, who had stopped trying to force their way into the phone booth, waited for him to emerge. Each took Russ by an arm, down the street, past the restaurant where Russ and Perry were to meet. Russ saw Perry laughing through the restaurant's curtain.

The provosts escorted Russ to a nearby parking lot, where several other Foresters were in the back of an army truck. "Climb in, we're leaving," one said. As the truck turned the corner heading towards the hill out of Owen Sound, they heard someone yelling and saw a soldier running after them. He slowly gained on the accelerating truck. He leapt, and those in the back pulled him the rest of the way in. The soldier came to his feet. It was Perry, and he was still laughing.

Once at camp, Russ, Perry, and the other AWOL soldiers received punishment — normally a day confined to barracks and loss of pay for each day's absence. For this extended absence Russ may have been given additional punishment — perhaps this was the time he was told to report to the drill hall with his toothbrush, where he was instructed to get down on his hands and knees and use it to scrub the floor of the cavernous room. If Russ's long absence was surprising, what followed in a few months surpassed it. In April 1941, he was appointed batman to the regiment's commanding officer, Lieutenant-Colonel Rutherford.

Becoming batman to the commanding officer was an honour. It would not have been given lightly, and must have reflected in some measure Russ's achievements in training. The appointment would help shape the remainder of his military service.

Being a commanding officer's batman is an appointment that is highly sought after. It can lead to quick promotion, but in the Foresters, it meant much more. Colonel Rutherford was greatly respected by his men, who had affectionately dubbed him "Uncle Tom." One of the Colonel's sons said his father felt towards the Foresters the way a father does towards flesh-and-blood sons,[13] and the affection was widely returned. Russ's choice as the Colonel's batman was no small matter.

Russ took charge of the Colonel's personal and professional needs, cleaning and pressing his uniforms, straightening his quarters, delivering messages, and anything else the Colonel needed. At the same time, Russ was required to perform well in all the training and exercises. Not doing so would have been an embarrassment to the Colonel.

On December 21, 1941, the Foresters were granted a two-week Christmas furlough. Most of the camp emptied. For Canadian families with soldiers home on leave, this Christmas was tinged with thoughts of the war. The Luftwaffe filled the air over Britain, and German submarine Wolfpacks roamed the North Atlantic, hunting Canadian ships carrying aid vital to the beleaguered island nation. The threat of an invasion remained high, and in the back of every Forester's mind was the knowledge that the regiment might soon be sent to England, and this could be their last Christmas at home for years to come.

FOUR

Auf der Suche nach einer Heimat
In Search of a Country

Frank was fifteen and had been in the Sudetenland only a few months when what was left of Czechoslovakia began to disintegrate. One after another, ethnic regions either declared their independence from the Czechs or were occupied by neighbouring countries. From Leitmeritz, Frank followed with interest any news from his old hometown, now part of the German Reich. He was happy his family and friends in Freistadt and Ostrau were finally safe. Whether those who had threatened Germans faced any consequences for their actions, either from civilians or the new German authorities, he had no way of knowing.

Although the Sudetenland had been annexed by Germany less than a year earlier, the Nazi Party already had a strong presence. It affected Frank's father's position as a court official in the prosecutor's office in Leitmeritz, which could only be confirmed after Franz produced documents proving he had no Jewish ancestry for at least two generations. The Nazis also made their presence felt through social clubs, which had a long tradition among Germans. Nazi clubs arose to compete with those run by social organizations or church groups. Franz joined one of those run by the Nazi Party, a car club, for those interested in driving. To join, he had become a member of the party.

Frank was angry when he learned his father had joined the car club. He believed his father joined the club only because he wanted to learn how to drive a car or motorcycle, something he had hoped to do for some time. Frank felt it was insincere, and if his father was going to join the Nazi party, it should not be to take advantage of the opportunity to learn how to drive or to gain an advantage at work. Later that summer, Frank's mother Josephina also took the pledge of allegiance and volunteered for a position with the local branch. For many, joining the National Socialists was a means of advancement, not a passion or a cause. For German emigrant Sebastian Haffner, who fled Germany with his Jewish fiancée to Great Britain (intermarriage was by then punishable by law in Germany), the "true" Nazis could be distinguished, as he wrote in 1940.[1]

German troops assembled in parade formation on the main square of Leitmeritz, October 12, 1938, shortly after the occupation of the Sudetenland.
(German Federal Archive [Bundesarchiv], Bild 146-2006-0017, photographer: o.Ang)

Who is a Nazi? How can he be recognized? Certainly not by his hanging a swastika flag out of his window; everyone does that in Germany today. It means nothing. Nor by his being a member of some Nazi organization or of the Party itself. Everyone who has a family to care for and cannot afford to lose his job is in one or another Nazi organization, and if he had the bad luck to pursue a calling in which membership of the Party is demanded, he joins the Party.

In Haffner's view,

The real Nazis, therefore, are not to be easily identified. There exist, however, a number of signs by which a man may know, until he has proof to the contrary, that he is dealing with a Nazi. Roughly speaking, the Nazis are found among the older SA or Storm Troop formations.... the lower Party functionaries, "leaders" of the Hitler Youth, and, above all, the SS or Black Guards.... But the Party badge ... is no sure proof — even if acquired before (the Nazi's seized power) in 1933.

But if it is not easy to recognize the Nazis from external signs and badges, there are some ... touchstones from which it is possible in every single case to establish whether a particular individual is a Nazi. Of these the most important and the most simple is the attitude to the policy pursued towards the Jews in Germany. Many people who are loyal adherents of the regime disapprove of the anti-Semitic excesses, others seek to ignore, to minimize, or, in border cases, to excuse them. All such are not Nazi. A Nazi is one who assents unreservedly to this general and permanent sadistic orgy, and takes part in it.

When Frank's family arrived in Leitmeritz in 1938, he found Germans from many different backgrounds. They were from Germany, from the Sudetenland, from Czechoslovakia, and from Austria. But they were all Germans. Back in his home in Freistadt, Frank's friends were not only ethnic German, but also Czech, Polish, and Jewish. In Leitmeritz, such friendships were frowned upon, especially if one's friends were Jewish. However, anti-Semitism was not restricted to Germany; it was also far from a uniquely Nazi characteristic. But the extreme anti-Semitic environment Frank was plunged into at the age of fifteen was far more pervasive and violent than anything he could have imagined, and it was now demonstrably a part of government policy.

In school, he learned about the German Reich of Bismarck, reborn under Adolf Hitler. However, it was not long before Frank realized that in the German Reich, this "pan-Germanic nation," there were two types of Germans: those from the homeland and those ethnic Germans from outside the nation's boundaries. He could see that Germans born in Germany viewed those from outside the homeland as somehow lesser.

This was made even clearer when he listened to those who had come from Germany to Leitmeritz to instruct the Sudeten Germans in what it meant to be a German. Frank knew what his German heritage meant and resented the idea he needed instruction to understand it. He and his family were just as legitimately German in their own way.

What was really being taught was what it meant to be part of Nazi Germany. This concept Frank and other younger people did not understand.

The teachers talked about the superior Aryan race of which they were a part, and how it needed to be kept pure. They were told the Nazi Party was necessary to protect the German Reich from its enemies, especially threats from Socialists, Communists, and Jews. And they also talked about Hitler in a manner that elevated him from a regular man and political leader to the personification of the German nation. Such an idea was not only foreign to Sudeten Germans, but for Frank at fifteen, was impossible to conceive.

———————◆———————

Frank's parents, however, were being drawn more deeply into Nazism. The first Christmas in the Sikora home in Leitmeritz began as any other. The Christmas tree was decorated and the special Yule-time dinner prepared. The Sikoras were a Catholic family, and after dinner, as was their custom, Frank, as the oldest son was expected to read a passage from the Bible. He prepared for that special time and privilege. But when it came time for the Bible reading, Frank's father announced, "This year we are going to do things differently.

"Now that we are in the German Reich," he told his wife and children, "we will do things as the Germans do. Tonight, Frank will read from *Mein Kampf* instead of from the Bible."

Frank was shocked. "Why should we change what we normally do?" he asked. "There's no reason we have to do this."

"Things are different here," his father insisted. "Here is the book, now read." Franz placed the book with Hitler's photograph on the cover on the table in front of Frank.

"Where should I start?" Frank asked angrily, not knowing what to say. He hesitated, hoping his mother would intervene. But she said nothing.

"It doesn't matter, just open it anywhere and read," said his father.

Frank reluctantly opened to the beginning of the book and began reading. But he read only a few sentences before pushing the book away. Scowling at the book on the table, then at his father he said, "This is so stupid!"

———————◆———————

Now that he was in German territory, Frank was required to attend meetings of the Hitler Youth (Hitler Jugend, or HJ). Meetings were held once or twice a week for about two hours, with boys fourteen to seventeen required to attend. Adults who had come to Leitmeritz from Germany were in charge of the HJ, and children of these Reich Germans were appointed the junior officers in the troops of local boys. On April 20, Hitler's birthday, a ceremony was held for new inductees, who took an oath of allegiance: "I promise to be faithful to my Führer, Adolf Hitler," they were required to recite in unison. "I promise obedience and respect to him and to the leaders he shall appoint over me."

Much of the time at HJ meetings was spent playing sports and in physical training, with an eye to preparing the boys for eventual military service. The training might involve throwing practice grenades or using small arms. The children also were taught the history of the Nazi party, its important people, places, and events. The story of the Felderrnhalle, the site of the unsuccessful Nazi coup attempt in 1923, was told. This occurred in Munich, where the Bavarian State Police confronted a Nazi march to overthrow the government. When Hitler, with Great War heroes Hermann Göring and Erich Ludendorff, led their supporters forward after being ordered to halt, the police fired on them, killing sixteen. After Hitler seized power in 1933, the Nazis who died there were declared heroes, and a memorial was erected at the Felderrnhalle.

The volunteers from Germany found the boys of Leitmeritz full of youthful enthusiasm. That summer in 1939, Frank was excited when his HJ troop leader, only a few years older than the rest, received permission from the Bannführer (the city's senior HJ leader) for a group from Leitmeritz to visit Munich. He decided they would go by "Autostopp" (hitchhiking, in German), a new method of travel in the Reich. The boys' parents had

During a Hitler Youth meeting in Odenwald, Germany, a young instructor describes how to use a rifle. He stands in front of a map of Europe with the inscription "Das Deutsche Reich Adolf Hitler's."
(German Federal Archive [Bundesarchiv], Bild 146-1973-060-53, photographer: o.Ang)

reservations about them travelling so far away without an adult, but none of the parents were openly critical of the idea. Even Frank's parents, who were Nazi party members, were afraid to express their concerns, lest it be taken as criticism of the Bannführer or the party.

When Frank's mother, Josephina, did speak with the Bannführer about the trip, it was to insist the boys wear their Hitler Youth uniforms while travelling: the brown shirt, red and white armband with swastika, black scarf with a leather thong to hold it in place, grey shorts, and the Hitler Youth knife with its inscription *"Blut und Ehre"* (Blood and Honour) at their side. The Bannführer agreed with Frank's mother, and all the boys were instructed to arrive the morning of the trip dressed in their uniforms.

On the day of their departure in the summer of 1939, Josephina gave Frank a postcard with their home address on it. She made him promise to mail it as soon as he reached Munich. He put the postcard in his jacket and left with his friend, Rudy Hoch. They met the other boys and went to the outskirts of Leitmeritz, divided into pairs, and stood in their uniforms waiting for a car to come. After a few minutes one approached. The boys watched expectantly, but the driver passed without even slowing. Soon another came, but it also passed, the dust it stirred stinging their eyes. One car after another left them standing there. After an hour, not one group was picked up. Their HJ leader decided they'd take the train to the town of Eger to try their luck, about 165 kilometres away, nearer the German border.

They wondered if their Hitler Youth uniforms might be causing motorists to be apprehensive, so they decided to change into their street clothes. When they went to the roadside at Eger, uniforms in their knapsacks, the first pair of boys was picked up within minutes. Soon they were all on their way. Frank and Rudy, who were travelling together, made great progress, but with little knowledge of the roads or the geography, they became lost, and rather than arriving in Munich they instead came to Vienna. It was a wonderful mistake. They spent the rest of the day exploring the old city. It was the largest Frank had ever been in, with ornate architecture and palaces, but what he marvelled at most was for the first time in his life hearing nothing spoken but German.

The next day, Frank and Rudy made their way back to the highway and reached Munich that evening. There they found the rest of the boys, who had been waiting impatiently. When Frank and Rudy excitedly told the others about Vienna, the rest of the group was jealous.

Now that they were in the heart of Nazi Germany, they donned their Hitler Youth uniforms and began their tour of Munich. Their HJ leader took them to the sites of important early Nazi events. They stood before the Felderrnhalle on Odeonplatz, where they were told Nazism had started. Meeting people in the streets, the group from Leitmeritz extended their right arms in the Nazi salute. The people they met responded not with a matching salute but by laughing at them. They met with similar reactions at other sites important in Nazi folklore. What had started out an exciting trip, visiting places Frank had been taught had a larger meaning, was becoming a disappointment, if not a joke. It was clear that even their HJ leader had no real interest in what they were seeing.

Disappointed with Munich, Frank was glad when the HJ leader decided they should travel south to Berchtesgaden. Maybe there, Frank thought, he would feel more inspired. They would visit the Obersalzberg, the area above Berchtesgaden where Hitler and other senior Nazi party leaders had their country estates. When they arrived, they found the mountains impressive, but Berchtesgaden was an unremarkable small town, and Obersalzberg

Map of western and central Europe showing the approximate route of Frank Sikora's trip across the German Reich in 1939. Cities and towns named are those mentioned in Frank's story. National boundaries are those in 1938, including changes brought about at that time by German expansionism and aggression. German city names are used although Czech and Polish names of cities in Czechoslovakia were used concurrently. Based on a map reproduced with permission from Stanford University's Spatial History Project on "Building the New Order: 1938-1945."
(www.stanford.edu/group/spatialhistory/cgi-bin/site/pub.php?id=51&project_id=)

was inaccessible, the tight security zone around the Nazi leaders' estates preventing the boys from seeing the homes. They had hoped to be lucky and see some of the famous German leaders in person, but once again were disappointed.

The group could not decide what to do next. Some wanted to head back to Leitmeritz while others suggested climbing the hiking trails on nearby Watzmann Mountain. The second highest mountain in Germany, the Watzmann was not a climb to be taken casually. Although Frank was the youngest in the group, he had previously climbed a two thousand-metre mountain. He knew that in street shoes and summer clothing, they had no chance of reaching the summit. The others disregarded his warnings and went ahead anyway, Rudy among them, leaving Frank by himself.

Alone, he wondered what he should do. They might be gone all day, and if they were fortunate enough to reach the Watzmann House, an inn high up the mountain, they might have to stay there overnight, leaving him stranded in Berchtesgaden.

The longer he sat there thinking back on almost every stage of the trip, the angrier he became. He was disillusioned and upset. The planning for the trip was poor, and no one they met seemed the least excited by the "glorious German Reich." He was angry at all the time spent in HJ meetings, the meaningless political slogans they were taught, and the indifference of the people they had met in Munich. The travellers had not spoken about it, but Frank was certain he was not the only one feeling that way.

What was he to do? He was fifteen, far from home and his parents for the first time. He wanted to explore Germany, and if the others were not interested, then he would go on his own. He decided to travel west as far as he could. He went to the roadside, stuck out his thumb, and in a few minutes a car pulled over. He was on his way, not sure where he was going, but excited about discovering Germany for himself.

Frank took leave of his ride at the Swiss border near Lake Bodensee. He unfolded his map and spread it out. Before him was all of Germany. Everywhere were borders: France, Belgium, Holland, Denmark, Poland. Within those boundaries Germany waited. He returned to the highway and continued his journey.

From Lake Bodensee he travelled to Karlsruhe, then to Cologne, Hamburg, Rostock, and Berlin. He met many people along the way, some providing rides, some offering a place for the night, and still others giving him dinner. At one point he stopped and helped a farmer, fulfilling a pledge all German boys were to carry out during their summer school break. The further he travelled, the more apparent it became that Germany was more or less the same as home and not nearly as exciting as it had been made to seem by the HJ leaders.

When the other boys returned to Leitmeritz after a week, all they could tell Frank's parents was that he was gone when they had come down from the mountain. They had returned to Leitmeritz expecting to find him there. Two weeks later, Frank showed up at home. He looked ragged, and when his mother saw him she nearly collapsed.

"Where have you been?" she demanded, relieved but exasperated. "I reported you missing to the police, and they are looking for you!"

It was only then that he remembered. Reaching into the side pocket of his jacket, he pulled out the postcard his mother had given him.

"I am starved. What is for dinner?" Frank asked, handing her the postcard.

That night, Frank's mother spoiled him with a local specialty, a dumpling made around a plum and sprinkled with sugar. Normally, three or four was enough for a meal. Frank ate twenty-one. He was not punished by his parents for leaving the travel group. On the contrary, they admired his spirit and resourcefulness and wanted to hear all about his trip. They were impressed that he had seen Germany. He had even seen Berlin, which they never had. His trip had taken him completely around the country, from the Alps in the south to the Baltic Sea on Germany's northern coast, covering thousands of kilometres.

Frank kept his disappointment about the earlier part of the trip to himself. The Bannführer in Leitmeritz, his friend Karl Habel's father, heard about Frank's trip and thought so highly of the fifteen-year-old's initiative and resourcefulness that he asked Frank if he would be willing to be a troop leader for the Pimpfe, the Hitler Youth for ten to fourteen-year-old boys. Leitmeritz was divided into two distinct social groups. The north side of the city was wealthy and the children well-behaved, the south was poorer and the boys had a reputation for being wild. Frank, who lived in the north, agreed to be "Troop Leader South." The Bannführer presented him with the green and white cord for his uniform, signifying his position.

The first meeting took place in the main square of Leitmeritz, where he planned to teach the boys to march and to stand at attention. As the boys arrived in the public square and Frank called to them to stand in line, some of the older ones began to loudly mimic Frank's Czech accent. Many were barely younger than he, and soon it was clear they had no intention of taking orders from this outsider. Frank was helpless as the boys he was supposed to lead broke ranks and ran wildly around the square, yelling and laughing, ignoring Frank's shouts to return.

From behind where he stood Frank heard an adult say, "Someone should be in charge of these hooligans and get them under control."

Turning, Frank saw it was his schoolteacher, and his face flushed. He had been proud when the Bannführer asked him to be a leader. Now he felt only embarrassment. The next day, he returned the green and white Hitler Youth cord. Frank blamed himself, but his vision of turning the boys into a well-trained troop had always been doomed to failure. He should have received help from someone older.

But Frank's enthusiasm had gotten the better of his common sense.

———◆———

Frank's exploration of Germany happened the summer before Germany invaded Poland. On September 1, 1939, Germans were told the invasion of Poland was necessary to protect fellow Germans in Poland from attack. Hitler also declared in the Reichstag and through German newspapers and radio that attacks by Polish forces on German territory had taken place the evening of August 31, precipitating action by German forces.[2] German troops invaded Poland from the north, west, and south, and Polish resistance collapsed after Russia invaded from the east on September 17.

France and Britain were treaty-bound to come to Poland's defence. An ultimatum was issued that if German armed forces were not withdrawn from Poland, war would be declared. Hitler ignored the threat, and Britain and France formally declared war on Germany on September 3, 1939. People in the German territories were not anxious to go to war. However, after a few weeks without a major attack from the west, the mood relaxed, and by the end of September, Poland was subdued. The quiet seemed destined not to last, as Britain and France assembled their forces and German troops no longer needed in Poland rushed westward. For the moment, the countries did little beyond firing verbal assaults through their leaders.

———◆———

Since joining the Nazi party in Leitmeritz in 1939, Frank's father had always worn a Nazi party pin on his lapel. But during a family vacation to Freistadt in 1940, Frank noticed it was missing.

Frank asked, "Where is your Party pin?"

Without saying anything, Frank's father turned over the lapel of his jacket to reveal pin.

"While in the Beskydy Mountains of our ancestors," his father explained, "it is only important we be ourselves, not Party members."

"You are such a cheater!" Frank said accusingly.

————◆————

On May 11, 1940, German newspapers reported the opening of the offensive by German Army West through neutral countries Holland, Belgium, and Luxembourg. The Nazis called it a preventive strike, needed because Britain and France were planning to attack Germany through those countries. In coming weeks, the military seemed nearly indestructible. The victories were rapid and the setbacks few.

Daily reports through May and June told of success after success. May 14 — Liege falls, German paratroopers in Rotterdam. May 15 — Holland capitulates. May 18 — German troops enter Brussels. May 19 — German Army West advances into the heart of France, Antwerp falls. May 20 — 110,000 prisoners taken. May 28 — Dunkirk in flames, Paris airport bombarded. May 29 — Half a million Belgian soldiers surrender. May 31 — Great air attacks on British troops fleeing Dunkirk. June 4 — 330,000 prisoners taken at Flanders. June 5 — Over 1.2 million prisoners taken; weapons and materiel for 80 divisions captured. June 6 — Dunkirk falls, 40,000 prisoners taken. June 11 — Italy joins the war on the side of Germany against England and France. June 18 — France is finished. Petain requests peace. June 22 — France capitulates.

A message issued by Hitler to German newspapers, published on June 25, 1940, reads:

> German people! Your soldiers have in just under six weeks fought an heroic battle in the west against a brave enemy, which has now reached an end. Their deeds will go down in history as the greatest victory of all time. We thank God for this victory. The flags will fly throughout the Reich for ten days and the church bells will ring for seven days. Signed Adolf Hitler.

The newspapers also described the fate of some found guilty of listening to enemy radio reports. The newspaper *Rheinische Landeszeitung* in Düsseldorf[3] reported:

From Berlin 28th June 1940 comes the following report:

In recent days more radio criminals have been charged by the courts for listening to enemy propaganda and passing it on to others.

Andreas Kottke was convicted of listening to enemy hate-news and passing it on. He was given four years prison and four years loss of honour.

In Magdeburg, Otto Schulze was sentenced to five years prison and ten years loss of honour. Schulze listened to the enemy radio and passed on hate propaganda at least ten times between October 1939 and January 1940.

Otto Watzrodt talked his work colleagues into listening to foreign broadcasts, which the supervisor then allowed them to do. All these criminals received tough sentences.

These traitors listened to and passed on the lies broadcast by our enemy: by committing this crime, they destroy the spirit and morale of the whole German people! There is only one thing to do with such traitors, and that is to make them a head shorter! Give these creatures the death penalty.

As 1940 drew to a close, Frank readied himself for the last semester of high school. On turning eighteen after graduation, he would enter compulsory military training. Beyond that, his mother had plans for him to attend university. He was young, healthy, and like most boys at seventeen, felt indestructible. He was anxious to begin the next phase of his life. However, Frank had no way of knowing how chaotic and difficult the next few years would be.

FIVE

Trooper
Panzergrenadier

As far as most Foresters were concerned, Christmas furlough ended far too quickly. They returned to Camp Borden, and if not reluctant, they arrived with little of the excitement that had heralded their enlistment the previous June. There was instead a determination to get on with the job, which most expected would result in going to Britain this year.

Their return in 1941 was greeted by bitter cold. Some January nights dropped to near -20 degrees Fahrenheit, turning their poorly insulated huts into iceboxes. The fire in the lone wood stove in each barracks had long died out by morning reveille, and the air inside the huts was so cold, the mens' breath looked like white smoke. It was painful to come out from under the warmth of their blankets. Though the sun only faintly tinged the morning sky by the time breakfast was done, the heat of the mess hall and the warm food had rid them of the morning chill.

By the time they returned to their huts, the freshly stoked woodstoves had removed the worst of the chill. The windows were crude thermometers — one could tell how cold it was by whether the ice grown on the inside of the windows overnight had begun melting after morning mess. Most had lingered as long as possible in the warm mess hall, so they now hurried to straighten their huts. On hearing the trumpet sounding roll call, the thousand men of the Foresters rushed outside for morning inspection and the day's orders, the sound of their boots crunching the dry snow like fingers on a chalkboard as they ran to the parade square.

On all but the coldest days, the regiment trained outdoors, receiving instruction in cross-country skiing, taking weekly route marches through the snow, and bivouacking overnight under canvas. By March, the Foresters had completed elementary training and busily studied for tests in map reading, scouting and patrols, field engineering, and small arms. A transformation had taken place. The four companies, which had started with a natural rivalry based on where they were recruited, were now a single-minded regiment with pride in being Foresters.

In April, the regiment relocated from Camp Borden to the Canadian National Exhibition in Toronto. During the war, the annual fair and exhibition was cancelled, the buildings instead housing troops and the grounds used for training. The Foresters were assigned the Horse Palace as their barracks, and they bedded down in the stalls where the strong equine odour soon permeated their bedding and clothes. With Toronto to provide entertainment, the CNE was a welcome change. Soon after arriving, the regiment was assembled and addressed by Colonel Rutherford, who broke the news he had been asked to take command of the 1st Canadian Armoured Brigade. Though reluctant to leave, it was his duty to accept the new posting. The Foresters lost a well-loved commanding officer, who for most personified what it meant to be a soldier.

They had scant time to dwell on their loss, since towards the end of May, they were ordered to prepare for relocation to Nova Scotia. Rumour had it they would soon travel overseas. The regiment marched through Princes' Gate at the entrance to the CNE grounds, seeing atop the gate the statue of Nike, Goddess of Winged Victory, clasping a single maple leaf in her hand. Russ and Perry marched in the Foresters column through Toronto's streets, travelling east along Lake Ontario. In Cobourg, large placards greeted their arrival. "Gala military celebration at Cobourg on Victoria Day and Sunday," it read. "Come and bid farewell to a crack Canadian Regiment on its way to war!"[1]

They marched as far as Trenton, where trains waited for them. They arrived several days later at Camp Aldershot near Kentville, Nova Scotia. There was no fanfare as they descended from the train into a cold drizzle rain to walk through the muddy roads to their tents in the large, hastily expanded military camp. Despite the sombre weather, spirits in the regiment were high as the men considered this a temporary billet before sailing for England.

While the Foresters waited in Nova Scotia with word they would travel to England, Russ prepared to return to Camp Borden. He was rejoining Colonel Rutherford, who had given him the choice of staying with the Foresters or returning to Camp Borden. With army efficiency, Russ had been forced to make the trip to Nova Scotia while waiting for his transfer to be made official. After only a few days, he bid the Foresters farewell. It was difficult to leave. He and Perry had played together with the Georgians, decided to enlist together, and shared a year of training with the Foresters. Now they were going separate ways. Perry expected to head overseas soon, while Russ boarded a train back to Camp Borden to join the fledgling Royal Canadian Tank Corps.

Russ's new regiment was the Prince Edward Island Light Horse, a tank regiment whose job was Headquarters Squadron for the Fifth Canadian Armoured Brigade. The Headquarters Squadron protected and provided logistical support for the commanding officer and his staff. As a tank regiment, they were expected to be among the elite of the Canadian Army.

Tank troops were viewed with admiration usually reserved only for fighter pilots. That reputation came largely from the successes enjoyed by German Panzer forces on the western front in 1940, when their Blitzkrieg tactics overwhelmed the British and French.

The British army realized after its failure in 1940 that it needed tank forces to counter those of the Germans. Canadian Brigadier Frank Worthington had long advocated a strong tank corps for Canada's army. Worthington had been ignored for years, but German successes had at last opened eyes to the need. Worthington commanded the Canadian Armoured Corps Training Centre, a separate camp within sprawling Camp Borden.

A higher level of physical and mental fitness was required in tank regiments than in almost any other branch of the army. In the PEI Light Horse, Russ would receive extensive training in weapons, anti-gas, camouflage, tank maintenance, and tank tactics. Any trooper unable to keep up would be transferred back to the infantry.

Having largely ignored Worthington, in 1941, Canada was in the position of having tank brigades, but almost no modern tanks.[2] The only tank available at Camp Borden was a Great War American antique, the M1917. These were purchased from the United States for two hundred and forty dollars apiece, under the guise of scrap metal bought to get around U.S. neutrality laws. The M1917 held only two men, a driver who sat in front and a gunner in the turret. The tank's top speed was no faster than a brisk walk, and the mechanical unreliability provided ample opportunity for the crews to practice repair and maintenance. But to one of the instructors, Jim Derij, these clanking creations were things of beauty.

Any trooper who dared complain about working on a broken-down tank would be met with an intense stare from Jim's dark brown eyes. If they didn't like tank work, he would tell them, they should try mucking out a horse stable. He knew what he was speaking of. Jim had left high school to enlist in the army at sixteen, joining the Strathconas' mounted cavalry regiment in Winnipeg. He even carried a picture of Margorie, his first cavalry horse, in his wallet. He had been fond of the big mare and enjoyed telling how in his first year with the Strathconas, she had thrown him off, putting him in the hospital for a week.

When the Strathconas converted to an armoured regiment after horse cavalry was phased out in the 1930s, Jim eagerly applied to train as a mechanic, seeing it as a chance to move up. By 1941, at twenty-six, he was already a ten-year army veteran and a qualified motor mechanic. He was a member of the tank school at Camp Borden, teaching mechanics and tank driving.

When Russ first climbed into an M1917, Jim was among the instructors telling the troopers how the tank was driven — the two levers in front controlled the tracks on either side of the tank; you pushed in the clutch pedal at your right foot and then pushed the right lever forward, and when the clutch pedal was released, the track on that side would turn forward, likewise for the pedal and lever on the left. To go in reverse, you pulled the levers back.

Shouting instructions so he could be heard over the noises of the engine and the clanking treads, Jim walked beside the tank as Russ manoeuvred through the course. At first, Russ found it awkward to coordinate the two tracks using both hands and both feet, especially if one was being put in forward motion and the other in reverse. When Russ brought the tank back to its starting point and climbed out, Jim gave him a curt nod and motioned the next man to climb in.

While coaching each man through basic tank driving and maintenance, Jim's mind must have drifted to his wife, Maria and son Roger. She was at their apartment on Dunlop Street in nearby Barrie with their infant son, and as soon as each day's training was over, he left Camp Borden to join them. When war with Germany was imminent, Jim had signed on for overseas service, knowing this could mean leaving his wife and son in Canada.

Jim Derij and Margorie.
(Photo courtesy of James Derry)

When orders were received in October, 1941, sending the PEI Light Horse to Britain with the rest of the Fifth Canadian Armoured Division, Jim was told he was being left behind to continue training recruits at Camp Borden. Russ would head overseas. It was a year since Russ had enlisted, almost all that time spent at Camp Borden. When he had enlisted in 1940, it was expected the Germans would shortly follow the British evacuated from Dunkirk across the English Channel. People in Britain and Canada waited for the worst. Had Russ been sent to Britain at that time, he would have embarked knowing there was a good chance that the division would be fighting German troops on English soil.[3]

However, by mid-November, 1941, when the Fifth Armoured Division boarded trains for Nova Scotia, the risk of invasion had subsided. Hitler had chosen not to invade Britain that fall of 1940. Instead, in June the following year he turned eastward, attacking the Soviet Union. By November 1, German troops were deep inside Russia. If Hitler finished off the Russians, he could again turn his eyes towards Britain. In the lull on the western front, Canada was rushing men, equipment, and supplies to reinforce Britain against an invasion that could come as early as spring.

The PEI Light Horse arrived at Camp Debert in Nova Scotia, where the men waited another week before boarding a train for the three-hour trip to Halifax. When they arrived, they found ten large troop ships moored in Bedford Basin, the four-mile-long inlet. They dwarfed the largest lake-going ships Russ had seen docked in Owen Sound. The regiment went on board the *Orcades*, built in 1937 to be a luxurious cruise ship of the Orient Line. Other ships in the harbour had likewise been converted to troop carriers, all filling with Canadian troops headed for Britain.

The convoy was going to cross the North Atlantic at a time when German U-boats prowled the ocean, sinking millions of tons of shipping.[4] But few of the Canadian soldiers spoke about U-boats. No one wanted to dwell on what would happen if they were torpedoed, sending them into the cold North Atlantic waters. Most were excited at the prospect of an ocean voyage aboard one of the huge ships and of seeing England when they arrived.

Each man boarding the ship received a card giving the deck number of his bunk. Russ followed in a line led by a Naval NCO through a doorway to a narrow iron ladder. Down ladder after ladder they went, ever deeper into the centre of the ship. Finally, they reached their compartment. Conversion from luxury liner to troop ship had removed every convenience and any hint of comfort. In place of paying customer accommodations were a series of steel-bottomed compartments, each holding about two hundred troopers.

Each man was assigned a canvas hammock, slung three high at right angles to one another.

Russ slept in a bottom hammock in the lowest deck in the ship, just above the ship's bilge. The sweating hull continually deposited cold water on the floor of the compartment. Drain holes drilled in the steel floor weren't adequate, so an inch of icy water perpetually sloshed about their boots. There were no portholes to provide fresh air, and light was provided by two large, bare bulbs which did little to dispel the gloom. For the next three days more and more troops came aboard, until the *Orcades* was filled with three thousand soldiers. While the troops had to endure the dark and crowded bowels of the ship, officers were housed in relative elegance. Russ was one of the few enlisted men allowed near officer's quarters. He reported daily to Colonel Rutherford, who was quartered in a stateroom on the upper decks.

The convoy escort arrived in Halifax on the afternoon of November 13. Troops standing topside watched a huge U.S. battleship sail into Bedford Basin, cast anchor, and come to rest. Following it were two heavy cruisers and eight destroyers. It was the eve of the repeal of the U.S. Neutrality Acts, so for the first time in the war, American warships were to escort a British convoy showing the U.S. flag.

As evening approached, the American destroyers left Bedford Basin, sweeping the sea for lurking German submarines. Tugboats nudged the large ocean liners from their moorings, pointing them towards the exit from the harbour. The departure was led by the *Duchess of Athol*, regimental bands playing on her deck and men lining the ships' rails as they slowly steamed through the steel submarine nets at the harbour entrance. When the *Orcades'* turn came, the departing troopers felt a sudden increase in the engine's volume, and a vibration ran like electricity through the ship.

The ships made their way to a rendezvous — the Halifax Ocean Meeting Point — where they formed into a convoy. They headed into the night and the open sea, surrounded by their American escorts. Below decks the hammocks swung like metronomes with the motion of the ship. Russ lay in his hammock, the one light left burning casting grotesque swaying shadows on the sweating hull.

The next morning, the troops coming up from a night below decks saw the convoy spread across the ocean. It was the largest body of troops yet to sail from Canada in the war.[5] In the distance, the long grey shapes of their American escorts patrolled the perimeter of the convoy. Overhead an airplane from Newfoundland hunted for U-boats, but the convoy's zigzagging northeasterly course soon took it out of range of those patrols. Other planes launched periodically from the American cruisers searched in front and to the sides.

The troops went through daily drills for abandoning ship, making their way above decks as quickly as possible. On some ships the soldiers were ordered to keep their boots undone. If their ship was torpedoed and sank, the boots could be kicked off.[6] It was a futile gesture to the troops on the lower decks. Russ and others waiting in line to make their way up the ladders realized that should the need arise to abandon ship, those in the lowest hold would never make it out.

The ocean remained calm the next day. Many of the troopers came to the main deck in search of fresh air and sun, watching the grey ocean waters sliding by. On its fifth day at sea, the convoy was met by six British destroyers, prompting the American warships to turn west and sail back to America. The Americans were soon lost from view on the western horizon, the six British ships seeming a puny escort compared to the powerful American force. They were now closer to the war in Europe than to Canada. The wind rose and the waves grew larger, the ships pitching and rolling in the worsening sea. By nightfall the winds were blowing at sixty miles an hour, the ships crashing through waves twenty-five feet high.

The convoy pressed on through the rough seas, passing three hundred miles south of Iceland. The storm transformed the bowels of the ship into a nightmarish scene. The ship plunged while the hammocks swayed in disorienting fashion. The smell of two hundred unwashed bodies, coupled with the rancid odour of vomit, was enough to disturb the stomachs of even the hardiest sailors, let alone the soldiers sequestered deep in the hold. After the first night of rough seas, nearly everyone had been seasick in the water rolling at their feet. The lack of ventilation made the stench overpowering.

The rough seas and strong winds kept up through the next day. Overnight in the gale, one of the troop ships fell behind the convoy. Two destroyers went searching for her, and there was relief when the missing transport at last appeared over the western horizon.

Lying in his hammock, Russ watched a sergeant slosh through the compartment where the Headquarters Squadron endured the voyage. Without warning, he shouted, "Colombo, get up on deck. They need an emergency lookout." Russ made his way from the compartment. Halfway up the second ladder, he met the ration crew coming from the ship's galley with the evening meal.

Leading the group was a pair carrying a huge black pot filled with steaming stew. The left side member of the pair was obviously not well.

His face was chalk white, his eyes were rolling and his steps unsteady. Russ watched carefully, ready to duck on a moment's notice. About five steps away, he saw the man's eyes widen, his cheeks bulge and then, despite a desperate effort to hold it back, he threw up violently — right into the middle of the stew. His companion took the ladle without blinking an eye and gave the stew a couple of vigorous stirs.

A horrid thought crossed his mind, but Russ dismissed it and continued up the ladder. Seconds later, his worst fears were confirmed as he glanced down and saw the kitchen crew place the stew pot at the head of the serving tables. As he watched, the first soldier held out his mess tin and received a generous dollop.

When Russ finally reached the deck, he was met by a sailor who guided him to the ship's galley, where he received a slice of dry bread, topped with a piece of cheese as hard as a rock. Hurried along, Russ gulped down his rations and went on deck, where he was issued a cape-like coat and shepherded to the rear of the ship, where a pair of monstrous binoculars was bolted to the ship's rail.

After receiving brief instructions, his eyes were glued to the binoculars in search of hostile vessels. The violently windswept mixture of sleet and wet snow felt like thousands of pins hitting his face. He stoically kept his eyes stuck to the binoculars, helped along by a naval NCO who stood behind him, shrieking if Russ shrank from the task for a second.

Four hours later, Russ descended the steel ladders to the murky but windless confines of his quarters. Even the inch of icy water on the floor couldn't dampen his relief at being out of the howling gale and biting sleet.

Russ bemoaned to anyone who would listen the stale bread and lump of cheese that was his dinner. In turn, his mates commiserated with him for missing the stew that was the main course of their evening meal. In their words, "the stew had had everything in it and for a change was reasonably well seasoned." Russ never cracked a smile while screaming inside with laughter.

Later, lying in his dank hammock, he could not help quietly laughing to himself. But he also realized that had the mishap been reported, the guilty party would probably have been punished, perhaps spending the rest of the crossing in the brig. In addition, it was late November 1941, and the ship was on strict rations, even though the convoy carried thousands of pounds of Canadian food, including sides of beef, which was needed to help with the food shortages in Britain. If the incident was reported, the stew would have been thrown out and two hundred soldiers would have gone hungry.

On November 20, a week after departing Canada, the wind slackened and the troops began reappearing on deck. The following day they sailed into the Irish Sea, coming to a halt off the River Clyde in Scotland. Four of the troop ships put into Glasgow. The remaining ships, one the *Orcades*, sailed south to the mouth of the Mersey River, where they waited while the river was swept of mines.

About midday on November 22, the ships moved upriver. The troops crowded the decks, watching the English countryside and the masts standing in the water where ships had been sunk by German mines or aircraft. As Liverpool came into view, war was evident close-up for the first time. Six months before, Liverpool had received the most concentrated bombing of any British city outside London. The German air force's high explosive and incendiary bombs had destroyed factories and rail lines, along with schools, hospitals, and homes. Despite the effort to close Liverpool's shipping, the docks were fully operational within weeks.

The troops were naturally anxious to disembark but were forced to stay on board an extra day, waiting for a welcoming party. To entertain the men a church service was held, followed by a boxing match. Finally, at five p.m., the *Orcades* was towed into dock and the troops told they would disembark — but not until the next day. Frustrated by the ongoing delay and despite a cold, steady rain, many stayed on deck late into the night, watching the activity on the docks and calling to the dock workers, whose thick accents made them practically unintelligible to the Canadians.

After two days on board ship in Liverpool harbour, following a ceremony by a group of British and Canadian dignitaries, the troops on board *Orcades* were finally allowed to disembark. Russ marched directly onto a waiting train as darkness fell. The blackout blinds were pulled down, and although some risked peeking outside when the train slowed to pass through towns, they found railway station signs had been removed. This had been done in 1940 to confuse the Germans in the event of an invasion.

As the train chugged southward, most men fell asleep, save those joining card games to pass the time. In the early morning, the men were abruptly wakened by NCOs passing through the cars, yelling at them to get their gear together. When the train finally stopped, the lights inside were extinguished and the soldiers descended into the military town of Aldershot, which like the rest of England was under strict blackout.

In the dark, the NCOs organized the men into their platoons. The column marched through the darkened streets, led by an officer of the advance party, sent ahead from Canada to prepare for the regiment's arrival. It wasn't far to the nearby military base, where the PEI regiment was brought to a halt in the parade square in front of Talavera Barracks. The rising sun on a grey English morning revealed the outline of two three-storey brick buildings. Running the length of the two barracks blocks were balconies. The troops were told to find a bed in the top two floors. They would have a few hours' sleep before being called back to the parade square. While the other men climbed the steel grate stairs, Russ left to put the Colonel's quarters in order, while the Colonel met with the advance party and the Brigade's officers and NCOs.

Once finished his task, Russ climbed the stairs to the rooms where the troopers were settling in. He walked along the balcony, searching for an empty cot. There were ten rooms for the troops on each floor, each housing twenty-four men. Twelve narrow beds lined each wall. Finding the rooms his platoon was assigned and seeing a free cot, Russ put his backpack down on a small chest at the foot of the bed. A fire had been started in the small fireplace at the end of the room, filled with coal from a small pail; they hadn't realized the coal was their entire daily ration. The room was cold enough to see their breath, and Russ doubted the small stove would do more than take the chill out of the air. He settled under his blanket, the cold making it difficult fall asleep.

Following reveille and breakfast that morning, the troops were taken on a route march around the military base and the outskirts of the town. It included a march up Round Hill, atop which sat Wellington's Statue, the victorious Duke of Wellington sitting atop his horse, Copenhagen. Standing thirty feet high, it was cast with bronze from captured French cannons melted down after Napoleon's defeat at Waterloo.

Talavera Barracks was constructed in the mid-1800s, named for a famous victory in Spain fought by Wellington against the French. The streets were lined with horse chestnut trees, and in front of each barracks was a parade square where the troops drilled. Civilian Aldershot offered movie houses, pubs, and music halls. Most weekdays, the training was finished by five p.m. and troops were allowed in town until ten at night without a pass, although they had to carry their helmets and gas masks at all times. Weekend leave was given once a month.

The arrival of the Fifth Canadian Armoured Division in Britain in late November was a major event for the Canadians and British, but it would quickly fade in significance following events on December 7. That day, Japan attacked Pearl Harbor and declared war on the United States. Germany declared war on the Americans four days later, drawing the U.S. into the war in Europe. Britain and Canada no longer stood almost alone against

Germany. These events, though momentous, received no mention in the PEI regiment's war diary.

———————◆———————

Russ was given a five-day landing leave in mid-December. It had been delayed because the men could only take leave as space became available and finding accommodation was difficult in cities. Russ received a railway pass, a ration card and cash allowance for food, and an address for the billet assigned to him in London, thirty-five miles east of Aldershot.

As the train entered the outskirts of London, the damage from the heavy bombing unfolded before him. Street after street contained bombed-out buildings, partially collapsed walls enclosing piles of debris. Sometimes all that was left of entire city blocks were piles of brick and wood. It seemed every building had signs of damage, the brickwork pockmarked where chunks were knocked out by shrapnel from bombs or machine gun bullets from planes.

Russ was seeing the results of the German Blitz that hit London between September 1940 and May 1941. Though the worst of the bombing seemed over, the high-low wailing air raid sirens still sounded frequently, sending people running for the nearest Tube station or backyard bomb shelter. People with homes no longer slept every night in air raid shelters as they had during the Blitz, though the platforms of Tube stations were still lined with beds for those whose homes had been destroyed.

Grey barrage balloons floated over the city, holding thick wire ropes intended to slice the wings off low-flying aircraft. Windows were taped to reduce injuries from flying glass, and sandbags stacked in front of doors and ground-floor windows to stop shrapnel from exploding bombs. At night the city was under strict blackout, with no street lights, thick curtains drawn shut, traffic lights fitted with shields leaving only a small cross of light, and white bands painted on lampposts, mailboxes, along curbs, and up stairways to prevent pedestrians from tripping over them.

Canadian soldiers on leave picked their way through the damage to see London's historic sights: Buckingham Palace, Big Ben, Piccadilly Circus, and other famous places, as popular in wartime as they had been before. Canadians were then the most common foreign soldiers in Britain. English attitudes towards the Canadians were mixed, as were those of the Canadian troops towards the English. Drunkenness and public rowdiness by some Canadian troops had brought attention from the press, although the behaviour was likely no worse that that of British soldiers. While admiring British civilians for their courage under German bombing, some Canadian soldiers complained that they felt unwelcome, as if the English did not appreciate that Canadians had left jobs, family, freedom, and comfortable homes to come to their aid.[7]

Returning to Talavera at the end of his leave, Russ settled into the routine of training. The regimen consisted of small arms practice, radio training, armoured tactics, principles of artillery, and tank mechanics. Tank crews were trained to march under the direction of semaphore flags (thought potentially useful in combat if radio contact between tanks was knocked out or to avoid interception by the Germans). And there was always a general toughening up of the troops taking place. In early February, the regiment was proud of completing a ten-mile route march through the English countryside over four inches of slippery snow, in only three and a quarter hours.

The Canadian Armoured Corps at last were training using modern tanks, a year and a half after the war began. In place of the antique M1917s they had used at Borden, they were given Canadian-made RAM I tanks, named for the ram sheep prominent on Brigadier Frank Worthington's family crest.[8] The RAM was produced in Montreal and shipped to Britain, where it became the main training tank used by Canadian troops. However, ammunition for its small two-pounder turret cannon was used sparingly, so when practice firing was allowed, it was usually with the tank's 30-calibre coaxial machine guns. The troopers got a sense of what it was like to take live fire by having rifles and pistols fired at the tank's hull while they were inside.

———————◆———————

In August, the regiment moved from Aldershot to the town of Hove, a seaside resort on the English Channel near Brighton. Life in Hove carried on, though it was a regular target of the Luftwaffe. Located on the southeast coast, it was often the first place German planes arrived and the last they flew over when departing. Soon after the start of the war, soldiers and civilians learned to run for cover at the sound of any low-flying aircraft, since Brighton and Hove were the last chance pilots of stray German planes had to use up leftover ammunition.

Air raid sirens and roaring plane engines often kept people up until dawn.[9] During one night raid on Brighton, three Focke Wulf 190s made a low-level attack on the city's power plant. On another, an air raid siren had barely sounded before several planes swept over the city, dropping bombs and machine-gunning the streets. When a German bomb hit a house in Brighton's Grosvenor Street, Canadian soldiers stationed in nearby St. Mary's Hall in Eastern Road ran to help. Digging in the wreckage with their bare hands looking for survivors, they found a young mother and her child under the rubble, both killed by the explosion.

One raid especially stood out to Canadians stationed in Brighton and Hove. It happened shortly after noon on October 12, 1942, when four German fighter-bombers came in low, machine-gunning the waterfront and scattering Canadian troops who had assembled in Hove's Brunswick Square. The German planes then swept over the train station, dropping two bombs, causing damage and civilian casualties. Sergeant Gordon Bannerman of the 76th Field Battery described the attack:

> C.D. Howe, Minister of National Defence Canada, was to visit. All Canadian units in the south east command were forming up at approximately the same time all over the area. The 76th Battery were lined up on one side of Brunswick Square when just over the waves came a cannon-firing German plane! Those nearest the coast side saw this plane coming in so low they thought the fire from his cannon was that the plane was on fire. The soldiers rushed into the doorways of the houses a split second before the plane roared over our heads. The cannon shells cracked into the pavement that we had just left.... The plane went up and over us and dropped a bomb a couple of streets over. None of us were hit — a miracle. Many German fighters came into the area at wave top level that day. Their spies must have sent word out that troop concentrations were to take place and to get a crack at us.[10]

On August 19, 1942, troops in southern England were placed on twenty-four-hour alert to prepare coastal towns for raids. However, this time, Brighton and Hove were not targeted. The reason for the order was made clear when BBC radio announced that Allied forces had raided the French port city of Dieppe. Word soon spread that the attack had gone poorly and Canadian casualties were high.[11]

Canadians had waited almost three years for a combat role in Europe, and the result at Dieppe was disastrous. The raid was the first offensive action by Canadian troops in the war, and only the second major Canadian action to that point, the other being the courageous but doomed defence of Hong Kong. However, the general reaction to Dieppe among Canadian troops in England was, based on the PEI regiment's war diary, a renewed sense of determination. They resumed training for what all knew was the inevitable large-scale invasion of France, though they didn't know it was still more than two years away. But as months dragged on, the routine of military life offered little to lift their spirits. They were separated from friends and family, training in mud and cold rain, with the occasional military exercise thrown in, leaving little to cheer about. Most Canadian soldiers were anxious to get on with the invasion.

Russ, however, was not idly waiting to enter combat. He had applied to become an officer in the Royal Canadian Armoured Corps. In January, 1942, the first step was ceasing to be the Brigadier's batman. By the end of the summer of 1942, he had completed a two-week "pre-officer training course," designed to weed out those lacking the necessary aptitude. He passed the written exam in September and was appointed an acting corporal with the PEI regiment. In October, he applied for and received approval to attend officer training school.

The regiment began training in several new types of tanks in addition to the RAM. One of these, the Crusader, was an earlier British design. They were also introduced to the Churchill and Sherman, both of which had a fifth trooper, like the RAM, to load the main gun. Of all the tanks they trained in, the Sherman was the fastest and most reliable, requiring a fraction of the maintenance of the Churchill. Troopers also appreciated the Sherman's mechanically-driven turret, an improvement over the Churchill's hand-cranked one.

On New Year's Day, 1943, Colonel Rutherford was called to a meeting at Fifth Armoured Division's headquarters, and he was told to bring the Brigade's unit commanders with him. It was an unusual command for New Year's Day, and there was a sense something serious was coming.

When they returned, someone let slip that the news was bad. Several days later it was announced the brigade the regiment belonged to was being broken up. The news was taken badly by all. The PEI regiment was victim to the ever-shifting realignment of forces as plans for military action were made and remade.

Russ, however, was already preparing to leave the regiment. He had been accepted into the Canadian officer training program. The next course was a general pre-officer training school, where he was mixed with potential officer candidates from other branches of the army. The course lasted the first six weeks of 1943. At the end, it was his leadership qualities that had stood out to the instructors. The examining officer summed it up, saying, "This cadet is clean and neat in appearance with a quietly friendly (perhaps reserved) manner. He has worked very hard throughout the course and has shown that he can handle men; has ability, initiative and common sense, and with further training and experience in his own branch of the service, will make an officer." Russ was approved for a pre-officer training course specifically for Armoured Corps officers. He passed the course, which ran from May to mid-August, and completed yet more qualifying exams. After a series of final screening interviews, on August 22, 1943, Russ was accepted into the officer training course for the Royal Armoured Corps at Sandhurst.

◆

In September, 1943, the young man from Owen Sound arrived at the revered Sandhurst Military Academy, the epitome of British military tradition and the English upper class. He didn't know if he was the only soldier from Owen Sound to have attended the academy, but it capped an amazing three years in his life. He'd never imagined when eating beans and fatback pork at McFadden's lumber camp a short time ago that he would one day attend this historic school. Five miles north of Aldershot, the massive Old College stretched a full quarter mile, looming over the parade ground. The white building looked like a grand mansion, with eight bronze cannon captured at Waterloo standing in front.

The new officer candidates assembled on the parade square. An officer of the British Guards Regiment addressed them. He explained that in the next six months, not only would they be tested physically and mentally, but they would be taught the decorum an officer was expected to show. There was no hazing ritual and no demeaning treatment. The candidates had passed tests of their psychological preparedness, mental abilities, and physical strength and stamina just to reach this point. In this final step, sterner tests awaited, but demeaning treatment was not part of that routine.

Reveille was at precisely ten minutes to six in the morning, followed by a shower. Even showering had a protocol. The cadets were instructed to start their showers hot and end them with a blast of cold water. Classroom instruction stopped precisely at four in the afternoon for afternoon tea, served with scones and jam. Training resumed until six thirty, when dinner was served accompanied each night by the playing of the Guards Band.

The first months at Sandhurst were a stern test. The training was intense and relentless, testing both mental and physical endurance. To some it was the worst time of their life. Exhaustion was so severe, some cadets suffered hallucinations. The only free time they had was a few hours on Saturday and Sunday. Saturday afternoons and evenings the cadets were allowed off the college grounds, but they had to be back by ten p.m., while Sunday afternoons they had to return no later than six p.m.

Cadets needed to be more than just physically fit to withstand the endurance exercises and the physical demands. Claustrophobia was a severe issue for some, with training designed to weed out those unable to cope for prolonged periods inside highly confining armoured vehicles. Much of the time was spent under canvas in the cold, wet English winter. Forty-mile marches across the fields after a full twenty-four hours of other training put the cadets under stress to see how they performed when hard physical demands were placed on top of lack of sleep.

Cadets were required to pay close attention to even the smallest detail of their equipment and uniforms. Each metal button, boot, and bayonet was to be buffed until it shone like a mirror. Several hours each night were spent polishing between dinner and lights out. Those not meeting the exacting standards would be sent with full packs to the stairs, where they would run up and down for an hour without break.

The cadets were divided into four companies competing to be Champion Company. One of the key competitions was the drill challenge. Each platoon of cadets spent hours on the parade ground under the supervision of the officer and sergeant-major overseeing their training. Any cadet slightly out of step or moving sloppily instead of sharply was ridden mercilessly. The Champion Company received the Red Lanyard, a cord worn around the left shoulder. This company had the coveted privilege of leading parades and escorting the flags bearing Sandhurst's colours.

Gunnery instruction was an important part of training, which included maintenance of the tank's main gun. While Russ was cleaning the breech of a Sherman tank's 75-mm gun, the lever holding the breech block open slipped from the hand of the cadet assisting him. The breech snapped shut, pinning Russ's finger between the breech block and the breech ring. The other cadet quickly opened it, but the damage was done.

Russ waited for the pain he knew was coming. As the initial shock of the injury wore off and the pain mounted, he was surprised there was so little blood. One finger was fractured and the outer skin peeled off his fingers, exposing the ligaments. An operation repaired the fracture, and Russ returned to full training after three days. He was fortunate not to have lost the fingers.

As the months at Sandhurst passed, some men disappeared from Russ's platoon. They left without a word, some leaving voluntarily, finding the training too difficult, others leaving because they were quietly invited to do so when failing to measure up to the standards of intelligence, mental toughness, physical strength, courage, and leadership.

In March, 1944, Russ's company assembled on the parade square as usual. The officer in charge of the company addressed them. He congratulated them for having satisfactorily completed all the tasks and challenges. They were now at the end of their training and would soon graduate from Sandhurst. They were expected, he said, to continue to perform to the highest standards and to carry on in the tradition in which they had been trained. At the end of the ceremony, the officer gave permission to the sergeant to dismiss the men.

"Troop! Dis-missed!" he shouted. A spontaneous cheer erupted from the men, who clapped one another on the back and shook hands. Two days later, the Sovereign's Parade took place. Russ was one of the several hundred new lieutenants, mainly British and Canadian, who marched onto the parade ground in front of the Old College. In a ritual carried out for over 150 years, they were led onto the parade ground by an officer on a white horse, while the Guards Band played on the college steps.

Newly commissioned Lieutenant Russ Colombo, Royal Canadian Armoured Corp, Sandhurst Royal Military Academy.

The newly commissioned officers stood for inspection and then marched in formation around the parade ground. Dignitaries addressed them, and awards were given out. Finally, with the band playing "Auld Lang Syne," the Colour Guard marched the flags inside the college, followed by the new officers, and finally the officer astride his white steed. Only after the doors to the college closed behind them were they the cadets considered officially commissioned.

In a picture taken in February, 1944, Russ stands with his graduating platoon against the north wall of the Royal Memorial Chapel at Sandhurst. His jaw is set firmly and there are heavy black lines under his eyes, while the corded muscles in his neck show his physical strength. Most of the twenty-two new lieutenants in Russ's graduating platoon would be posted to combat units in the Royal Canadian Armoured Corps. They realized they would take part in the Allied invasion of Nazi-held Europe, which everyone was certain must happen before summer ended.

SIX

Fallschirmjäger
Paratrooper

The fall of 1941 was a time of tremendous military success for Germany, unparalleled in modern European history. In the course of a matter of weeks in 1940, Germany had defeated the combined armies of Britain and France. The British were forced to a desperate withdrawal from Dunkirk, while France was broken in half, with Paris and northern France under German occupation. German troops occupied Czechoslovakia, Poland, Denmark, Norway, the Netherlands, Belgium, France, and much of North Africa. Britain and her Commonwealth alone stood against Germany in the west. Almost a year later, Germany attacked the Soviet Union in a front running from Norway to Romania in what was described by Hitler as a pre-emptive invasion, striking against Bolshevism before the Soviet Union could invade Germany. By September, Germany held most of the Ukraine and was planning the battle for Moscow. The final act enlarging the war occured following the invasion of Pearl Harbor by the Japanese, when Germany declared war on the United States. It was, Hitler said, due to extreme provocation by the Americans, who had made open acts of military aggression against Germany, including attacks against German U-boats and seizure of German merchant vessels in international waters.

Frank and his friends heard adventurous stories about the war from friends returning on leave to Leitmeritz in late 1941. They had joined the military after graduation the previous year and arrived home in their uniforms, talking at length about the "glorious war."

Frank and other boys in his class were still months away from graduation. They feared the war would be over before they had a chance to take part. They could not volunteer for the military before turning eighteen, unless they had graduated from high school. But the Bannführer, the father of Frank's friend Karl Habel, a local Nazi Party official, wanted his son to volunteer for enlistment and arranged for the entire senior high school class to be given the chance to write exams early, in March. Those successful could volunteer for the armed services. The final exams lasted three days, and all but three of the class graduated early.

Frank's parents did not disagree with his volunteering at the age of seventeen. They knew that on his eighteenth birthday he would be drafted regardless. Volunteering might cause the boys to be looked on more favourably and at the very least give them a better chance to get into their preferred branch of the service.

As soon as their school graduation was confirmed, Frank, Rudy, and Karl went together to the Recruitment Centre in Leitmeritz. There were three doors, each with a sign indicating a branch of the military: one for the Waffen SS, another for the Luftwaffe, and a third for the army (recruitment for the navy was in another city). Frank and most of his friends chose to join the Luftwaffe, hoping to become fighter pilots.

———————◆———————

When the three friends passed through the door marked "Luftwaffe," a clerk rose from his desk to meet them. Hearing they wanted to enlist "to be pilots," the clerk smiled and gave the boys enlistment forms. As if in a competition for the final pilot's position in the Luftwaffe, they raced to complete their forms and return them to the clerk. Frank finished just before Karl, and he jumped up and walked briskly to the clerk's desk. The boys waited to be interviewed and were called one at a time into the office of the Luftwaffe officer in charge of recruitment.

When Frank walked into the office, the recruiting officer sat at his desk examining the completed forms. Frank tried to appear calm as he stood before the officer, who had not acknowledged his presence. On the wall behind the desk were two pictures. One was of Adolf Hitler, the other Hermann Göring, head of the Luftwaffe, Reichsmarshall of Germany, Hitler's second-in-command. Göring was a larger-than-life Nazi whose exploits as a fighter ace in the Great War were well known.

Finally, the recruiting officer looked up from his paperwork. Before him was a young man, thin but tall, his blond hair swept to one side, his large blue eyes giving the appearance that this one was in reality too young to enlist.

The officer asked Frank questions to confirm that what he had written was accurate. Seeing the records from Frank's high school, he was surprised to find the boy was indeed seventeen, not the fourteen- or fifteen-year-old he appeared. After verifying the information, the officer stamped Frank's papers and put them aside. As he was about to tell Frank he would be contacted shortly and told when to report for a physical examination, Frank spoke up.

"Sir, I have something to show you," he said.

The officer raised an eyebrow as Frank held out an envelope. The officer removed a sheaf of photographs. He looked at the pictures of military aircraft one at a time.

"Where did you get these?"

"Sir, I went to the Luftwaffe base at Oschatz and photographed the planes as they were taking off and landing." Frank was proud to show his initiative. But instead of expressing admiration, the officer said nothing, his expression changing only with a protracted raising of one eyebrow. Reaching the last picture, he put the stack in a pile face up in the centre of his desk. Finally, he looked up.

"Young man, a camera is not part of a recruit's basic equipment."

Frank's unease grew. He had expected praise for his initiative, and that was clearly not forthcoming.

"Besides," the officer continued "taking pictures at military airfields is strictly prohibited. Take your photographs with you, candidate Sikora. You will be notified by letter of the date and location of your physical examination."

He stamped Frank's enlistment papers then returned to reading a document. Frank realized the interview was over.

Gathering up the photographs, Frank flushed with embarrassment. As he turned to leave, he glanced up at the photograph of Göring, the Iron Cross on his chest and a string of medals across the left breast of his military jacket. Around his throat on a black and gold ribbon hung the Blue Max, the Pour le Mérite, the highest military award from the Kingdom of Prussia during the Great War. Göring looked so self-assured. Frank felt heartened as he made his way from the office. However, his dream of becoming a pilot, perhaps an ace like Göring, was crushed as the doctor at his medical examination in Dresden a few weeks later found him "Not Suitable As Pilot." He would instead be enlisted in the Luftwaffe's land forces.

With his enlistment taken care of and only the call to basic training left, Frank's parents encouraged him to take a skiing vacation near the old family home of Teschen. Frank thought it a wonderful idea. Shortly before he was to leave, his father took him aside. Warning Frank not to tell anyone what he was about to say, including his friends, he handed his son a bag containing screwdrivers, pliers, and a chisel. He asked Frank to visit the cemetery in Jablonkau, the city east of Freistadt where generations of their ancestors were buried. He instructed Frank to find the headstone of one particular ancestor from the nineteenth century.

"Search for the headstone in our family's plot," Franz explained to his son, "that has a Polish name."

Frank was told to remove the metal nameplate from that headstone and bring it back. He took the tools. He understood why it was important to hide the fact they had a Polish ancestor. If Nazi Party officials learned they were not purely German, it might mean his father would be overlooked for promotion or, in the worst case, that he would be kicked out of the party, which would cost him his job. Now he understood the real reason his parents had encouraged him to travel back to Freistadt.

Frank was happy to be back in Freistadt. It was a time to relax and celebrate. He had graduated from high school, itself an accomplishment since many boys dropped out of school to work. He was proud to tell old friends and relatives in Freistadt that he'd been accepted as a recruit in the Luftwaffe. Any seventeen-year-old boy would be optimistic about his future.

One night during his visit, Frank woke to the sound of yelling. Looking out his window, he saw a group of men dragging a boy about his age down the street. The next morning he asked the relatives he was staying with what the yelling had been about. He was told the German army was forcibly recruiting all German men fit for military service, and one of the boys hadn't wanted to go. Frank could not understand the boy's desperation and wondered how "German" this person could be if he did not want to serve his country. How different he and his friends were, having gone out of their way to enlist early.

Returning to Leitmeritz following his vacation, Frank was again taken aside by his father.

"Did you do it?" Franz asked anxiously.

Handing the bag of tools to his father, Frank said, "It was not a problem."

Mixed among the tools was the metal nameplate from the headstone. It was a secret they would never again mention. In the dark that evening, Franz Sikora carried the bag and shovel into the yard behind their house. He dug a hole in one of the flowerbeds. Taking one final glance around, Franz placed the bag in the hole and quickly covered it.

———◆———

In April, 1942, the call came for Frank to report to basic training. He was glad the waiting was over. He was to report to the military base at Oschatz, a town in the eastern part of Germany, about one hundred fifty kilometres from Leitmeritz. Basic training lasted three months. The recruits were all between seventeen and nineteen years old, and at first basic training felt like a form of sport. However, it soon turned into one of the hardest physical and mental tests Frank had ever experienced. The trainers were Luftwaffe corporals and sergeants who revelled in brutalizing the new recruits.

Frank was among those who were special targets for abuse, because of their "arrogance" at being high school graduates. The instructors wanted to break their will by stressing them physically and mentally. The training was so severe that several of the recruits died. One was killed when a shell in the heavy ammunition belt he was forced to carry around his neck went off, ripping a large hole in his neck. Other recruits were so weakened by the hardships of training, they caught serious infections or fell ill. A few chose to desert rather than continue. When these boys were caught, they were jailed, where the treatment was even worse, as they were now considered disloyal and cowardly. After months of abuse in jail, they would be sent back to basic training, where the trainers, knowing their history, would make them even greater targets for abuse.

During basic training, Frank was occasionally assigned to guard prison work gangs. One such occasion was in the town of Quedlinburg, and the prisoners were from the concentration camp at Buchenwald. Frank observed several distinct groups within the work gang. Each group kept to itself and was distinguished by the colour of a patch sewn on the upper arm of their shirts. There was a group with red triangular patches, Frank had not seen before. He approached one elderly man.

The old man hesitated. He had seen too much brutal treatment of the prisoners at Buchenwald to take lightly any interaction with someone in a uniform. Was this skinny boy like the guards at Buchenwald?

Dutifully, the old man explained to Frank that the red patch meant he was a political prisoner. He explained he had been arrested in 1937 for belonging to the Communist party and had been at Buchenwald ever since. Then the elderly man shuffled away and Frank returned to watching over the work gang, with his rifle slung over his shoulder. It was just routine duty.

Shortly after the conclusion of basic training, in the summer of 1942 Frank's unit was ordered to Finland. They would join their new allies, the Finns, who were fighting to protect disputed territory from the Soviet Union. In 1939, the Soviets fabricated a military incident by shelling their own Russian village near the Finnish border then accusing the Finns of an unprovoked attack. When the Finns refused to cede territory, the Russians invaded.

Despite being greatly outnumbered, the Finnish army badly mauled their attackers. Some reports put Soviet dead at more than a quarter million, compared to fewer than twenty-five thousand Finns. In the lull that followed, Soviet demands for Finnish territory increased, leading to German troops being invited to take up positions in northern Finland. The invasion of the Soviet Union by Germany in Operation Barbarossa in late June, 1941, was followed within days by joint Finnish and German attacks in the north. The German goal was to capture the Soviet Union's Arctic port of Murmansk and to secure access to nickel mines in northern Finland. Soviet resistance stopped the attack at the Litsa River, fifty kilometres west northwest of Murmansk, where the Germans dug in and built a defensive line.

Frank's unit travelled in freight train cars to Insterberg in East Prussia, and then on to Estonia, spending four miserable nights packed in a passenger train, sleeping on the benches, lying on the floors, and even in the luggage racks. When they reached Estonia, they were loaded onto a ship to Finland. Frank was assigned a spot in the lowest deck. During their voyage to Finland, the ship's alarm rang incessantly, and when it did everyone on the ship had to race up the narrow ladders to the main deck and wait until the all-clear signal was given. Then they all filed back below decks, only to be called back again.

After docking at the southern Finnish city of Turku, the men were loaded into freight cars, twenty men to a car. The cars had bunk beds, straw covered the floor, and in the centre sat a stove. A metal bucket was provided for their sanitary needs, but as with all men, they preferred the boyish pleasure of peeing from the open door.

Meals were provided daily, but butter, cheese, and ham were obtained by bartering with the local people when the train stopped. The soldiers were willing to trade virtually anything they owned — with the exception of their rifles and ammunition. Men who had travelled this route before had come prepared to trade, bringing women's nylon stockings, soap, and cosmetics. Most trading was for fresh food, but sometimes an exchange was made for a few moments of "tenderness behind the wood pile."

The recruits were young, optimistic, and most were excited by the adventure of travelling for the first time outside Germany. Frank was struck by the wild beauty of the landscape. The rail line passed through deep forests, the dark green spruce and pines broken by stands of white-barked birch trees. The doors of the freight cars remained open day and night, and the further north they travelled, the longer the days became and the closer Frank felt to nature.

Finally the train reached Rovaniemi in northern Finland, the end of their rail journey. Stepping from the train, Frank saw a weathered wooden sign announcing they were at 66 degrees north latitude, the edge of the Article Circle. They boarded buses and continued northwards, stopping at the town of Kirkenes, Norway, for a few weeks before being sent to the southern end of the front in the Petsamo peninsula, between Kirkenes and Murmansk near the Arctic Ocean. On the northern coast lies the frigid Barents Sea. It is a land of barren tundra out of which rise hills of barren rock covered only by moss and lichen. Inland are steep hills whose rocky slopes rise above the swampy land. Hundreds of rivers and streams flow through the peaty bogs, the Arctic backdrop broken only by short, gnarled trees and low bushes. Further south, where Frank's unit was positioned, the tundra was interspersed with dense pine forests that broke the winds sweeping across the desolate landscape.

Frank was stationed in northern Finland from August 1942 until June 1944. His unit was part of the more than fifty thousand troops of the XIX Mountain Infantry Corps, occupying a strongpoint northwest of Murmansk, about two hundred miles north of the Arctic Circle.[1] The corps was commanded by the legendary and dreaded General Ferdinand Schörner. The troops' dislike for him was due to the extremely harsh punishments given under his command for even minor offences. Later in the war he gained even greater notoriety for ordering any soldier found behind the front lines without a written order executed on the spot, without trial.

A famous signpost for German soldiers in Kirkenes, Norway, in 1941.
(Bundesarchiv, Bild 101 I-092-0257-18, photographer: o.Ang)

In 1942, there was a stalemate at the front in northern Finland. The Germans were unable to capture Murmansk, and the Soviets could not capture Kirkenes, the Arctic port used by Germany. For the moment both sides carried out only local and long-range reconnaissance patrols and small operations.[2]

The German strategy was a defensive one, designed around a system of strongpoints. Steel-reinforced concrete bunkers were built in positions chosen for their commanding view of the countryside. These were supported by trench systems, allowing unobserved troop movement. There were strategically located ammunition and supply depots, and the entire front was laced with rows of barbed wire and minefields. Three belts of such strongpoint defences were built, each prepared as a fallback position if the one in front was overrun. Typically, a division would have ten strongpoints, each manned by a company with thirteen light machine guns, four heavy machine guns, two 80-mm mortars, two light infantry guns, and two 37-mm antitank guns. Artillery support could be called on by forward artillery observers from positions behind the front.[3] Such highly organized defensive networks were examples of the deadly force the Germans were able to bring to bear in defending their positions all across Europe.

Winter in Kirkenes came early the year Frank arrived. To survive the Arctic winter, something he wouldn't have thought possible, they were given prefabricated huts made of ill-fitting plywood and paperboard sheets. There were no nails to hold the structures together, and the pieces failed to fit snugly, leaving large gaps through which the cold air blew. From time to time Laplanders visited their camp, wearing colourful clothes, watching silently as the soldiers built their poorly designed structures. They tried to explain with gestures that the huts needed to be dug deeper into the ground. Looking at the roofs, they would only shake their heads. As long as it was warm, the structures were fine. But once temperatures dropped, the problems became evident. The poorly engineered huts were heated by wood stoves, but the wood the soldiers were given was green, and when burned it filled the huts with smoke. In the three-month-long winter darkness inside the Arctic Circle, the temperature outside dropped below -45 degrees Celsius, and everything inside the huts froze.

Everything, that is, except for hordes of body lice that infested Frank and his companions during winter. The tiny lice crawled about their bodies, especially where clothing was in contact with the skin, in their underwear, armpits, waistline, neck, and shoulders. Two days after feeding on a soldier's blood, each female insect laid as many as three hundred eggs in the seams of their clothes. Within a week, the eggs would hatch and nymphs emerge. They caused tremendous itching. The torment was worst at night, when the soldiers settled into their bunks to try to sleep, causing ceaseless scratching. The blood-feeding lice also raised fear of the spread of disease, especially typhoid. The only way Frank could deal with the lice was to bury his clothes and underwear in the snow, the cold killing the adults but not all of the eggs, which would hatch to begin the infestation over again.

Conditions in summer were no easier. Mosquitoes swarmed incessantly around their heads, getting into eyes and noses, being breathed in and swallowed live. The sun did not set for three months, and temperatures reached almost 40 degrees Celsius. The warm temperatures caused the soil to thaw and the groundwater to rise, flooding the ground so that boards were needed inside the huts to reach the bunks without wading through water. Anything falling on the ground inside the huts would be soaked in the stagnant water, which soon began to give off the smell of rotting eggs as organic matter decomposed.

The two years in northern Finland failed to live up to the stories of exciting military adventures Frank had heard. The conditions were harsh, the men isolated, and the time was spent mostly in tedious activities. Summer or winter, their only interesting task was when they patrolled the Arctic tundra. From time to time, a Soviet patrol would be seen in the distance, although combat with one was rare. Frank was now nineteen, and the war was far from the adventure he had imagined it would be as a seventeen-year-old.

SEVEN

Lost Innocence
Verlorene Unschuld

The drive from Sandhurst to Blackdown Barracks in March 1944 was only twenty miles, but to Russ it was like entering another world. No longer crammed into barracks with other troopers, now Russ was saluted by them, shared a room with a lieutenant in the officers' quarters, and ate meals in the officers' mess.

Blackdown Barracks was near the town of Woking, midway between Aldershot and London, and home to the Third Canadian Armoured Corps Reinforcement Unit. Known as 3 CACRU, when Russ arrived there on temporary assignment in April, 1944, one of the first things he did was find Colonel Rutherford. The Colonel had been made commander of 3 CACRU when the Fifth Canadian Armoured Brigade was dismantled over a year before. Rutherford's support had played a large role in Russ pursuing officer's training, and the Colonel must have felt as proud of Russ as he would have of his own son. Their reunion lasted only a few weeks, as orders arrived sending Russ to a unit stationed near a southern English town with the bleak name of Coldharbour.

Many transfers from 3 CACRU happened that spring. Canadian units across England were being brought up to full strength in preparation for the coming mobilization. They would be needed within weeks as Allied Army Headquarters put finishing touches on Operation Overlord, the secret plan for the invasion of Nazi-occupied Europe.

At Coldharbour, Russ found the other tank troop commander was a familiar face. Jim Derij, the former driving and mechanical instructor at Camp Borden with the PEI Light Horse, like Russ had become a lieutenant and was himself recently assigned to this unit. They were now part of the Headquarters Squadron of the Fourth Canadian Armoured Division. Chance had brought them back together in the same tank troop, each commanding a squadron of four tanks to defend the general staff and Headquarters. They were the only purely combat troops in the Headquarters, everyone else having duties in communications, supply, or other jobs supporting a division of nearly fifteen thousand men.

This was Russ's first command, and he remembered the axiom Colonel Rutherford had used many times, that an officer is best served when he has inspired the respect and affection of the men he leads. After four years in the army, Russ had seen many approaches to leadership. Some officers chose to force discipline by punishment for not observing strict rules. Other officers had been lax, failing to correct all but the most extreme breaches of conduct, preferring to coax men along rather than expecting them to perform to a high standard. Russ entered his first command believing an officer could only obtain the best from his men he commanded by treating them fairly, giving them respect while holding them to high standards.

Training in the Fourth Armoured Division was taken seriously. Everyone realized they were being prepared for the coming invasion. Field exercises emphasized movement, the Squadron taking to the road through southeastern England. Exercise "Jill" in April was described in the unit's war diary as "a pleasant drive through the English countryside," the Squadron vehicles "merrily rolling along on the great adventure." The day went off without major complications, a welcome change, since there was usually confusion as the men and vehicles negotiated the unmarked English country roads and towns.

Russ (second from left) with unidentified Armoured Corps officers at the Second Canadian Tank Training School in England.

When not on field exercise, Russ was assigned to carry out routine duties and oversee training. As junior officer, he was given the least-liked jobs, including taking troops to the firing range, and seeking volunteers for the Divisional Sports competition held at the nearby town of Groombridge. But the most disliked job in the unit was likely that of censoring letters. Troopers turned over their letters and information related to troop strength and locations was removed, as were statements critical of the army and England. This "pain in the neck" was the duty of the unit's junior officers like Russ and Jim. But it gave a glimpse into the attitudes of the troops, which, if for no other reason, made the job of censoring important.

Morale-building was important to senior officers. The troops had been in England for as long as five years, most without any activity other than training. One way they tried to boost morale was allowing newspapers to be produced by Canadian units. It was hoped this would build camaraderie and bolster a fighting spirit while providing a diversion, but it was also an informal means of communicating with the troops. The newspaper of the 18th Armoured Car Unit was named *The Staghound*. An article published January, 1944, shows the feelings of *The Staghound's* writers about Canadian troops expected to soon head into battle. It was titled "Ortona."

ORTONA

In the days of peace, few Canadians knew anything of sol-diering. Few of us had ever seen a military uniform, and had no conception of war, except for the lurid, but infrequent tales of our fathers who had been in the last fracas.

So different from our enemy, who is bred for battle, reared on the martial exploits of his race, taught constantly of his superiority over all other men.

Yet at Ortona, described by Alan Moorehead[1] as the bitterest, most terrible fighting of the war, our lads whipped them, and whipped them well.

The guys from the farms and the woods, and the cities of Canada, who knew nothing of soldiering before, took on the best of the Aryan supermen — AND BEAT THEM!

What does this prove?

It proves that volunteers will smash conscripts every time, and it proves that the spirit that made our boys volunteer (and that not one would admit having) is still inside them.

This is the spirit that wins the battles.

It proves also, that Canadians are as good fighting men as any in the world.

If Canadian troops were confident about their coming combat role, feelings towards their political leadership could be outright hostile. In May 1944, Canadian Prime Minister Mackenzie King visited England to take part in a conference of Commonwealth prime ministers. He also took time to visit Canadian troops stationed in southern England. On the day of his visit to the Fourth Division, a heavy rain fell, dampening a demonstration planned for the prime minister of the Division's military drills and exercises. Unlike almost all other officials visiting the troops, the prime minister made no formal speech, despite knowing that within weeks these soldiers were to take part in the invasion of Northwest Europe.

The reason King chose not to address the troops was obvious. During a previous visit to England, the prime minister had been loudly booed by some when he took the microphone. This time King took no chance, even though the troops were warned to be on their best behaviour. The reason for their dislike of King and the government was the creation of a second class of soldier — non-combatants who the troops in Europe labelled "Zombies."

These were soldiers allowed to sit out the war in Canada, given a choice of whether they would fight, while those who had volunteered for overseas service had agreed to put themselves in harm's way. King's Liberal government felt it could not ignore the strong sentiment in Quebec that Quebecers should not have to fight "England's war." The solution implemented to try to satisfy both English Canada and Quebec was embodied in his clever election slogan "conscription if necessary, but not necessarily conscription." Under tremendous pressure from the rest of Canada, King's government finally imposed conscription, but to satisfy Quebec, it promised that the conscripts would serve only in Canada. They would not be forced to risk their lives.

In late May, word came that a new commanding officer was taking over the Headquarters Squadron. His name was Clarence Campbell. The tall man who stepped out of the jeep at Coldharbour in late May had been a well-known and at times controversial referee in the National Hockey League during the 1930s, with a reputation for losing his temper.

Major Clarence Sutherland Campbell was thirty-nine when he came to Coldharbour and had accomplished far more in his lifetime than most men.

When only nineteen, he had completed a law degree at the University of Alberta. He was selected a Rhodes Scholar and attended Oxford. Returning to Edmonton in 1930, Campbell began practicing law, but also took up refereeing in the professional Western Hockey League. Before long, his work on the ice led to an invitation to referee in the National Hockey League. He began refereeing during winter and practicing law in summer.

He held his NHL job until 1939. It ended in controversy after a game at Maple Leaf Gardens. When Toronto defenseman Red Horner was struck over the head with a stick and Campbell called only a minor penalty, Leafs owner Conn Smythe was so incensed that he insisted Campbell not referee any more games. It resulted in Campbell spending the last few months of 1939 in the league head office assisting NHL president Frank Calder. Campbell's contract for the 1940–1941 season was not renewed, and in August 1940, he enlisted with the Edmonton Fusiliers. His education enabled him to join right away as a second lieutenant. By 1941, he had risen to captain and switched to the Active Force, and by 1944, he had served in several branches of the army and been made a major.

Campbell's hope was to attend Senior Officers' training at Camberly and then take command of an infantry company and eventually a battalion. He had by this time impressed many with his "serious example of soldiering."[2] But he would not get the chance to attend Camberley. Instead, Campbell was assigned command of the Headquarters Squadron of the Fourth Canadian Armoured Division. Plans for the invasion of France were progressing rapidly, and the Division was to join the assault several weeks after it began. The Headquarters Squadron needed its commanding officer in place. For Campbell's backers among Canada's senior officers, including Major-General Frank Worthington, this command was as close as they could get him to a front line unit. The Headquarters Squadron officer cadre was now complete, and they, along with the rest of the Fourth Canadian Armoured Division, waited for the invasion to begin.

———•———

Before the sun rose on June 6, 1944, most Canadian troops in southern England realized a large military operation was underway. Many were awakened during the night by waves of planes flying overhead towards the English Channel. At sea an armada sailed towards France that by dawn began the assault on Normandy. Before the day was over, the troops in England and people across Britain and North America received news that the long awaited invasion of Hitler's stronghold in mainland Europe had started.

The invasion provoked great excitement in the Headquarters Squadron, raised a notch further when word came to be ready to move to France at any time. Rumours spread quickly about when and to where they would move. Training helped take the edge off the excitement, especially the daylong trips to the firing range to sharpen skills with Bren guns and rifles.

Exactly one week after D-Day, a new weapon appeared in the skies over London. It was the first V1 rockets launched by the Germans. Their flight paths took most of the V1s directly over the Headquarters Squadron's lines in Coldharbour. These "pilotless planes," as a war diarist called them, passed overhead at a height of only two to three thousand feet and "caused a tremendous sensation." Called V1s, Buzz Bombs, or Doodle Bugs, the distinctive pulsating engines alerted troops of their imminent arrival. When one was heard approaching, everyone stopped, scanning overhead until it appeared, puffing its exhaust trail across the sky.

Their low altitude and straight line of flight made them a favourite target for anti-aircraft guns in Coldharbour. If the path happened to be directly over the regiment's area, shrapnel from the exploding airburst shells landed among the troopers. Shrapnel often came to earth still hot, splinters of metal up to four inches long and three quarters of an inch thick propelled down at high speed by the exploding shells, like a red-hot metallic rain.[3] Smashing into the ground or bouncing off buildings, they threw off sparks and careened in any direction, potentially causing serious injury. The shrapnel regularly ripped the regiment's tents and broke windows, sending glass flying into houses. People quickly became used to the interruption, taking shelter before carrying on what they were doing. Most exciting for those on the ground was to see a fighter close in on a V1, giving the regiment a grandstand view of a Spitfire shooting down a Buzz Bomb.

Two weeks after the invasion of Normandy, the Squadron was still geared up for a move to the front lines in France. However, no order to move came, and day-by-day the troopers' impatience to join the invasion grew. For a month, they sat in camp at Coldharbour, ready to go but without orders. To make the situation worse, they were confined to camp — no passes were being issued for any reason. According to the Squadron's war diary, the morale of the men continued to slide as their "personal D-Day" seemed as far away as ever. It did not help to hear about others taking an active part in the war, especially in the American press, which routinely overlooked the actions of all but U.S. troops.

The Staghound commented on this perpetual oversight in an article titled "An Open Letter to American Newspapers," which went on to say:

Dear Friends,

(It has been noticed that) the U.S. papers ... feature almost exclusively, the American part in battles. Many other reports report that British Tps. are mentioned sometimes — Canadians hardly ever.

It took Walter Winchell to open the eyes of his country-men when he wrote an admirable and widely read article on Canada's part in the war efforts, but we could not help but notice the touch of amazement that even Winchell brought into his writing when he discovered that others were fighting too!

Walter returned to New York, marvelling as if from a voyage of discovery. He wrote his article with the gusto that comes from complete surprise.

We have a story that should be told, and we are proud to tell it ... Every man serving overseas (in our army) is a Volunteer. We are small in numbers, we represent a great nation.

The Canadian Volunteers took up battle stations years before Pearl Harbor. After Dunkirk, our red-patched First Division stood along the edge of this "aircraft carrier off the coast of Europe," and was, in those fierce, critical days, the only organized formation on the Allied side that was capable of battle.

Had your headline writers sailed with any of our hundred ships manned with ten thousand of our sailormen, who sailed against the Germans on "D" Day, they would have seen that other men were fighting.

Canadian paratroops were among the first to hit French soil, and our soldiers raced with yours and the British against the beach defences. Together, they stormed and took them, while our RCAF helped you and the British to rule the skies.

While our magnificent American soldiers are sweeping up on Cherbourg, British and Canadians hold five crack Panzer Divisions down towards Caen and Tilly. There is a bitter battle there.

A little nationalism is natural — we are guilty of it too! To play up and report firstly on your own troops is natural, but we raise, right now our little voice, against the misleading inaccuracies of some of your journalism.

Good-humoredly, and with no malice, we recall the handling of the important and vital Dieppe Raid news. In all too many of your papers the banner headlines proclaimed, "Americans land in France." Surely this was in bad taste? Surely it was an injustice? Surely your people know now that four fifths of the Dieppe soldiers were Canadians? The Rangers who were there fought bravely, but they were only fifty odd, only a handful among thousands.

Send your headline men to our formations in battle line, and they will come back, as Winchell did, with wide-eyed amazement, and will then realize that there are a few more guys in there pitching.

Our Allied soldiers fight and die together. Yanks, British, Canadians and the rest of us are in it side by side.

We Canadians do not want publicity — our deeds will speak — but we do protest against injustice. And, being Canadians, we are not too modest to step right up and tell you so!

After more than a month confined to barracks, the weather perpetually grey and raining, rumours resumed that the Fourth Division was about to move to France. Skepticism, however, was strong by this time and the news was met largely by disbelief. But on July 14, 1944, orders came to send an advance party to France to prepare the way for the Headquarters Squadron. The Fourth Canadian Armoured Division prepared to at last join the fighting in Normandy.

———————◆———————

Russ and Jim got no sleep the night of July 17 as they had hundreds of details that needed looking after. Though they had known for than a month this moment was coming, it seemed the last-minute preparations would never be done. Vehicles were marshalled into line in preparation for the move, and at precisely 3:15 a.m., the Headquarters Squadron left Coldharbour, headed for London's East End docks.

Russ's tank was fifth in the column of eight winding its way through the streets of London. They were part of the convoy of trucks, tanks, and half-tracks led through the blacked out streets of London by Canadian military police on motorcycles. They reached Tilbury dockyard just after seven a.m., parking their tanks in the marshalling area. Russ and Jim were assigned one among the thousands of tents jammed into the nearby camp. They were issued rations to last two days, a lifebelt and seasick bags, and their first pay in French money. There was pleasant surprise at not being confined to camp after being restricted to Coldharbour for more than a month.

Overhead, the continual stream of V1s unsuccessfully targeted the dock-yards where the Fourth Division waited to embark, while below the docks hummed with activity, day and night. Soldiers and sailors frenziedly loaded every imaginable army vehicle onto all sizes of ship in the Thames River. It took two days for all of the Headquarters Squadron vehicles to be winched into the air by derricks and lowered into ships' holds. The Squadron's tanks were hoisted onto open-topped "Landing Craft Tanks" (LCTs) or driven into large "Landing Ship Tanks" (LSTs).

The men's anticipation of immediate departure died as the ships remained firmly moored to the dock. When they did finally pull away it was only to anchor in the river. There was little to do and no one knew how long the wait would be. The officers tried to keep the troops occupied, but mostly the men sat aboard ship, playing cards and watching the work on the docks and ships moving in the river.

Four days after the troops arrived, ships carrying the Headquarters Squadron weighed anchor and moved slowly downriver, past the masts and funnels of ships sunk earlier in the war, heading towards the mouth of the Thames. By midnight on July 22, the convoy was at the mouth of the English Channel off the coast at Dover. The ships were blacked out, and in the darkness a steady stream of V1s passed overhead on their way to London. Orange and red tracer fire from guns on the ships chased the V1s, painting the night sky and leaving a luminescent afterglow in the eyes of the troops watching on deck.

As the convoy passed the narrowest point in the English Channel, the massive fifteen-inch guns of the German batteries on Cap Gris Nez in France opened fire. From the French shore less than ten miles away, each heavy shell weighed nearly a ton and sounded like a freight train as it raced overhead. It created a tense hour until the ships had passed out of range.

Early that morning they arrived off Juno Beach, near the town of Courseulles-sur-Mer. No one had slept as their convoy drew nearer France, and thoughts turned to what awaited. Most had enlisted four or five years earlier and trained ever since. Now they were to have the chance to use that training.

Russ stood at the ship's rail with the men of his tank squadron. Their ship sat offshore among vessels of all types and sizes, from merchant vessels bringing supplies, to hospital ships bearing large red crosses, and landing craft running back and forth, ferrying men and equipment to shore. Overhead floated grey barrage balloons suspended to discourage low-flying enemy aircraft. Waves of Allied planes roared in from England to engage German targets a few miles inland. All along the beach, lines of vehicles and soldiers waited to move inland.

When its turn came, the LST Russ was on headed towards shore. To the surprise of the soldiers, the two large doors making up the ship's bow slowly began opening while they were still offshore. Their first thoughts were that it was a mistake, that water would rush inside and sink the ship. Instead, the ship picked up speed. Russ and the men in his squadron braced for a sudden

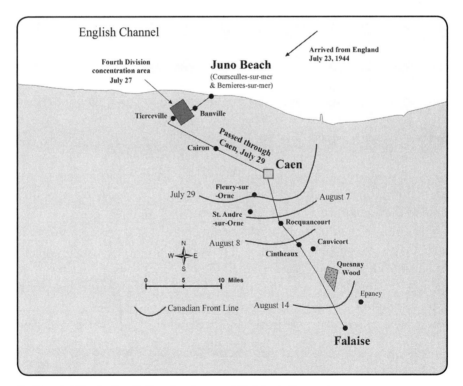

Positions held by the Fourth Canadian Armoured Division in Normandy.

Based on a map reproduced with permission from Stanford University's Spatial History Project on "Building the New Order: 1938–1945" (*www.stanford.edu/group/spatialhistory/cgi-bin/site/pub. php?id=51&project_id=*).

jolt, but instead, the ship's captain cut the engines at the last moment, bringing the flat-bottomed ship to a gentle stop as its bow rose and ran aground. Russ and the rest of the tank troops made their way to the ship's hold while sailors unwound the heavy cable lowering a ramp to the sand. The tanks were now free to drive from the ship, the last twenty or so feet through the surf.

Up and down Juno Beach, the Fourth Canadian Armoured Division's regiments were coming ashore. The first to land was the Governor General's Foot Guards, followed by the South Alberta Regiment, the Canadian Grenadier Guards from Montreal, and finally the British Columbia Regiment. The Division's Motor Battalion, the Lake Superior Regiment from Port Arthur and Fort William in northwestern Ontario, disembarked at Red Beach near Grave-sur-Mer. The Fourth's infantry regiments, all from Ontario, also were unloading. There was the Lincoln and Welland Regiment, called the Lincs, from the Niagara Region, the Algonquin Regiment from central and northeastern Ontario, and Hamilton's Argyll and Sutherland Highlanders. They were soon joined by the Division's four artillery regiments, the 15th and 23rd Field Artillery, the Fifth Anti-tank, and the Eighth Light Anti-aircraft.

The Headquarters Squadron began disembarking on July 24 but was slowed by the frequent collapse of the derricks unloading vehicles. It took three days for the Squadron to fully disembark and assemble with the rest of the Division at the marshalling area between Banville and Tierceville, spread out two to four miles southwest of Juno Beach.[4]

Five days after arriving, all regiments had assembled and the Fourth Division was ready to move inland. The Headquarters Squadron moved out for the front lines on July 29. The day was hot and the roads dusty, the dull thud of shelling growing louder as the column moved inland.

Nothing in their training or experiences thus far had prepared them for what they were about to see. As they approached the city of Caen, the wreckage from Allied bombing shocked even these soldiers, used to the extensive damage in London. Most of the city had been destroyed, and rubble from Caen's buildings had fallen into the roads. In places the bricks, stone, and wood were piled twenty to thirty feet high where Canadian and British Engineers had bulldozed paths through the wreckage.

The troops were enveloped in a pervasive foul smell as they entered Caen. They soon realized it was from bodies buried in the collapsed buildings. Gagging troopers held their noses or put handkerchiefs over their faces. Some estimates put the number killed by the Caen bombings at five thousand civilians, most buried in the rubble by misdirected Allied bombing.

From the turret of his tank, crawling through the streets, Russ saw one of the few structures not badly damaged by the bombing. It was Église Saint-Étienne at the Abbé des Hommes, a large church with thick stone walls and tall Gothic spires that still stood in the centre of Caen. Thousands of civilians who had sought refuge within miraculously escaped the repeated Allied bombings. Three weeks earlier, Canadians had first arrived at the Abbé, among them war correspondent Matthew Halton. He later described that day.

> Our high command had planned and hoped to take Caen on D-Day, but in fact it was a month later before we got it. And in that month, the people of Caen learned the meaning of Hell.
>
> During that terrible month some two thousand people had taken refuge in a famous church, the Abbé des Hommes. The whole month they have lived there. Some had died there, babies had been born there; the sanctuary was turned into a hospital. By some miracle not one bomb and only one shell had hit the church.
>
> We heard fantastic stories. Stories such as this, for example. There was no electricity to run the great pipe organ. So every day the small boys and girls climbed up a loft and pumped the bellows with their hands and feet. And so every day, the music … went swelling through the church.
>
> … I'll never forget the scene when the people swept out into the little square outside and sang "La Marseilles" as I'd never heard it sung before, in tears, and yet, in joy.[5]

The Fourth Division fanned out south of Caen to the front line. The Headquarters Squadron went about two miles south of the city on the highway to Falaise, stopping near the village of Fleury-sur-Orne. Canadians had cleared the village of German troops about a week earlier, and it showed scars of the fierce battle to take a bridgehead south of the Orne River.[6] Nearby was a German Tiger tank, destroyed in the recent battle. It was the first Tiger the Squadron's troopers had seen up close and was the subject of considerable interest.

Standing beside the massive German tank, Russ and Jim realized how puny their Shermans were. Two features immediately impressed them: the Tiger's long 88-mm cannon, overhanging seven feet beyond the front of the tank, and the heavy armour covering the massive vehicle. The Shermans they drove weighed barely half of the Tiger, and the Canadian tank's 75-mm gun looked pitiful compared to the menacing 88. Both men thought the same thing: their Shermans would stand little chance in a tank-to-tank fight against a Tiger.

At Fleury-sur-Orne, Jim and Russ were less than fifteen miles from Juno Beach, a meagre advance in the almost two months since D-Day. The fierce German defence in Normandy had kept the Allies penned up with their backs against the English Channel. Although the Germans had recently been forced to relinquish Caen, they still held Verrières Ridge, the strategically important high ground south and east of the city. From that vantage point, Generalmajor Kurt Meyer, thirty-four-year-old German commander of the 12th SS Panzer Division, had a clear view of the rolling countryside and the Canadians below.

The 12th SS was a Hitler Youth Division, assembled in 1943 and given to Meyer and his cadre of veteran SS officers and battle-hardened NCOs. They had trained their seventeen- to nineteen-year-old recruits well, and in the month since D-Day, the 12th SS had repeatedly fought the Canadians, earning a reputation as unrelentingly fierce opponents.

———◆———

When the Fourth Division deployed into the front line, a deceptive calm existed. Both the Canadians and the young soldiers of the 12th SS knew the quiet would not last. In the meantime, the Germans shelled the Canadians. The lack of rain and the chalky earth made any trip by a Canadian vehicle south of Caen a harrowing experience, German spotters only two or three miles away on the ridge bringing down artillery fire when they saw clouds of dust. There was also random shelling of Canadian lines, which was why the Canadians brought only armoured vehicles to the front line, vehicles with tires instead of tracks with sandbags or bricks stacked to protect the tires from shrapnel. In one case, two shells from German 88s landed in the Fourth Division's artillery headquarters. Fortunately, both shells failed to explode.

The German 88s doing much of the shelling had proven themselves deadly to Allied tanks in Normandy. Though its role was as an anti-aircraft weapon, it proved deadly when fired on targets on the ground. On the wide open plains south of Caen, the gun could be aimed over "open sights," the German gunners looking directly along the cannon's barrel through a high power telescope, aiming the powerful weapon the way a hunter uses a rifle's sights. It was highly accurate when used this way. The effect of the high velocity shells on armour was devastating. Switching to high-explosive rounds against infantry, the 88 was likewise terrifyingly efficient.

Not long after moving into the front lines, the Fourth Division began seeing German soldiers brought in as prisoners of war. One early instance was described in *The Staghound*:

> These prisoners were taken by "D" Sqn. during the recce patrols, and Cpl. Hoffman was used to interrogate them.
>
> "When I arrived at RHQ, I saw them standing there with a group of our men looking them over curiously. Although as nervous perhaps as they, I went over with Lt. Calcutt to the first one.
>
> "He was a little fellow who looked a little ludicrous because his clothes were far too large for him. As soon as I spoke, he began to cry like a child (in fact, he didn't look a day over 17) but he finally stopped and spoke to us a little when he saw we meant him no harm.
>
> "One of the other two looked like the real, original Hitler Aryan with blonde hair, blue eyes, etc. He was pretty sure of himself and eyed me suspiciously. He gave me the creeps, that one.
>
> "The third one was shaken pretty badly, but he was able to talk. He seemed glad of the chance to talk, and words tumbled over one another when he finally got going. We learned from him that they had been trying to give themselves up for some time and that they did not like the German Army any more.
>
> "They did not impress me as being so tough. Our men are a hell of a lot tougher, to my mind. The second one did have some of that Hitler stuff that we have been reading about for so long.
>
> "It was a good and interesting experience for me to question these men, for these were the first live Germans that I have come into contact with. The only others that I have seen, have been dead, or else marching past as prisoners."

Despite the frequent harassing shellfire, a sense of normality soon developed. The first Saturday at Fleury-sur-Orne, many of the troopers took time to bathe using buckets of water drawn from the village pump, which to their surprise the Germans had left in working order. With few duties the next day, many of the men stripped down and sunbathed.

While troopers in the Headquarters Squadron relaxed on the front lines, the same could not be said for senior military staff of the First Canadian Army, including the senior officers of the Fourth. They were involved in planning the Fourth's first major combat operation, Operation Totalize. It was to be a massive attack against the Germans on Verrières Ridge.

The Canadian troops in Operation Totalize were to push south through the Germans on Verrières Ridge, their objective the crossroads at a French village named Falaise. They were to meet there with American forces coming north, in doing so encircling the German Seventh Army.

The Germans had stymied British Field Marshall Bernard Montgomery's plans for almost two months. Under Montgomery's command, repeated Canadian and British attacks had made little progress. After the war, Montgomery would say that Canadian soldiers were not at their best in large, planned operations. They were, he said, better "in the fluid type of battle, where he can crack about and kill Germans. They're better at that than in a set piece battle."[7] But after nearly two months, Montgomery had little success expanding the beachhead.

The gains by Canadian and British forces in Normandy had come at the cost of heavy losses of men and tanks. It was claimed the repeated and costly operations by Montgomery's forces on the left wing of the Normandy front were a strategic success, since it forced strong German forces, especially the Panzer divisions, to stay near Caen, instead of opposing the Americans to the west. But Montgomery's goal must surely never have been merely a holding action. He must have wanted a breakout.

Had he been able to orchestrate this in the two months after D-Day, Montgomery would have collapsed the entire front. The Germans viewed the stalemate south of Caen as a strategic success, since it kept open the supply lines to the German Seventh Army. Now that force was being pushed back by the Americans, who had broken the stalemate on the western end of the Normandy front. The German High Command was aware of the necessity of holding the position south of Caen, but in early August they had no choice but to weaken their forces on Verrières Ridge, sending Panzer units to reinforce the front facing the Americans. In early August, conditions were ripe for Montgomery's breakout and Canadians were to be the spearhead of the assault.

Though weakened, the defences opposing the Canadians were still formidable, particularly the anti-tank forces. The 12th SS Panzer Division was the best of the units facing them, and it was bolstered by units from the German 15th Army and the twelve thousand-strong 89th Infantry Division. Most importantly, the 89th brought additional artillery, anti-tank guns, and the dangerous 88s.

The battle lines were thus set, strong German anti-tank defences facing powerful Canadian tank forces. In the looming Operation Totalize, one was bound to break, and on that outcome hung the immediate fate of the western front.

While Russ and Jim waited with the Fourth's Headquarters Squadron near Fleury-sur-Orne, to the northwest of Caen, their division's commanding officer, General George Kitching, arrived at Château de Rots, in the Normandy countryside near the village of the same name.[8] Kitching and his staff joined other senior officers of the Second Canadian Corps, waiting for Canadian General Guy Simonds to brief them on plans for their upcoming attack.

The tall, gaunt General George Kitching was a British-born commander of Canadian troops. He had trained and served as a British officer before resigning to join the Canadian army, seeking advancement that he felt would be slow or non-existent in the British army.

Kitching had served with the Canadian forces under Montgomery during the Sicily and Italian campaigns in 1943. He was a young general whose sole combat experience came when commanding the 11th Canadian Infantry Brigade for several months in Italy in 1944. Only thirty-three when given command of the Fourth Canadian Armoured Division, Kitching had been in the Canadian army for five years, and as recently as 1940 was a lieutenant in the Royal Canadian Regiment. He had been promoted past hundreds of officers and commanded one of only two Canadian armoured divisions.[9]

Kitching's commanding officer was Canadian General Guy Simonds. Simonds was also British by birth, but his family had immigrated to Canada when he was only eight. Simonds graduated at the head of his class from the Royal Military College in Kingston and was considered a prodigy, perhaps the best officer ever to have come out of Canadian officer training.[10] However, Simonds too lacked extensive combat experience, his only battle command prior to Normandy coming during six months in 1943 in Sicily and Italy.

Montgomery treated Simonds almost as a protégé, identifying him as one who "had the makings of a future army commander."[11] Seeing Montgomery and Simonds together, one was struck by their physical similarity, with their slender builds, straight dark hair, and pencil-thin moustaches. Simonds had high expectations for Canadian troops in the coming battle he named Operation Totalize. Although the German soldier was very good, Simonds said, he was no match for the Canadian, who was brought up with a different mentality, was an individualist and imaginative.[12] As he began his address to the officers assembled in the Chateau for his briefing, Simonds read from a note he had earlier sent to all units under his command. In it, he cited the recent example of Canadian Major John Mahony, awarded the Victoria Cross for his actions in Italy.

Reading the citation aloud, Simonds stressed that although Mahony's regiment had just entered its first major action, his leadership had held a bridgehead against overwhelming odds, fighting off repeated German counterattacks. Simonds told the assembled generals they and their officers needed to show the same leadership in the coming battle, pushing beyond what they might believe possible. There was to be no excuse for anything but veteran performance from the Fourth Canadian Division, despite the operation being its first.

Operation Totalize was planned in the aftermath of unsuccessful assaults by British and Canadian troops on Verrières Ridge. Operation Goodwood and its Canadian partner, Operation Atlantic, had gained important ground near Caen, but with losses of large numbers of British tanks and Canadian infantry. Of the nearly seven hundred British tanks sent into action, almost half were destroyed. That rate of loss was unsustainable and required a new approach.

The plan Simonds described was innovative but risky, because the opening assault, Phase One, would be at night, an unheard of tactic for tanks. When someone told him, "But it's never been done before," his reply was simply "That's why I'm doing it."[13] Night fighting was considered highly risky for tanks, since enemy infantry could easily get close enough to use hand-held anti-tank weapons.

In daylight, the long field of view from Verrières Ridge allowed hidden German anti-tank guns to pick off Canadian tanks before they could find and destroy them. From the range of a mile on Verrières Ridge, just a few concealed German 88-mm and 75-mm guns were capable of destroying a half or more of a Canadian armoured regiment's sixty tanks before they could be dealt with. And the Germans had more than a hundred anti-tank guns hidden along the ridge, dooming to failure any frontal assault. A night attack was supposed to take away this threat.

The plan also included heavy bombardments preceding Phase One. When that ended, four hundred massed tanks would move forward, so large a force that even if many were destroyed, the attack could continue. To prevent German soldiers infiltrating among the tanks during the night attack, Simonds would send Canadian infantry with the tanks during Phase One, carried in newly improvised armoured troop carriers dubbed Kangaroos.

To keep the armoured columns on course, artificial moonlight, a tactic from the Great War, would be provided by searchlights aimed at the clouds. Anti-aircraft guns would fire tracer rounds along the line of the attack, and a radio beacon would provide a loud signal when the tanks were on the proper line of attack.

Phase Two would be a conventional daylight attack by two fresh armoured divisions, one the Fourth Canadian and the other the First Polish. Both divisions would advance overnight during Phase One and take over the front in the morning. It too would begin with an aerial bombardment, and a barrage by Canadian artillery. Concealment from the deadly German anti-tank guns in Phase Two would be provided by smoke shells.

If successful, the Fourth and the Polish would meet up with the Americans advancing from the south under General George Patton. They would trap the German Seventh Army in Normandy.

With the briefing over, the generals and staff of the Second Canadian Corps returned to their own headquarters. As General Kitching's car left, back in the harbour near Fleury-sur-Orne, Russ and Jim watched as the last of the fuel cans were emptied into their tanks' twin fuel tanks. The two lieutenants did not realize the coming battle had the potential to bring the war to an early end, making Simonds and Kitching two of the most famous generals of the Second World War, and the Fourth one of its most heralded divisions.

———◆———

The rising sun cresting Verrières Ridge on August 7 dissolved the fog that had settled above the wheat fields. The mist gave way to a day dubbed "beautiful" by the Headquarter Squadron's war diarist. But before this day was finished, the beauty of the French countryside would be replaced by the wrenching sights and sounds of battle.

At divisional headquarters, Russ and Jim were busy making sure the eight Headquarters tanks were fully loaded with ammunition for the 50-calibre machine guns and shells for the main gun. Shells were loaded through the top hatch, passed by a soldier from the ground to another standing on the deck of the tank, to one more in the turret and then to one inside the hull, who placed the shells in racks on the inside of the tank. The shells were colour-coded to distinguish armour-piercing rounds from anti-personnel, high-explosive, or smoke. The two lower ammunition racks, one on each side of the hull, held a total of eighty-four shells. A rack in the turret held a further six.

The Germans on the ridge seemed unaware of the imminent attack, doing nothing beyond their routine artillery harassment. One of their shells found a slit trench where the driver of a Headquarters gasoline truck was resting. He was the Headquarters Squadron's first casualty. Two other troopers were wounded when a lone Junkers 88 aircraft bombed and strafed the Squadron.

As the day progressed, the armoured regiments that would lead Phase One moved into pre-start positions, joined by infantry troops in Kangaroos. The rolling hills kept the assembling forces largely hidden from direct sight of the Germans, but they put so much dust in the air, it was surprising they did not attract shelling. Were the Germans asleep, or lulling the Canadians into a trap?

The Fourth Armoured Division, part of Phase Two, waited south of Caen for the order to move into position. They would come forward overnight behind the tanks taking part in Phase One. Russ and Jim were with Fourth Division command, their job to provide a defensive shield for General Kitching and his staff. If the General needed to see firsthand what was happening else-where on the battlefield, he could send one of his staff officers forward in the command tank, equipped with a strong radio. Otherwise, the General would follow behind the main fighting forces and provide direction to the armoured regiments as the battle developed.

There was a nervous energy among the tank crews. For most it would be their first time in battle and the long, drawn-out wait was almost painful. They fell into familiar training patterns, checking and rechecking weapons and equipment, but mostly they just waited quietly. Troopers glanced repeatedly at their watches as the minutes slowly ticked by, while the Padre passed among the men, offering to pray with them. Major Campbell was keeping his eyes on both the tank troops and the General. Campbell would be part of the group accompanying Kitching as the Fourth advanced during Phase Two.

———————————————•———————————————

Sunset arrived at nine thirty on August 7. As it did, armoured vehicles taking part in Phase One fired up their engines and slowly moved forward, pacing themselves so the lead vehicles would cross the start line on time.

As the massed Sherman tanks of Phase One began advancing, a handful of Canadian artillery fired shells over German positions on the ridge, a sound heard across the Canadian lines. At Headquarters, Russ saw the shells explode high in the air, base plates blowing off ejecting flares leaving trails of coloured smoke as they floated down, red to the east and green to the west. A continual stream of flare shells identified the targets for two approaching lines of British and Canadian bombers.

Canadians and Germans alike stared skywards as the heavy drone of approaching bombers grew louder. The Germans ran for cover, jumping into slit trenches, knowing the flares meant Verrières Ridge was in the line of attack. Coming towards them were two streams of heavy bombers, over a thousand four-engine Lancasters and Halifaxes from airfields in England, about two hundred and fifty of them from Royal Canadian Air Force Squadrons.

The bombardment when it came was ferocious. The Germans on the ridge could only shelter in their slit trenches from the terrifying concussion and flying shrapnel. On top of the intense aerial bombardment, German positions were pounded by shells from Canadian artillery. More than three hundred and fifty guns spread out south of Caen fired onto suspected German positions. Each exploding bomb and shell lit the sky like a flash of sheet lightning, the sound of the explosion following seconds later, the concussion waves reverberating in the chests of the watching Canadians.

Shortly after midnight the bombing stopped, but the artillery continued firing unrelentingly for another hour. By the time the carefully planned barrage was over, more than sixty thousand shells had exploded on the ridge.

With the departure of the Allied bombers, the Canadians lit their searchlights, shining the beams on the clouds. Bofors guns began firing orange-coloured tracers, marking the lanes where the columns of tanks were to advance. Four hundred tank engines roared to life, adding to the noise of exploding artillery shells.

When the order came, the tanks and troop carriers of Phase One began slowly moving, their columns each a twenty-yard-wide armoured battering ram, four tanks abreast and dozens of tanks deep, grouped so closely one could almost jump from tank to tank. At the head of each column came a flail tank, swinging steel chains attached to a spindle on the front of the tank to beat the ground and explode mines buried by the Germans. The flails raised great clouds of dust from the dry earth, enveloping the advancing columns in a gritty fog. The dust clouds were made worse by the tank treads kicking more dirt into the air. Tank drivers quickly found their vision obscured. They had closed their hatches to allow the turret to rotate, and even in the best conditions the periscopes provided poor visibility. In the dark and the clouds of dust, their vision was so poor, drivers saw little beyond the small light at the back of the tank in front of them.

Amid the noise, the flashes of exploding shells, and the clouds of dust, tanks lost their way. Some drove into bomb craters, where they were trapped. In a few instances Canadians fired on other Canadian tanks caught out of position. But other than tanks setting off mines and a few being hit by German anti-tank guns, there was little contact with the enemy. Tanks on the front or sides of the advancing columns occasionally fired their guns when a tank commander thought he had seen Germans. But mostly the massed armoured columns continued steadily forward onto Verrières Ridge, past pockets of German opposition. The German front lines were pierced. Simonds's plan for Phase One had worked.

Shortly before two a.m., word was given to the Headquarters tank crews to mount. For more than two hours, Russ and Jim and their crews had watched the flashes from the explosions on Verrières Ridge. Now they were to move.

Jim, more than most, may have felt the importance of this moment. He had wondered as a teenager in the militia in Winnipeg if he would one day be in battle. Now he was about to fulfill all those years of training. In the turret, he might have thought how unpredictable life was. It seemed so improbable he was here, in this dusty field in France, the engines making the tank quiver like a hound ready to hunt. In Russ's tank, his thoughts may have turned to the quiet street in Owen Sound where Blanche and Jack were at that moment likely sitting on the front porch after dinner. Were they thinking of him and what he might be doing?

Finally, over the tank-to-tank radio, Russ heard the order to begin their advance. The noise of the idling tank engine changed from a low throb to a throaty growl as the engines revved loudly. The tank jerked roughly into motion, clouds of blue smoke from the twin Ford engines filling the air.

As the tanks accelerated, the loud squeak-squawk of their bogey wheels and the clank of the tracks was muffled by Russ's tanker's helmet. Each tank commander stood with his upper torso out of the turret. For now, they would travel "unbuttoned," with the top tank hatch open, allowing the tank commander to scan for targets much faster than he could with it closed. But standing there, he was also exposed to rifle and machine-gun fire and shrapnel.

Russ's and Jim's tanks formed a hollow square, inside which General Kitching, Major Campbell, and the headquarters communications centre moved forward, pacing themselves to reach their starting point shortly after dawn. They followed the route taken earlier during Phase One, the path cleared of mines and marked by white tape and amber and green lights on the ground.[14] From time to time they passed Canadian tanks, casualties of a mine or anti-tank fire, but the only signs of battle other than the firing of their artillery were occasional pockets of Germans who continued fighting the Canadian infantry assigned to mop them up.

On Verrières Ridge, many of the German troops were in a state of shock from the bombardment. When the artillery barrage finally lifted, they heard the ominous sound of hundreds of Canadian tanks approaching. Some panicked and ran, believing their lines destroyed by the devastating barrage they had somehow survived. Others stayed to fight.

By dawn the armoured columns of Phase One had reached their forward objectives. There they simply stopped. They stopped not because of casualties or because of stiffening German resistance, for there was little of either. It was decided days earlier that they should stop here. Now the plan called for the Fourth Canadian and the First Polish Armoured Divisions to move forward and execute Phase Two of Operation Totalize.

By six a.m., the Fourth reached the front line north of the village of Cintheaux. They were to wait a full six hours, unless told otherwise. A wave of Allied bombers was to carpet-bomb the area ahead. The Canadian officers who had been present at Simonds's briefing in Château de Rots may have realized the irony of the delay. His earlier imprecations to show "strong leadership in battle" and to "push beyond what they might have believed possible" seemed absurd now that Simonds abandoned any initiative built up from Phase One.

Kitching knew Simonds had three hours to cancel the bombing preceding Phase Two. He had even warned Simonds this opportunity would arise. The day before, he and the First Polish Division's General Maczek both told Simonds he should let their divisions begin their attacks without waiting for the next wave of bombers.[15] But as the clock ticked inexorably on that morning, Kitching knew Simonds had failed to send the message to call off the bombing.

Simonds chose caution, despite knowing ULTRA codebreakers had intercepted German messages saying their second line of defence was weakened when Panzers were transferred against the Americans in western Normandy.[16] His misjudgement would cost the lives of many Canadians and Poles and decimate a large part of the Fourth's tank forces.

———————•———————

The person helped most by Simonds's questionable decision was Kurt Meyer, commander of the 12th SS. Through the early hours of August 8, Meyer had watched the artillery and aerial bombardments of Verrières Ridge, but reports from the battlefield were confused. The gravity of the situation became clear as he drove north in the morning to assess the situation. Streaming past him were groups of fleeing German soldiers, something he had never seen before. The Allied attack had broken the German front, although from the sound of small arms fire in the direction of Verrières Ridge, it was clear some German units still held. Meyer jumped from his car and stood in the road as shells from Canadian artillery exploded nearby.

"Before me," he later said, "making their way down the Caen-Falaise Road in a disorderly rabble, were the panic-stricken troops of the 89th Infantry Division.[17] I realized that something had to be done to send these men back into line and fight. I lit a cigar, stood in the middle of the road and in a loud voice asked them if they were going to leave me alone to cope with the enemy. Hearing a divisional commander address them in this way, they stopped, hesitated and then returned to their positions."

Continuing forward, he surveyed the front lines. The fields to the north of Cintheaux were filled with hundreds of Canadian and Polish tanks. Why didn't the massive tank forces put in an attack and press their advantage home?

That question was answered by the sound of an approaching plane. It was a lone American B17 bomber. He realized it must be the prelude to another aerial bombardment, this one aimed at the defensive positions he was forming near the farms and woods around Cintheaux. Immediately, Meyer ordered a recently arrived Panzer force to attack. He wanted them to go forward as quickly as possible, away from the defensive line the bombers would be targeting.

Roughly fifty Panzers and Tigers headed north to engage seven hundred Canadian and Polish tanks. The massive tank forces they were going to attack, made up of men poised to enter their first engagement, were about to learn firsthand the cruel uncertainty of battle.

———————•———————

Waiting was torture to the Canadian troops north of Cintheaux. Most sat quietly, looking at pictures of their wives or sweethearts, rereading their letters. No one wanted to embarrass himself by showing fear. They hoped their nerves would hold once the shooting began, but some felt sick to their stomachs, their bowels loose. Others chain-smoked cigarettes with shaking hands. In all of them, adrenalin poured in great torrents through their veins. Many were finding the thought of lowering themselves into the claustrophobic and highly explosive interior of their tank a test of their will-power. The inside of the Sherman is suffocatingly small. And sitting inches from explosive rounds of ammunition it is very dangerous. The armour surrounding the men in the turret seemed sufficient until one saw the effect of a high-velocity armour-piercing German shell. There were enough burned-out Shermans littering the fields of Normandy for the Canadians to know an 88 shell could easily eviscerate their thinly armoured, high-silhouette tanks.

Worse than the thought of dying instantly if hit by a shell was that of fire. The speed with which the crew compartment in a Sherman could burst into flame when hit left the image of being horribly burned to death.

In the Fourth's lines, the quiet was broken by the crack of a lone German cannon, followed by an exploding shell somewhere in the direction of the Polish Division. From Kitching's headquarters it sounded as if the Poles were beginning their attack ahead of schedule. They had not — it was Meyer's Panzers attacking. German tanks now suddenly opened fire in front of the Canadians, using the scattered farmhouses for cover. All hell was about to break loose.

———————◆———————

At nearly the same time as Meyer's tanks began their attack, the main force of bombers arrived overhead. They were Simonds's bombers, the ones he had made nearly seven hundred tanks wait three hours for. More than six hundred B17 Flying Fortresses of the U.S. Eighth Air Force were commencing their bombing runs, signalling the start of Phase Two. The bombing began at twelve thirty in the afternoon and, when it was completed, the Fourth and the Polish armoured divisions were supposed to start their attack.

The first bombs fell on target, and billowing clouds of grey dust filled the air, mixing with thick, black smoke where fires had ignited. The oily smoke drifted towards the Canadian and Polish positions. In a few short moments the Canadian lines turned from tense calm to embattled confusion as shells from the attacking German tanks mixed with exploding bombs. To Fourth Division troops waiting for the order to begin the attack, it sounded as though bombs were dropping behind them. Confusion turned to disbelief as the Canadians and Poles realized that some of the bombers were dropping their loads short. The Americans were carpet-bombing their own allies.

Troopers scrambled into tanks, some crawled underneath them, and still others flattened themselves on the ground. The ground shook as bombs exploded all around. It lasted only minutes. As the last of the bombers flew on, and Russ opened the hatch of his tank, the orderly assemblage of men and vehicles was replaced by burning Canadian vehicles, cries of wounded men, and the unwounded emerging from shelter. The medical corps began attending to the hundreds of casualties, and the ambulances, whose role would have been to take wounded from the battle with the Germans back to field hospitals in the rear, instead carried those wounded from the mistaken bombing. Those killed in the bombardment were placed in makeshift morgues in the fields.

Kitching's staff worked to re-establish contact with the headquarters of each of the division's regiments, to determine the extent of the damage. As far as Kitching was concerned, his orders had not changed. The Fourth was to begin the attack on the heels of the American bombardment, and it was his intention to carry out that order. The force of German tanks sent against the Fourth just before the bombardment had been eliminated by Canadian and British tanks, but the Poles, less than a mile to the east, were suffering badly from an attack by a strong force of Jagdpanzer armoured tank destroyers.

Despite the losses and confusion from the American bombing, the Canadians began their attack almost on schedule. However, Meyer had used his time well. In the precious six hours granted by Simonds, Meyer had created a strong defensive line of anti-tank guns and 88-mm flak cannons redeployed to the front from anti-aircraft positions. These were now concealed among the woods and farmhouses dotting the countryside.

When the Fourth Division's tanks began advancing, they faced the deadly formula of an exposed attack across open fields with long fields of fire from German antitank weapons. The smoke screen supposed to protect the Canadians was largely nonexistent, making the Fourth's tanks sitting ducks.

The Germans allowed the Canadian tanks to come well forward before opening fire. When they began firing, the effect was devastating. Tank after tank was hit by German anti-tank shells. In tanks hit and disabled without exploding or bursting into flames, the crews had a chance to bail out, but once outside the protection of their Shermans, they were exposed to machine gun and small arms fire. Some crews were cut down, while others sought cover in the fields.

The Fourth's tanks were forced back by the devastatingly accurate fire. By late afternoon, the attack had stopped, barely making headway beyond Cintheaux. The situation was no better for the Poles, who lost forty Shermans.

Montgomery, whose portion of the Allied front had stagnated for a month, ordered Simonds to renew the attack. Simonds in turn pressed Kitching to move the Fourth Division forward overnight. Kitching sent the Fourth's British Columbia Regiment make its way in the dark to a strategic hill from which German defensive positions could be threatened.

After sunset, tanks from the British Columbia Regiment moved forward, a detachment of infantry from the Algonquin Regiment riding atop. Relying on maps and compasses to negotiate the countryside in the dark, the Canadian force became lost. Finding a hilltop they believed was their objective, they were in fact on the wrong hill, miles behind German lines.

At sunrise on the morning of August 9, the Germans discovered this isolated Canadian force in their rear. Meyer unleashed his tanks. Trapped on the hill in exposed positions, the Canadians were helpless, lacking the firepower to seriously damage the German Tiger and Panther tanks assaulting them while their poorly armoured Shermans were vulnerable to the German tanks. One Canadian tank after another was knocked out while the surrounded Canadians radioed Kitching's headquarters for artillery and aerial support. But when the Canadian artillery fired on the coordinates given by the trapped Canadians, nothing reached the intended target. Not knowing their true position, the shells came down on a hilltop five miles to the west. Despite the desperate calls for assistance, no help came. By the end of the day the German Tigers and Panthers had destroyed forty-seven of the fifty-two B.C. Regiment tanks. Only a small force on foot was able to escape.

The next morning marked forty-eight hours since the start of Operation Totalize. With Simonds insisting the German defensive line be broken, Kitching sent a tank force against a German anti-tank stronghold barring the path to Falaise. The place was Quesnay Wood, and it was laced with German anti-tank guns, mortars, and small arms. The attack began concealed by early morning fog, Canadian tanks moving out in columns. They drove straight at the Germans in a frontal attack. The men in the lead tanks realized they were especially vulnerable, with nothing protecting them from the deadly German 88s but their thin armour and the thinning mist.

Suddenly the lead tank was hit. Barely had that tank been destroyed than more anti-tank guns in Quesnay Wood opened fire, taking out one tank after another. The Canadian tanks tried to find a target to return fire, but the woods provided a near perfect hiding place. From a distance of two or three miles, the edge of Quesnay Woods looked like a solid wall of leaves; picking out a cannon muzzle through the veil of foliage was practically impossible. Firing their 88s across open sights and flat fields, the Germans could hardly miss.

This was the last gasp of Operation Totalize. The Germans pushed back the attack on Quesnay Wood with heavy Canadian casualties. The Fourth had made little progress towards Falaise, still eight miles away. The chance to seize a victory that might have shortened the war was gone.

Crew of a Sherman tank loading shells. Spent shells lie on the ground. This tank was with Headquarters Squadron, the British Columbia Regiment, near Meppen, Germany, April 8, 1945. (Canada Department of National Defence/Library and Archives Canada. Photographer Captain Alexander M. Stirton. MIKAN no. 3396351)

While Simonds regrouped his forces, Russ and the four tanks in his troop rolled back up the Caen-Falaise highway, rejoining the Headquarters Squadron near the village of St.-André-sur-Orne on the evening of August 10. The village, then a few miles behind the front, had been liberated barely more than a week earlier and was on the Canadian front line until Operation Totalize. A burned-out Tiger tank near the village held considerable interest for the Squadron's troops, some of whom put their bedrolls underneath it, understandable since the hot dry weather made digging slit trenches in the chalky earth difficult.

Little was left of the once sleepy town of St.-André. Most of the buildings had been destroyed by repeated shelling. In the ebb and flow of attack and counterattack, there had been no chance to bury the dead. Many were men of the Queen's Own Cameron Highlanders from Winnipeg, who had driven the German defenders from the town and held off repeated counterattacks.

When the Headquarters Squadron arrived, there was considerable discussion as to whether they should take responsibility for burying the dead. No one wanted the job, but it was impossible to miss the smell. The next day Russ was ordered to assemble a work detail and bury the bodies from the wreckage of St.-André. With a truck and the men of his tank troop, Russ entered the village.

The troopers picked their way through the rubble, lifting bodies from the ruins and loading them into the back of the truck. After weeks in the summer heat, their bodies had swollen obscenely, stretching their stained and putrid clothing. The faces of the dead were black, barely recognizable caricatures. There was no dignity now in their deaths, and whether they had fought bravely seemed irrelevant.

The truck carried the bodies to the edge of town, where they were unloaded at the roadside, the Canadians separate from the Germans. The burial party checked each soldier's identity tag, removed and bagged their pocket contents, and filled out a form for each man. Just as graves were being dug, a jeep approached, coming to a halt near the burial party with a clergy officer in the back seat.

"Lieutenant, I need to speak with you," the reverend said.

Russ came to the jeep. "Yes, sir," he said, saluting.

"Have you had clergy approval to bury these men?"

Russ was surprised. "My orders came from Major Campbell, sir. I have no idea if a reverend or priest had anything to say about burying these men."

"Then stop burying them. Leave them where they are."

"With all respect, these men have been through enough, sir. They deserve to be buried."

"Lieutenant, you are to leave them where they are until the appropriate religious observances are held," the clergyman answered curtly. Seeing anger cloud the young officer's face, he added, "That's an order."

Russ saluted, turned, and walked briskly back to the waiting burial party. "Unload the rest of the bodies from the truck and lay them out in the field." Then under his breath, he added, "They'll have to wait for god knows how long to be buried."

The burial party pulled the remaining bodies from the rubble. They were brought to the field, and Russ's anger grew as the field turned into an open morgue. At the end of the day, the bodies were covered with canvas, still waiting for someone from the clergy to approve their burial.

———◆———

The Fourth Division waited for the inevitable order to resume their assault. They had helped move the Canadian lines eight miles closer to Falaise, though most of that was accomplished in Phase One. There were eight more miles to go. On August 13, the Headquarters Squadron moved from St.-André to the village of Rocquancourt. The Squadron was reminded of the need for slit trenches when during the next two evenings, German bombers came over the harbour, ringing it with flares and dropping delayed action bombs. Two of the bombs landed near the kitchen without detonating, forcing its relocation.

Montgomery ordered Simonds to capture Falaise as quickly as possible. The German Seventh Army still was engaged to the west, overextended and vulnerable to encirclement — if the Canadians pushing south could join up with American forces coming north. On August 13, Simonds met with his Division and Regiment commanders.

In describing the coming attack, Simonds dressed down his officers for what he felt were serious shortcomings. To Kitching the briefing was very tough and unpleasant.

> Simonds blasted armoured regiments for their lack of support for infantry — he quoted the heavy infantry casualties of the past month compared to armour. He demanded much greater initiative from armoured regiments — drive on — get amongst the enemy, etc. Forget about harbouring at night

— keep driving on. Arrange your resupply accordingly. Don't rely on the infantry to do everything for you! It was a real blast and it shook everyone up. […] I felt our commanders of regiments did not deserve such treatment.[18]

After criticizing his divisional and regimental commanders, Simonds described his new plan. Operation Tractable was to follow the same approach as Phase Two of Totalize. To get past the German anti-tank defences in daylight, two massed tank columns would attack on the heels of artillery and aerial bombardments. They would advance under cover of a smoke screen, the tanks moving as fast as possible, firing at German defenders only if they appeared as the columns sped by. The difference from Phase Two of Totalize was to be speed — this time they were to go as fast as possible and stop for nothing.

At about eleven thirty a.m. on August 14, a hot, hazy day, Canadian artillery fired marker shells for the bombers, followed by smoke shells fired on the flanks of the route the tanks were to take. Allied bombers swept in to attack German anti-tank defences.

The first wave passed over the Fourth Division and began releasing its bombs on German positions several miles to the east and south. With the drifting clouds of dust and smoke from the explosions blowing towards the Canadian lines, the next squadron of bombers found their targets obscured and began their bombing runs too soon. High explosive and fragmentation bombs intended for the Germans began falling on the massed Canadians tanks. Even a Spitfire pilot fired his cannons and machine guns on the Canadians.

Packed in their tight armoured columns in the open, there was no chance for Canadians to take cover. For those not in tanks, there were not even slit trenches to escape in.

General Kitching and his headquarters were in the middle of the bombing. Only luck allowed him to survive as bombs fell on either side of his command headquarters.[19] Caught with the General were Russ and Jim in the protective tank force, and Major Campbell, part of Kitching's staff. It was a terribly helpless feeling being bombed by their own planes. They could only sit and hope they were not hit. Shrapnel glanced off the tank hulls, and dirt thrown high in the air landed on the turrets. Then, as suddenly as it began, it ended. Once again the smell of thick, oily smoke from burning vehicles stung the troopers' nostrils and burned their eyes, while exploding ammunition sent shards of metal erratically through the air. General Kitching's radio communications were knocked out but in surprisingly short order, word came from the Division's armoured regiments they were ready to move forward.[20]

It was quickly apparent many of the bombs had hit their intended target of Quesnay Wood, where the phalanx of German anti-tank guns waited for Canadian armour to roll out. The bombardment had obliterated the guns hidden there and devastated the woods, uprooting oak and beech trees. The ground was cratered deeply, the German guns and vehicles tossed on their backs and ripped apart. The men attending those guns had been killed.

On signal with the departure of the bombers, Canadian artillery began firing smoke shells. With clouds of white smoke obscuring the fields ahead of the line of advance, the order to move came over the radio. More than three hundred Fourth Division tanks began advancing. They started out south of the village of Cauvicourt, east of the Caen-Falaise highway, arranged in a massive square, enclosing in its centre the lightly armoured command and support vehicles.

The head of the columns quickly reached top speed, followed by row after row of tanks. They crashed forward, racing across the ripening wheat fields. Inside the troopers were thrown violently about as the tanks lurched and bucked unexpectedly over rough terrain. The smoke screen did as much to obscure the vision of the advancing drivers as it did to hide them from the Germans. Dust kicked up by the tanks and the bombardment made visibility even worse. The tanks had to be steered through the haze towards the faintly visible glow of the sun.

German gunners took their toll, but the targets were seldom more than shadows appearing suddenly and disappearing just as quickly. On occasions when German soldiers running from anti-tank positions were seen, the tank crews fired on them. But with the order to keep moving and the tanks bouncing through the fields at high speed, hitting anything was pure luck.

The vanguard of the advancing Canadian tanks reached their first objective, the Laison River. They had pierced the German lines. Falaise and victory were seemingly in sight. But now Allied Intelligence sabotaged the Fourth. Intelligence had said they would be able to quickly ford the narrow stream without being held up. But when the tanks arrived at the creek, it turned out the banks were too steep and the bottom marshy, so any tanks entering it became stuck, unable to pull forward or back out.

What had been a race towards Falaise past the German front lines suddenly turned into a parking lot as the tank columns backed up three miles from their starting point. A few fords across the Laison were found, but as the tanks dribbled across, they ran into stronger German resistance. The Canadians paused to let more tanks come forward, but with daylight coming to an end, it was decided the advance should wait for morning.

Russ and Jim and their tanks had one main task during Operation Tractable and the earlier Totalize. They were to guard Kitching, his command centre, and his staff (including Major Campbell). They had screened the division's commander with their tanks, encircling Kitching's command centre as they moved forward. If an anti-tank gun somehow escaped detection, it would first have to fire at one of the Headquarters tanks. In this way, Kitching stayed not far behind his fighting regiments.

Though the Fourth again stopped short of Falaise, Operation Tractable had accomplished a key part of its objective. German lines were broken, and what remained before the Canadians were relatively weak defences. It was more than a week since Operation Totalize, and Falaise finally was at hand. But in breaking the German lines, the Fourth Division had lost more than a hundred tanks that littered the battlefields between Caen and Falaise.

The morning after Tractable ended was cooler, the sky cloudy. Rain was in the offing. This day the tank regiments fought not in fast-moving armoured columns, but in small battles to eliminate German strongpoints. The German defenders north of Falaise, some of them remnants of Kurt Meyer's 12th SS, faced a desperate situation. Ordered to hold their positions at all costs, they no longer had a fully cohesive front to defend, each German strongpoint ran the risk of encirclement. Some chose to make this their final stand, understanding that every hour they could keep open the gap between the Americans and Canadians, more of the Seventh Army escaped north.

On the second day of Tractable each regiment took on German strongpoints barring the way forward. Kitching's headquarters was no longer mobile, freeing the Headquarter Squadron's tanks for other support roles. Russ and Jim began taking their squadrons forward, answering calls for assistance and participating in direct roles in the fighting. Somewhere on that confused battlefield, one of the Squadron's tanks was knocked out by a German 88, fortunately with no casualties.

For two days the Fourth was caught up in this piecemeal fighting before at last taking the key crossroads at Falaise. The Germans continued their retreat. Many headed for one of the few remaining bridges north, over the Dives River at the village of St.-Lambert.

Seeking to close off the escape route, a small force of tanks from the Fourth's South Alberta Regiment and infantry from Hamilton's Argyll and Sutherland Highlanders moved toward St.-Lambert. On the afternoon of August 18, the Canadians approached the village from the west. Losing two tanks when entering St.-Lambert, the Canadians took up position on a hill overlooking the town. With only one company of tanks and fifty Argylls they held their position while thousands of Germans tried to get past them to St.-Lambert's bridge.[21] At one point the Canadians had to call their own artillery down on their position and fire their tanks' machine guns at one another to drive off the Germans who swarmed around them. Hundreds of Germans surrendered, creating a serious problem, as there were no men to spare to guard prisoners. The commander of the small Canadian force, Major David Currie, had his troops hold their ground against tremendous odds, inflicting heavy losses on the Germans passing below their hilltop position. It was three days before Currie's tiny force was relieved, by the end having close to two thousand prisoners. For his actions, Currie earned the Victoria Cross, the only one awarded to a man from the Fourth.

———————◆———————

As the retreat from Normandy turned into a rout, large numbers of Germans were surrendering. But just because a soldier had surrendered did not mean he was not a threat. In situations where the alternative was death or injury, there was no choice but to surrender. Or a soldier might surrender under extreme duress, tired, cold, hungry, and under near-constant attack. After getting dry and warm, being fed, and having rested, some German soldiers would have felt the prospect of going to a prisoner of war camp was untenable and would look for any chance to escape.

Many of the Germans surrendering to the Fourth came through the Headquarters Squadron on their way to the POW cages. The steady stream of prisoners added to the manpower shortage pressing the Headquarters troops since mid-August, when dysentery began spreading among the troops. Many who remained healthy were either guarding German prisoners or transporting them.

Dawn on August 20 came dull with heavy rain, the downpour turning the roads and harbours from dust bowls into mud pits. Two German prisoners had been brought to the Squadron towards the end of the afternoon, and rather than having to guard them overnight, Russ was ordered to take them to the POW cage. Taking his rain cape, he joined a driver waiting at the jeep. He was a stranger to Russ, a soldier from another unit. The two Germans sat dejectedly with their hands tied in the rear of the jeep. They were dirty and their uniforms were torn. Russ took the Sten gun from the driver and sat in the passenger's seat. As they drove into the gathering darkness, the temperature dropped. Both Russ and the driver wore rain capes, but the Germans had none and were soaked to their skin. It was a miserable night, the wind and rain whipping into the back of the open jeep, where the prisoners began shivering uncontrollably.

With an eye on the condition of the two Germans, Russ instructed the driver to stop. He pulled over to the side of the road in a wooded area. In the heavy rain and beneath the canopy of trees, it was black except for the dim light cast by the shielded headlights. The rain beat like a drum on the hood, and with the drops hitting the leaves and falling in heavy splotches to the ground, it was impossible to be heard without yelling.

Soldiers of the German 12th S.S. Division in a barbed wire prisoner-of-war cage in Normandy, France.
(Canada Dept. of National Defence/Library and Archives Canada/PA-131397. Photographer Lieutenant Ken Bell)

Motioning the Germans out of the jeep, Russ gave the Sten gun to the driver and shouted at him to keep them covered. In broken English, one of the Germans asked that their hands be untied so they could relieve themselves. Telling the driver he was going to untie them and to be alert, Russ released their hands. Satisfied that the driver had the prisoners covered with the Sten gun, Russ went to the jeep, where he took two rain capes from the floor. He walked to the Germans, and as he handed the first one a rain cape, the man grabbed Russ's outstretched arm. He pulled Russ forward and off balance. They began grappling, Russ's arms hindered by his rain cape. In the struggle, he managed to free his right hand and pull his pistol from its holster. The German fought for control of the gun, but as they wrestled Russ pulled the trigger, and the bullet struck the German in the chest.

The wounded man fell to the ground, but before Russ could react, the other man knocked the pistol from his hand, sending it skidding away in the mud, lost in the darkness. In the blackness broken only by the dim light of the jeep's headlamps, they fought, rolling on the soaked ground.

Coming to their feet together, each man struggled desperately for control, but the wetness and the mud made it impossible to get a firm hold. Both men had entered a place in their minds where survival in its most primal form was all that mattered. Gaining leverage for a moment, Russ sent the other man to the ground. As the German started to rise, Russ swung his leg and kicked him, knocking him back to the ground. He scrambled to rise again, and once more Russ kicked. Desperate, close to the end of his strength and teetering at the very edge of any form of control, Russ kicked again, striking repeatedly until the German stopped trying to get up. Finally, the man lay still. The rain was the only sound.

Russ staggered back to the jeep where he collapsed in the seat in a state of shock. He couldn't tell how long he sat there, but he eventually recovered enough to realize he hadn't seen the driver since the fight had begun. He called out. There was no answer, only the rain beating on the hood. Had the driver been killed, or was he lying injured? Walking to where the two Germans still lay, Russ looked for the driver. There was no sign of him. Russ realized that when the first German had jumped him, the driver must have panicked and run away.

Gathering his strength, Russ walked back to the Germans, who both lay where they had fallen. He carried their bodies to the jeep and laid them in the back. Then he had to sit again, his emotions too strong to continue. In time he recovered enough to drive back to Headquarters. He turned the bodies over to the duty officer, explaining what had happened. The officer asked if he needed help. No, Russ replied, walking to his tent. He collapsed on his cot, falling into a coma-like sleep. In the morning, he was disoriented, the memory of the previous evening somehow not in his conscious mind. He looked down and saw he was still wearing his boots, covered in dried blood and hair. The previous night came flooding back as Russ sat on his cot, reliving the horror.

———◆———

In and around Falaise, the German Seventh Army was frantic in its attempts to escape from Normandy. Squeezed from the north by the Canadians and British and from the south by the Americans, they fought to withdraw through a square of land only about four miles wide. The Canadians held three sides of the square and faced inwards, seventy thousand Germans fought to get past them. They came mostly on foot, funnelled into this narrow gap. Facing them were only seven thousand infantry, primarily those of the Fourth Canadian Armoured Division, and their allies the Polish. There was simply not enough infantry to prevent the Germans filtering through the area at night, and with the ring of encircling Allied troops constantly tightening, the Germans soon had no choice but to move during the day. Allied aircraft and artillery mercilessly hammered the retreating troops, the rocket-firing Typhoons and machine-gunning Spitfires and Hurricanes attacking anything moving on the ground, while the artillery rained shell after shell down on the desperate and concentrated Germans.

The area around Falaise became a killing ground. Helpless to defend themselves, the Germans had only two choices — surrender or push on. Those wounded or unwilling to go further took refuge in forested areas. As the stragglers among the German troops filtered past the thin lines of the Fourth, the Canadians turned to follow. They ran into the mangled remains of the German Seventh Army.

What the Canadians found shocked and sickened even the most veteran soldiers. The narrow lanes were choked with dead soldiers and horses and the twisted and burnt wreckage of German vehicles, their drivers and passengers also twisted and blackened and sitting where they were when killed. Countless dead horses lay bloated, still tied to the carts they had been pulling. At times, bulldozers were brought in to push the bodies, equipment, and vehicles aside. In spots, dead German soldiers lay piled in decomposing heaps, the overpowering smell sickening everyone who passed.

The end of August marked the end of General Kitching's tenure as the Fourth's commander. Despite his being well-respected, his removal is not mentioned in the Headquarters war diary. His replacement was General Harry Foster, who had commanded a brigade in the Third Canadian Infantry Division since D-Day.[22]

Foster was well known to Jim Derij. Like Jim, he was a Permanent Force soldier who was a long-time member of Winnipeg's Lord Strathcona's Horse regiment. Foster had the textbook look of what one imagined a soldier should be — lean body, piercing eyes, close-cropped hair, and thin moustache in the British military fashion. This was a general who looked capable of taking a rifle and joining the front-line troops in a firefight. The truth was not far from this. He had led part of Canada's D-Day assault on Juno Beach, coming ashore at Courseulles-sur-Mer commanding the Seventh Canadian Infantry Brigade. Foster was also veteran of Sicily and southern Italy, his brigade winning a reputation for performing better than others. He was simply one of the best generals in the Canadian army.[23]

Foster took command of the Fourth in late August as the pursuit of the retreating Germans picked up speed. It was a time of perpetual movement. Along with their British and American allies, the Fourth Division kept pressure on the Germans, giving them no time to rest, regroup, or establish defensive positions. Nearly every day the Headquarters Squadron advanced to a new location, from Epaney through fifteen miles of narrow roads to Coudehard, then the next day another ten to Ticheville, inching nearer the Seine River through towns named le Sap, Broglie, Le Muchery, Criqueboeuf, and Tostes. At each village the citizens came out to greet the Canadians. Cheering, happy villagers lining the roadsides waving French flags. Bottles of Calvados were passed to the soldiers, who left the children with chocolate and the adults with cigarettes.

The Germans did everything they could to slow their pursuers. Blown bridges, roads blocked by felled trees, and culverts removed halted the pursuing Canadians until the obstruction was removed or repaired. Deadlier strategies were also employed. Land mines were planted in the roads, some so large they could toss a forty-ton tank into the air. A few strategically placed rearguard troops could bring an entire Canadian division to a halt. Hidden snipers, a machine gun nest with a platoon of troops, or a well-concealed anti-tank gun meant the column had to wait while the threat was eliminated. But for each hour their pursuers were held up, the Germans lost just as much time by having to conceal themselves by day from Allied planes.

As Russ's and Jim's tank squadrons sped north, the bloody month of August, 1944, came to a close. It was a deadly month for the Canadian Fourth Division. For the Germans, however, the toll was far higher, with entire divisions obliterated. The Hitler Youth nemesis that had faced the Fourth south of Caen, the 12th SS Panzer Division, had lost all its tanks, and only a few hundred of its more than ten thousand troops made it out of the Falaise Pocket. Their leader, Kurt Meyer, was captured and would later face trial for the murder of Canadian prisoners of war.

Survivors of the 12th SS who escaped north would be integrated into other German units, to fight again against the Fourth's troopers. But for the moment, they raced north towards the Seine. In those days of pursuit, when it seemed the German army had all but given up, victory for the Allies seemed just around the corner. But it was an illusion. Yet more suffering by soldiers and, increasingly, by civilians, was to come as the battle moved into Belgium, Holland, and finally into Germany itself.

EIGHT

An einem strahlenden Wintertag
One Brilliant Winter's Day

Frank's romantic view of being in the military was long gone by 1944. Had he really believed the army would be exciting and adventurous? It was hard to imagine it after two years stationed north of the Arctic Circle. He had passed his eighteenth and nineteenth birthdays living in squalid conditions, the only break in the monotony was the occasional patrol across the tundra. These at least gave relief from the tedium of camp life, a chance to feel close to nature, to exercise, perhaps to see a hare or a fox, or at least their tracks in the pristine snow. Glimpsing wildlife seemed more likely than the possibility of seeing Soviet soldiers in January 1944, since there was almost never a report of their patrols being seen, and exchanging fire was rarer still.

Winter patrols were done on cross-country skis, the Finns having taught the Germans to run on their skis, barely using their arms. The men tired much less quickly using the Finns' method, and it made skiing the tundra a pleasure. In preparation for the day's patrol, Frank donned his all-white

Member of the German army in winter camouflage clothes and skis.
(Bundesarchiv, Bild 146-1969-140-57,
photographer: Blaurock)

camouflage suit and pulled the white hood over his head. With his ears inside the hood, all sounds were muffled, and the freezing temperatures made the suit rustle loudly. Combined with his heavy breathing, practically nothing else could be heard.

For the most part they travelled on trails made by previous patrols. The parallel tracks looked like a narrow railway line in the otherwise untouched snow, packed down by dozens of previous skiers. Their route wound through patches of trees and across stretches of open ground. The line of soldiers in Frank's patrol moved like an inchworm, backing up at the bottom of hills as each man took a run up it, spreading out when they went downhill, tucked down to coast as far as possible before resuming the steady push-slide, push-slide. Even at -20 degrees Celsius, the men produced enough heat that they would be sweating freely. The strenuous exercise in the Arctic cold created a kind of euphoria, making Frank feel incredibly alive.

Against the snowy background, his patrol was practically invisible in its white camouflage suits. Clearly visible, though, were the twin tracks they followed. The patrol followed the ski trail into another of the many wooded areas when Frank suddenly heard an explosion. He stood looking into the shimmering cold, seeing nothing unusual. Only then did he notice spots on the snow, spots of the most brilliant red he had ever seen. On the crystalline white surface, the red looked as vivid as on an artist's canvas. Then to his surprise, he saw more spots appearing, and only then did he realize it was blood, and that it was his, gushing from the right side of his chest and neck.

Frank collapsed on the snow, blood streaming from his wounds. He lay unable to move, but aware of everything happening around him. He heard more explosions nearby. He recognized the sound of German hand grenades and reasoned the other explosions must be Soviet grenades. Gunfire was exchanged, the rapid fire of submachine guns and the heavier, slower sound of rifles. Then, as suddenly as it had begun, the firing ended. For a moment everything was absolutely quiet.

Others in Frank's patrol stayed crouching among the bushes near the trail, waiting to see if their attackers still remained hidden among the trees. Finally they rose. The Feldwebel[1] sent several men to find the attackers, but they soon returned. There was no sign of the Soviet troops who had ambushed them, save for their ski trails. It was clear they had found the ski trail used by the Germans, perhaps even watched on previous days to see if it was used regularly or at a certain time of day. The ski tracks provided a perfect opportunity to plan an ambush. The Soviet troops had lain in wait as

Frank's patrol approached, then thrown their hand grenades and opened fire before quickly withdrawing.

Frank lay alone in the snow, his skis still on his boots and the leather loops of his ski poles around his wrists. His side and arm ached and he felt a sharp pain in his neck. A face appeared above him, saying something, then another face, then a third. They looked at him with what seemed curiosity. Then everyone began acting quickly. Hands tugged at his arms and legs, and he felt his skis come off and the straps of the ski poles removed from his wrists.

Frank felt the odd sensation of half a dozen hands roughly lifting him. They placed him on a makeshift stretcher made out of ski poles and a tent tarpaulin. He was aware his blood was collecting on the bottom of the tarpaulin while the company's medic worked desperately to staunch the bleeding. He pulled back Frank's hood, wrapped a dressing around his neck, and told another soldier to press his hand on the wound. Frank's coat was zipped open. Inside it was soaked red. A bandage was wrapped so tightly around his chest, it made breathing difficult. With his wounds treated as well as possible, the makeshift stretcher holding Frank was lifted and the patrol began making its way back to camp.

Frank fought to hang onto consciousness as a curtain began to fall over his eyes. First the treetops disappeared, then the trees themselves, and finally the faces of the soldiers carrying his stretcher. There remained only a narrow bright strip, a sliver of light just above the ground. He hung on to that light, willing himself not to lose consciousness, believing it was his only remaining connection with life. Frank was still a boy, only nineteen, and he did not want to die.

When the patrol reached the camp, Frank was loaded in a vehicle and raced to the field hospital. His camouflage suit, clothes, and boots were removed. Naked, he was placed still-conscious on an operating table, covered with a thin blanket. Between the cold air and shock, he could not stop shivering. Two doctors came forward and bent over him. The older of the two removed the field bandages and examined the wounds. Frank watched the doctor take a pair of sharp tweezers and felt as he probed with them in one of the wounds. Carefully the doctor removed a splinter of shrapnel. He held it up to the light, examined it briefly, then showed it to his colleague and finally to Frank.

"Look what I found!" the doctor said before dropping it with a clink into a metal bowl.

As the older doctor continued to probe for shrapnel, the younger one began joking with Frank, still conscious as they worked on his wounds. Frank tried to laugh, but it was forced. From the corner of his eye, he noticed for the first time a nurse standing beside him. She was attractive, with long black hair. She held Frank's hand, looking in his eyes while the doctors continued to look for and extract shrapnel. The doctor pulled back the sheet. Frank lay naked before her. She looked for a long time at his body then looked into his eyes.

Squeezing his right hand, she held the index finger and thumb of her other hand close together.

"So small," she said. She might have been referring to the size of the wounds, although Frank found he had just enough blood left to blush.

When the operation ended, he was moved into a military hospital, where a long convalescence followed. When one of the two doctors visited Frank in the hospital ward, he said some splinters remained in his chest and neck, since removing them would be more dangerous than leaving them. By July, Frank recovered sufficiently to be released. He had regained full use of his right arm that had been seriously injured by the grenade.

"You can be happy," the doctor said, "the remaining fragments look to be immobile, and we don't think they will move to pierce either your carotid artery or your lung.

"However," he joked, "you will probably never play tennis again." Frank laughed and thanked him. Of the eight pieces of shrapnel he had been hit by, five had to be left in his chest and one in his neck (where they remain after more than sixty-five years). Frank was discharged from the hospital and set out to rejoin his unit in Lapland. He would soon learn they had left Finland, and he would not see any of them again.

NINE

Pursuit to the Maas
Und weiter an die Maas

The Seine River, symbolic of Paris, held a different meaning for the troopers of the Fourth than notions of the Eiffel Tower. To them, it signified a major step forward in the war, a sign that the tide had swung strongly in their favour, and victory might not be far off. Pushing north from Falaise, the Fourth's infantry regiments, the Algonquins, Argylls, and Lincs, began crossing the Seine in boats at a hairpin turn in the river, near the town of Elbeuf, seventy-five miles west of Paris.

The Germans chose retreat from the Seine rather than resistance. Establishing a bridgehead on the north bank of the river, Simonds's Canadians spread out across the web of roads lacing the French countryside, continuing hard on the heels of the German army.

The Seine River crossing at Elbeuf. Shown are Staghound armoured cars of the 18th Armoured Car Regiment (12th Manitoba Dragoons) on August 28, 1944.

(Canada Dept. of National Defence/Library and Archives Canada/PA-144143. Photographer Lieutenant Harold G. Aikman)

Russ and Jim's main role was once again protection of the Division's General and Headquarters. While racing ahead, the Fourth had to halt to deal with German troops left in their path, strategically placed to slow the pursuers in the most deadly manner possible. When the Headquarters passed through Airaines, the village had just been cleared of the enemy. Dead Germans and burning vehicles were everywhere. The following morning, the Squadron began another long trip under overcast skies, arriving late at night in what seemed a good harbour in a thick wood. However, they soon discovered the Germans were not far ahead, and with no other Canadian troops between them, the Squadron backtracked to a location near Bellancourt.

In the next few days, the Fourth reached the Somme near Abbeville, crossing at Pont-Remy.[1] Word came that the Division was to spend two days on the north bank of the Somme, regrouping and resupplying. It was a relief to pause from the constant travel and fighting, the mobile bath units providing a hot shower and clean clothes, followed by plentiful hot food and a full night's sleep. Major Campbell used the time to deal with charges against Fourth Division troops. As a lawyer and a member of the Division's Headquarters Squadron, he was a logical choice to be judge advocate general for the Fourth. He tried one case of a soldier "unfit for duty" and two others charged with being absent without leave.

The drive deeper into northern France resumed after a two-day respite. It was all the Fourth could do to keep pace with the Germans, liberating town after town, cheered on by French civilians happy to see the end of four years of occupation. Some places the Canadians passed through had been held by the Germans only hours earlier. It was exciting and tiring, driving long days and stopping only briefly at night to refuel and sleep for a few hours.

On September 6, the Fourth began filtering uneventfully into Belgium, heading toward the town of Eekloo. Any sense of accomplishment was muted by the cold rain. As they progressed across Belgium, the Fourth's troopers were often the first Allied soldiers seen since the Germans' hasty departure. The Belgians gave the Canadians an even greater welcome than the grateful French. The response was often almost hysterically happy. The column of vehicles was forced to a crawl as it wound through the narrow streets lined with cheering Belgians, the Canadians waving to the happy crowds. In places, so many excited people choked the streets that the columns were forced to stop, the men shaking the hands of the passing soldiers, slapping them on the back. The women kissed and hugged them. Grateful Belgians climbed on the jeeps, trucks, and tanks, throwing flowers and giving the soldiers wine, fruit, and cakes. In the face of this sheer joy, every man felt like a hero.

There was little the officers could do to maintain order in the happy mayhem, and so much wine was shared with the soldiers that at times it almost sabotaged the Canadian advance. The scene was repeated in practically every town and village the Headquarters passed through, and it became so serious orders were issued allowing only co-drivers to dismount when vehicles halted. Otherwise, when the celebrating civilians forced the column to a halt, the troopers would be pulled into the crowd, and when finally rounded up were often too intoxicated to drive.

The chase through Belgium soon turned deadly, the cheering crowds replaced by an enemy who had stopped retreating. The Canadians found Germans waiting for them on the far side of the numerous canals. Having blown the bridges across the waterways, the Germans on the far bank were prepared with artillery, mortars, and machine guns perfectly aimed at the approaches to the canal. German defences made each crossing dangerous, and many Canadians were killed in Belgium. Each time the Canadians forced their way across a canal, the Germans withdrew to the next, where they would wait for the Canadians to catch up.

It is perhaps surprising that at the same time as fierce battles at canal crossings were taking place, at Headquarters Major Campbell took time to prosecute what seems a minor infraction. When driving into the Headquarters harbour, he noticed two troopers in a nearby wood, firing captured German pistols at a tree. Firing enemy weapons was forbidden unless under the supervision of an officer. Major Campbell ordered the provosts to take the two troopers into custody and quickly convened a court. Within ten minutes the men were arrested, tried, found guilty, and sentenced.

After fighting across the Ghent Canal, the Fourth advanced north to the Leopold Canal. Some Germans remained south of the Leopold, and they were to be rooted out by the Fourth. This became a combined armour-infantry operation, as small battle groups of the Fourth's tanks and infantry companies spread out across this corner of northeast Belgium. Headquarter Squadron's tanks worked the area with the Lake Superior Regiment. "Everyone reports good shooting," reads the light-hearted description in the war diary. In reality, these battles were sharp and often unexpected exchanges against concealed German troops, anti-tank guns, and the ever-present threat of ambush, mortar bombs, and mines.

While the Fourth was mopping up in Belgium, the Allied High Command made a bold move to open up a path into Germany. Operation Market Garden began with high hopes on September 17, with landings by paratroopers deep behind German lines. At the same time, a British armoured division began fighting its way north, needing to advance seventy-five miles up a narrow corridor in only four days to join up with the paratroopers dropped along the route. But the operation petered out within a week when the armoured assault was stopped and the paratroops at the far end of the corridor killed or captured.

The Fourth's offensive was idle while most of the fuel and ammunition needed to continue operations were directed to support Operation Market Garden. For a few weeks, life at the Headquarters Squadron took on a more relaxed tone. Besides the daily trips taking captured Germans to the rear, it was a chance to relax and socialize in the Belgian towns. On September 18, the Headquarters Squadron Quartermaster went to draw fresh battle dress and boots from the supply depot. The war diary remarked that "the boys will really dress up for the Belgian women now, a decided improvement in general smartness and appearance has been noticed since the men have been allowed to proceed on short pass to 'Open Towns.'"

On October 12, Russ, Jim, and their tank troops were assigned to support the First Canadian Scottish Regiment crossing the Leopold Canal. The Scottish, recruited in Victoria, British Columbia, had held a small bridge-head on the north shore of the Leopold since October 6, but it was a tenuous position, with only a floating footbridge across it. They were joined across the canal by soldiers from the Royal Winnipeg Rifles and the Regina Rifle Regiment. But without a bridge letting Canadian armour cross, there was little chance to break out of the pocket.

With Headquarters tanks on the southern edge of the canal, the Canadian Scottish began moving an hour after midnight on October 12, concealed in the lee of the dike running along the north edge of the canal.[2] They made it to the main road running north, where at a break in the dike stood the remnants of a blown bridge. The Germans, seeing the Canadians had crept hidden by the raised bank of the dike, took up positions on the bank's north face. The two forces were only yards apart, Germans on one side, Canadians on the other, with neither able to do more than throw grenades over the dike. Any Canadian peering over the crest provided a perfect target for German machine guns. Neither could the Germans attack over the dike, since sitting on the southern edge of the canal were the Headquarters tanks. While their cannons were of little use, the Headquarters tanks each carried two 50-calibre machine guns, which could spray bullets along the top of the dike. The tense standoff lasted all the day.

The Canadian Scottish decided to try to break the stalemate that night. At ten p.m. the attack was put in. On signal, the Canadians all pulled the pins on their grenades and threw them over. After a second grenade volley, the Canadian Scottish stormed over the top and captured the north side of the dike.

Having captured the north shore of the canal, the Canadian Scottish advanced to the nearby town of Eede.[3] This gave Canadian engineers enough cover to finish a bridge. As soon as it was ready, the Headquarters tanks rolled across, relieving the Canadian Scottish and securing the bridgehead. The Squadron's diary notes in restrained fashion that "moving across the Leopold Canal several prisoners were taken and the troopers suffered no casualties."[4]

———◆———

In mid-October, the Fourth moved towards Antwerp. The city offered the promise of a deep water port and greatly shortened supply lines. Every piece of equipment and gallon of fuel had to be brought from the temporary docks at the Normandy landing sites. Supply shortages were handicapping the Allied armies' advance towards Germany. Even though the Allies held Antwerp, German artillery lining the shores of the thirty-mile-long Scheldt Estuary prevented ships reaching the port.

The difficult task of clearing the Scheldt was given to the Canadian army. The Fourth's role was to strike northeast from Antwerp to protect the rear of the Canadian forces once they entered the Beveland Peninsula on the north shore of the Scheldt. The Headquarters Squadron moved northeast from Antwerp to the town of Schilde, where several days were spent being resupplied for the coming offensive. The lull also allowed training in removing land mines, which the Germans used in great quantities to slow the Canadian advance.

Resupplied, the Fourth moved north. The swampy soil restricted the tanks to the roads, which were heavily mined and studded with roadblocks, making each mile slow and dangerous. The flat land of northern Belgium was ideally suited to Germans manning anti-tank weapons concealed in farms and woodlots with long fields of view to the approaching Canadian columns.

The Headquarters tanks were on the front lines, only a few miles south of the village of Wouwse Plantage. The village was a short distance inside the Dutch border with Belgium and was one of a series of dominos needed to topple German defences in the region. Taking Wouwse Plantage would flank Germans defending Bergen-op-Zoom.

Russ's tank troop took up position near Achterbroek to provide a defensive screen against German attacks while the troops to take part in the assault of Wouwse Plantage moved into position. The Headquarters tanks came under fire, but not from the Germans. Six British flail tanks of the British 49th Infantry Division beating nearby woods to clear it of mines somehow mistook the Headquarters tanks for Germans. Fortunately, British marksmanship was poor, and Russ and Jim's tanks were unscathed.

The fight for Wouwse Plantage began at eight a.m. on October 23, when a hundred men of the Argyll and Sutherland Highlanders set out on foot from the protective cover of a wood south of the village. With them came eight tanks of the Canadian Grenadier Guards. Three miles to the north across the fields lay the village. The Argylls were told to cross a mile of this flat, open country, then dig in. It was a battle plan well known to the troops, exposing the infantry and armour to mortar, machine gun, anti-tank, and artillery fire while crossing a long stretch of open land.

As soon as Argylls and Grenadier tanks left the woods, the small force heard the sound of artillery shells and mortars. The Germans defending Wouwse Plantage knew that when they were attacked, it would likely come from one of several woods, and their shells landed among the Canadians with deadly accuracy. All the Argylls could do was drop to their stomachs and wait for the shelling to ease up. It took nearly three hours for the Argylls to travel the mile to their objective. Left in the mud, the dead and wounded totalled nearly a third of those who had stepped out of the woods. The Grenadier tanks fared even worse. Forced by the mud onto the elevated roadbed, they were even more exposed than the Argylls. Anti-tank fire from the town and by guns hidden in farmhouses dotting the countryside made the Grenadiers tanks easy targets, and they were picked off one after another.

The Argylls had reached their objective that morning, although in reality they were trapped. Now it was time for the second wave of the attack to begin. They had seen what had happened to Argylls, yet the Company of Lake Superior troops were unhesitating as they raced forward in their tiny Bren gun carriers, accompanied by tanks from the Governor General's Foot Guards. From the moment they emerged into the open, German anti-tank and mortar fire began. The tanks and carriers tried to race to Wouwse Plantage, but German anti-tank gunners picked off the tanks.

It wasn't long before the armoured support was wiped out, leaving the lightly armoured Lake Superior troops by themselves. With the shelling now focused entirely on them, they were forced to abandon their carriers and take cover in the fields. Working their way forward on foot, they went a mile beyond the Argylls before being pinned down. They would spend the night a mile short of the village, shivering in the mud and a cold rain.

The next morning, two fresh companies of Argylls prepared to go forward with eight more Grenadier tanks. They were presented with the same plan that had already failed twice, an attack across open fields. At least this time the attack would start in the pre-dawn darkness.

The Headquarters Squadron tanks continued their support for the attack on Wouwse, moving under the command of first troop of the Eighth Canadian Light Anti-Aircraft Regiment. They held a section of the front near Stappensven, Belgium, protecting the eastern flank of the troops attacking Wouwse Plantage. Although not involved directly in the assault, the Headquarters' tanks were able to fire on German positions scattered around Wouwse Plantage, and were themselves subject to enemy fire. That evening one of the Headquarters tanks was struck by an 88. Trooper John Carter later died of his wounds.[5]

When the Grenadier tanks emerged from the woods to start their run up the road, they found the road slick from heavy overnight rain. Instead of a sprint forward, they were forced to crawl along to avoid sliding into the ditch. The sound of the Canadian tanks was enough to start the German guns.

The Grenadier tanks returned fire on the farm buildings. Their shells set some of the farm buildings on fire, and in the light provided by the flames, the German anti-tank gunners were able to pick out targets. They disabled the lead tank in the column, blocking the narrow road and, as had happened the previous morning, the infantry proceeded alone. Aided by darkness, this time the Argylls made it within half a mile of Wouwse Plantage.

To take pressure off the Argylls, a second attack was sent forward that morning. From east of the village, two companies of Lincoln and Welland troops and a troop of tanks from the B.C. Regiment pushed up the highway from Essen across the Belgian border. At first the attack made good progress, but the tanks bogged down on the muddy roadbed. The Lincs pressed forward, but heavy artillery and small arms fire forced them to retreat. That afternoon the Headquarters tanks moved again, placed under command of "A" Squadron of the 18th Armoured Car Regiment, within sight of Wouwse Plantage between Spillebeekweg and Huijbergen. The ring of Canadian troops was tightening, though none had yet made it to the outskirts of the village.

Mist formed over the fields as the third day of battle dawned. The fog was a welcome sight to the troops preparing to renew the assault. The attack this day would be three-pronged. One company of Lake Superiors would drive from the east to draw fire from German defenders. A second company of these northwest Ontario men would drive north to take a brickyard south of town. Meanwhile, two companies from the Lincoln and Welland Regiment would drive straight up the main road in Wasp flamethrowers. Supporting the Lincs would be tanks from the Governor General's Foot Guards, as well as covering fire from mortar crews and artillery batteries.

When the attacks began, the morning fog shielded the Canadians from view. Hearing the Canadian vehicles coming, all the Germans could do was fire blindly. Wisely, the Canadians held their fire, concealing their positions as long as possible. The Lincs reached the edge of Wouwse Plantage and the Wasp flamethrowers and tanks finally engaged the German defenders at close range. Flaming liquid spouted from the front of the Wasps, laying burning oil into the German lines in the woods bordering the town. This feared weapon broke the defenders' resolve, forcing them to withdraw into the village rather than face the horror of the sheets of flame.

From the east, the Lake Superiors advanced to the crossroads and established a defensive line to fight off counterattacks. With the Argylls pursuing the Germans into the village, the Lake Superiors reached the brickyard and forced its defenders to retreat into town. The battle turned into a building-to-building fight. Other Canadian troops attacked Germans in the isolated farmhouses dotting the countryside.

Although it seemed clear the Germans in Wouwse Plantage could not hope to hold the village, they did not withdraw. Perhaps they believed they would be relieved by a counterattack that never came. Losses on both sides in the house-to-house fighting were high. By the end, two thirds of the forward platoons of the Lincs were killed or wounded. The town would not be declared captured until late that afternoon.

Russ and his troop of Headquarters tanks came forward to support two companies of the Lincoln and Welland Regiment holding Wouwse Plantage against counterattack. Jim brought his troop forward later that afternoon.[6] With Wouwse Plantage taken, the Fourth Division turned west towards the city of Bergen-op-Zoom. Russ's tank squadron provided a rearguard, protecting the bridge at Wouwse Plantage on the Canadian eastern flank.

The South Alberta Regiment's tanks and the Division's infantry units pushed west. Theirs was no set-piece battle, as was the case in Operation Totalize or Tractable. It was not even a smaller organized attack such as at Wouwse Plantage. Instead, as the Division moved towards Bergen-op-Zoom, it found the roads and fields deadly from mines, roadblocks with hidden anti-tank guns, and pockets of infantry waiting in ambush. The consequences were as deadly as any major battle.

Having fought its way to Bergen-op-Zoom, the Fourth protected the approach to the Beveland Peninsula. This prevented a major counterattack to support German troops trapped on the northern shore of the Scheldt.

However, the Germans there fought on, preventing Allied shipping using Antwerp. Opening the Scheldt would require some of the hardest fighting Canadians faced during the war, the Germans trapped there refusing to surrender until November 8.

———————————

The beginning of winter in 1944 was harsh even by Canadian standards. It was not the cold temperatures, for Canada's north was far colder. It was the waves of wet, freezing air sweeping off the North Sea that made it impossible for the troops to stay warm. Dark clouds scudded in off the sea, grey with heavy loads of rain or wet snow. One storm after another was pushed inland by the incessant winds to buffet the Canadian troops now stationary along the Maas River in southern Holland.

A Canadian offensive across the Maas was forced to wait. With Antwerp's port still not fully operational, there was an ongoing shortage of supplies. Instead of sending fuel and ammunition to the Canadians, the British and Americans fought over them, taking turns attempting to break through into Germany. First Montgomery had failed to create a breakthrough with Operation Market Garden. Next the Americans took their turn, throwing themselves against the Seigfried Line at Aachen, further south. Like Montgomery's failed attempt, the American offensive also ground to a halt. All the while the Canadians waited in southern Holland.

Canada's generals' best hope was that sufficient fuel and ammunition could be stockpiled to resume their attacks before the spring thaw made the roads and fields impassable. However, just as crucial as the shortage of supplies was the lack of adequate numbers of reinforcements. By 1944, the supply of men enlisting for overseas service had slowed to a trickle.

As strong as the response had been in 1940 when things were darkest, the call for overseas volunteers was now going almost unanswered. In 1944, there was no threat of Britain being invaded, as in 1940. Then Britain had stood alone with Canada and other Commonwealth countries, facing a German army that had crushed every opponent.

Now, Germany was retreating on all fronts. Britain and Canada were joined by the United States and Soviet Union. By late 1944, Italy had swung from the Axis to the Allies, Russia was on the offensive, German cities were being laid to waste by Allied bombing, and the U-boat menace had been throttled. It seemed clear it was only a matter of months until the war in Europe ended.

Another factor in the lack of reinforcements was that most men who stayed in Canada were rewarded with well-paying jobs. Emerging from the Depression, steady work was something many younger Canadians had never known. No one could say if these jobs would end when the war was over, and giving up a good job to join the army at this late juncture seemed senseless. For Canadian troops in combat, it meant there were never enough replacements. Not that there weren't plenty of soldiers in the army, for there was a large, well-trained contingent of Canadian soldiers sitting at home. The problem was very few of them were willing to join the troops overseas.

Tens of thousands of trained Canadian soldiers refused to go to Europe. Some had enlisted for home service only, and others had been conscripted. Neither group could be sent overseas without their agreement. And very few were willing to make such an agreement. This was the so-called "Zombie Army," hated by many of the men fighting in Europe. It was tremendously controversial for Mackenzie King's Liberal government.

French Quebec was overwhelmingly against conscription, and English Canada was even more overwhelmingly in favour of it. For many on both sides of the issue, pre-existing tension between English and French undoubtedly intensified feelings of dislike over the issue.[7]

Many troops in front line units viewed politicians at home as cowardly for not supporting them. They viewed the "Zombies" (formally called home defense troops) as "gutless wonders."[8] Some Active Force volunteers (also called general service men) training in Canada before heading overseas were stationed at the same army bases as those drafted but unwilling to volunteer for overseas service. At Currie Barracks in Calgary, animosity between the groups turned violent.

> ... (S)ome 150 men were involved in a battle ... and "rifles and bayonets were brandished." ... The ... fight started in the canteen when the home defense troops started to sing "It's better to be a zombie than a general service man."
>
> Tables were overturned in the fight which followed ... and the home defense troops ran to their hut and grabbed their rifles and bayonets to repel the general service men who resented the implication of the words of the song.
>
> Then the home defense troops barricaded themselves in their hut and the general service men ran for their arms ... the general service men milled around the home defense stronghold for about two hours.[9]

Some troops in combat also resented able-bodied men in Canada who chose not to enlist, and the army itself was criticized for failing to send active service troops in rear echelon positions in England and Canada to the front lines, or to transfer to the army those who enlisted for overseas service in the Royal Canadian Air Force and were not needed there. But most despised were the "Zombies."

———————◆———————

In November, the Fourth's role was to protect a large section of the front running south of the Maas River in Holland. On November 10, Russ and Jim took the Headquarter Squadron tanks to the town of Lith on the Maas River, under command of the Fifth Canadian Anti-Tank Regiment. They were allotted an area to defend on the Canadian side of the Maas. However, Russ gained a reprieve when he was selected for two days leave in Antwerp, a room waiting for him at the famed Excelsior Hotel. Five other ranks also received leave, their destination the smaller city of Ghent. They were selected because Major Campbell decided the combat troops should receive leave before any others in the Headquarters.

With the Canadian army in a holding position, General Simonds appointed a new General in charge of the Fourth. Major General Harry Foster, who had taken over from George Kitching in France, left the Division in a downpour the morning after the announcement. Every officer in the Headquarters and a large number of other ranks lined the courtyard in the pouring rain to wish him godspeed and give him three cheers. His replacement, Chris Vokes, arrived the following day from command of the First Canadian Infantry Division in Italy. His reputation of being rough around the edges and tough in his speech and attitude, made the troops feel he was one of them.[10] He was in those ways the opposite of Major Campbell.

When Russ's leave was over, he returned to patrol duty on the Maas River with the Headquarters tank troops. They rotated out of the front on November 25, joining the rest of the Squadron in the rear. With the Fourth's activity reduced to shelling and patrols along the Maas, efforts were made to keep the troops occupied. Concerts by military bands were organized, as were movie nights and live travelling shows by the likes of The Haversacks. Regular dances provided opportunities for the troops to spend time with Dutch girls. In late November, the batmen for officers of Headquarters Squadron's "F" mess were granted the use of the dining room for a dance. "Quite a good time was had by all," according to the war diarist, "except for a few uncomfortable minutes when one of the batmen escorted a young lady in who had formerly run around with the Jerry soldiers and was considered an outcast by the other young ladies."

———————◆———————

On November 26, Headquarters moved to the village of Vught. It was an unimportant city militarily, but its name carried a sinister meaning to the Dutch. The Germans had made Vught the site of a major concentration camp.[11] It was part of the extensive Nazi network of thousands of concentration camps, spread from France to Russia.

Prisoners were sent to the camp in Vught starting late in 1942, and in little more than a year and a half, thirty thousand people passed through its gates. Hundreds died during the first few months due to mistreatment, many Jewish children among them.[12]

The camp was divided into two sections, one part holding Jewish prisoners prior to their being transported to the Nazi death camps at Auschwitz and Sobibor in Poland, the other for Belgian and Dutch political prisoners. Starvation and disease were commonplace, made worse by the routinely brutal beatings and torture, vicious dog attacks, hangings, and shootings by the SS guards.[13]

The camp was liberated by the Fourth on October 26, 1944, when the 96th Anti-Tank Battery, part of the Fourth's Fifth Anti-Tank Regiment arrived.[14] The liberation was recalled by one of the camp's survivors. "(T)he Canadians troops came over the hill right up to the wall fighting the Germans. The Germans were evacuating from the camp and left a rear guard action to fight the allies. They were fighting and running at the same time. As you entered the camp into a courtyard there were 500 bodies lying in a pile and these poor people were just executed that morning. They were just thrown in a pile. There were around 500–600 live prisoners left who had been set up for execution that afternoon, but the Canadians arrived instead so they were spared. The people were in the most horrible condition, starving to death, ill, and very badly mistreated. When the Canadians arrived they were standing around in the courtyard. Not in any barracks just standing around while the fighting was going on."[15]

The Headquarters Squadron was mainly billeted in private homes in Vught. The Dutch were happy to take Canadians into their homes, not only in gratitude for liberation, but for the food the Canadians brought. Food had been scarce for years and the Dutch still faced shortages. The Headquarters kitchens were favourite sites for the Dutch, especially children, and they were often invited to share army rations.

As December neared, Canadian troops in the Netherlands planned to hold Christmas parties for Dutch children, a practice that had become a tradition when the troops were in England.[16] The Headquarters Squadron planned to host a Saint Nicholas Day party on the sixth of December, part of the Dutch celebrations.

On Saint Nicholas Day, the hall filled with children six- to eight-years-old from Vught and from towns evacuated from the Fourth Division's front along the Maas. The soldiers entertained the youngsters with a puppet show, by singing Canadian children's songs, and playing musical instruments. Before long the laughter of the three hundred children would have filled the hall. It must have been wonderful for the Canadian troops, especially those like Jim, who had a son in Canada he had not seen in years.

The highlight was the arrival of Sinterklaas. The Canadians had planned this to perfection. Sinterklaas, in his red robe, arrived with nine attendants, called *Zwarte Piet* (Black Peters). They were driven to Vught in a decorated armoured car, accompanied by provost outriders on their motorcycles. With Sinterklaas listening, the children sang Dutch Christmas songs for him and the troops. Then a large lunch prepared by the Headquarters cooks was served. The crowning feature was the Sinterklaas cakes, made by the Sisters of the Order Chenoinessis de Saint Augustin using flour and sugar from the army. Finally, each youngster received a Christmas parcel from Sinterklaas, containing a chocolate bar donated by the troopers, a wooden toy, and drawing materials.

Across the Maas River, Dutch children trapped behind German lines were not so fortunate. Food shortages there were critical. Electricity and heating fuel were in short supply, and as the winter turned colder, the Dutch took wood wherever it could be found, burning furniture and stripping wood from their homes. The worst was the lack of food; the Dutch were slowly starving. Over the winter the daily ration would be repeatedly cut. That winter in occupied Holland, nearly thirty thousand civilians died of malnutrition and its complications in what the Dutch came to call the "Hongerwinter."[17, 18]

About a week after the children's Christmas party, the Germans markedly increased the number of V1 and V2 rockets targeting Antwerp. "(T)he hellish machines roared over … in an endless procession day and night … hundreds of V2s were seen to streak skywards from the north of Holland"[19] towards Antwerp's port. Then word arrived of a new German offensive through the Ardennes Forest.

When the Ardennes attack[20] began, few believed the Germans had the resources to conduct a large-scale offensive, so at first it wasn't considered a serious threat. However, the severity of the situation sank in a week later, when General Vokes returned from a Christmas Eve meeting at First Brigade Corps Headquarters with orders that the Fourth was immediately moving to counter "the great probability of enemy action."

The Headquarters Squadron was on the road by five thirty in the evening on Christmas Eve, headed to the town of Ulvenhout, just south of Breda. On their arrival, the troops were briefed on the threat. As many as twenty German divisions were attacking American forces in southeast Belgium, with the suspected goal of retaking Antwerp. If they recaptured the port, it would dramatically cut supplies to all Allied troops and, far worse, would encircle Montgomery's 21st Army Group, of which the Fourth Canadian Armoured Division was part. The Fourth was in Breda to stop the Germans if they broke through American lines in the Ardennes.

Not only did the Fourth have to contend with the possibility of stopping the main thrust if it broke through, but Allied intelligence reported the Germans planned an attack by a paratroop corps. If a paratroop attack was launched, it was expected to cross the Maas by boat and in air drops, creating havoc behind Canadian lines. Intelligence also warned that the enemy planned to use English-speaking German soldiers disguised as Allied troops. In preparation, anti-paratroop patrols began, and the Division was put on ten minutes' notice to move.

Christmas morning in Ulvenhout was spent with the troops grimly preparing for an attack. They had to make do with hastily prepared rations on Christmas night, after which they were ushered into a large, unheated chicken coop and shown a movie "very much appreciated by the troops."[21]

When Christmas dinner was finally served a day late, more than two hundred troopers sat down to a "wonderful meal" in the dining room at St. Lorenz Gesthuis Hospital. The hall was decorated and the tables had white linen table-cloths and chinaware. The Mother Superior and Principle Sisters of the hospital sat down with the troopers as special guests. Russ and Jim, if not on patrol duty, would have joined the Squadron's officers serving the meal, assisted by the Senior NCOs. Major Campbell was the emcee for the dinner, presenting the senior officers of the Headquarters Squadron to the troops. When Sergeant Tully, in charge of the kitchen, and his staff were introduced, they received a tremendous ovation. The officers donated extra beer, "which was really appreciated by the boys." General Vokes and his senior staff officers visited during the meal, expressed their good wishes for the future, and autographed many menu cards.[22]

The next morning shortly before seven a.m., a V1 was shot down and exploded near Headquarters. Though the ground shook and windows were broken by the explosion, there were no casualties. A German paratroop attack, not V1 rockets, was still the main threat, and a double strength perimeter guard was maintained, with warnings that if and when the Germans came they would be dressed in Canadian battle dress. However, as the week passed, gradually, the Ardennes offensive petered out and in early January came to a halt as American forces attacked from the south.

With the threat ended, the Fourth resumed its holding duties in southern Holland. When they returned to Vught, they found that other units had taken over the Headquarters troop's previous quarters. This forced part of the Headquarters Squadron into buildings badly needing repair. They had no heat due to the large number of broken windows that had caused the hot water pipes to burst. Repairs were undertaken, and when time allowed, repairs were extended to civilian homes in Vught. It raised Major Campbell to the status of a sort of Santa Claus to the townspeople, especially the success in making the electricity supply more constant.[23]

With the situation in southern Holland returned to a holding operation, there was need again for activities to keep the troops occupied. The day after relocating to Vught, Major Campbell attended a meeting at the ice rink in Tilburg of the First Canadian Army's Hockey Committee. A series of games among the units was planned, and the Major was the Fourth's member on the committee. The Hockey Committee assigned rink allotments and practices to start on January 17. Though it was not far from the front, a hockey tournament was planned to keep up the troops' morale until action resumed.

By February, however, conditions were ripe for epidemic levels of colds, flu, and more serious diseases, causing a steady stream of men to be dispatched to the field hospital. Coal supplies for heating were practically non-existent, and the troops operated in freezing temperatures, both inside and out. Diphtheria and pneumonia were circulating through the Squadron, and the spread of disease was now a more serious threat than the Germans, compounding the lack of reinforcements.

In late January, Jim was found unconscious in his bed with a high fever and was taken to hospital. Like most, he had a bad cold, but doctors told Major Campbell that Jim had been suffering from pneumonia for some time. Under antibiotics Jim quickly recovered, returning to the Squadron in little more than a week.

Russ was also felled by serious illness. It started in early February with a headache, dizziness, and dysentery.[24] Strong chills were followed by a burning

fever. The doctor's initial diagnosis was a case of severe meningitis or enceph-
alitis, either extremely dangerous. He was evacuated to hospital, where two
holes were punched in his spine to collect spinal fluid for signs of bacteria.
Russ was visited in hospital by Major Campbell, who reported him "still fairly
ill, but his ailment has not yet been diagnosed." Five days later, the fever and
chills were gone, but the ongoing dysentery and the aftermath of the infection
left him "washed out."

While Russ was recovering in hospital, the Rhineland Campaign
began. It was a major offensive by Canadian, British, and American forces
into western Germany. The initial objective was to drive the Germans from
west of the Rhine. It began with a joint Canadian and British attack east
from Nijmegen in Holland into Germany. The Americans were to begin
their offensive further to the south, pushing northeast to create a pincer
movement, meeting the Canadians and British at the German town of
Wesel on the Rhine.

In late February, the Fourth Division received orders to join the Rhineland
Campaign with the Second Canadian Corps near Kleve, Germany. Russ,
though still suffering the after-effects of weeks of persistent dysentery, was
released from hospital to rejoin the Headquarters Squadron for the move
into Germany.

Two days before his release, a replacement, Lieutenant W. Ellery, was
attached to the tank troops. Lieutenant Ellery's appointment to the tank troops
may have been because of uncertainty about Russ's ability to rejoin before the
Headquarters Squadron moved out. The war diary does not indicate whether
Russ regained command of his tank troop after returning from hospital.

The Headquarters Squadron moved out of Vught for Germany under brilliant sunshine at noon on February 22. The move was an event the Squadron's
war diarist said was something "most of the troops had been waiting five and
a half years for…." The buildup of Canadian and British troops heading to
Germany was so great, there was no hope of finding buildings to house the
men, so the tents came out of storage in a harbour a few miles south of Kleve.

Shortly after the Squadron had set up camp, Field Marshall Montgomery
and his staff arrived to brief General Vokes and the Division's senior officers
on the role of the Fourth in Operation Blockbuster. The plan was for the
Second Canadian Corps to attack along a front eight miles wide in a series of
frontal assaults towards the Rhine at Wesel. The first phase of the attack would
be carried out by three infantry divisions, the Canadian Second and Third and
the British 43rd. They would be followed by the Fourth Canadian attacking
through the Hochwald Forest.

Behind the front lines, Canadian and British troops waited for the break-through at the Hochwald. The area became congested as more units poured in with incessant German artillery fire adding to the mayhem. During one recce Major Campbell was caught in an enemy artillery barrage and quickly withdrew, realizing the area was unsuitable as a harbour.

The battle for the Hochwald Gap was among the hardest fighting any-where during the war. In the end, the attempt to push the Fourth's armour through the Gap was unsuccessful. It took the Second and Third Canadian Infantry Divisions to drive the Germans from the Hochwald. As one veteran later wrote, "the final cannon-fodder efforts at the gap (were) … like … mad-ness; "… it looked like a large graveyard for tanks."

Finally passing through the Gap, the Canadians continued east, meeting strong German resistance at every strategic point along the way. On March 5, the Headquarters Squadron moved forward to an area just behind the infan-try and ahead of the 25-pounder guns of the artillery. The perimeter guards were on their toes that night because of the threat of German infiltration and counterattack. General Vokes' tactical headquarters moved out in the morning on Operation Blockbuster, accompanied by a troop of Squadron tanks under Jim's command.

At Headquarters Squadron the next day, Staff Sergeant Shore was walking through a field adjacent to the harbour when he stepped on an enemy mine.[25] His left foot was blown off. Within minutes a member of the Signals Corps was on his way to help the injured sergeant, but he too stepped on a mine, also losing a foot. Others came to help. Just as the injured Signals trooper was being placed on a stretcher, one of those helping, Trooper Hancock, stepped on yet another mine. This blast was stronger than the previous ones, blowing Hancock's right leg completely off, while the injured Signals officer who had already lost a foot had his other leg fractured. Two other men who had come to help, Private Litchfield and Trooper Cleveland, were only slightly injured. Now three men lay badly injured in the field, and two others were wounded and trapped.

Running to the edge of the field, Russ ordered everyone to stay exactly where they were.[26] No one else was to go to help, he ordered, and the men already in the field were not to move. Alone, Russ stepped out into the farmer's field, making his way towards the injured men. He knew he had to act quickly. He followed as best he could the faint tracks of footsteps leading to the injured soldiers. Reaching the soldier whose leg had been blown off, Russ hoisted him across his shoulders. He told Privates Litchfield and Cleveland to follow him out of the minefield, stepping exactly in his footsteps.

At the edge of the field, Russ lowered the injured trooper to the ground, where medics began attending to the terrible wound. Russ walked back into the minefield, following his own footsteps to another of the injured troopers. This man too he carried to safety. In all, Russ made his way into the minefield three times, each time carrying out an injured soldier. All the injured men were evacuated to medical facilities and survived.

With the Canadians in possession of the Hochwald, the Germans had no choice but to withdraw to defensive positions further east. They were harassed mercilessly from the air and by artillery as they withdrew. The Canadians advancing after them found a repetition of the scenes from Falaise, with scores of German dead lying along the roads.

The Canadians' pursuit was hampered by the saturated fields, which forced them to stay on the mud-covered, mine-laden roads. Many mines were buried deep enough to be missed when the roads were swept. As a result, tanks and other vehicles were casualties. Each city the Fourth reached was defended desperately by the Germans, making cities in east Rhineland such as Keppeln, Sonsbeck, Xanten, and Veen, synonymous with deadly street-to-street and house-to-house fighting.

Fighting their way east, the Canadians finally came within sight of the German city of Wesel. On March 10, the German rearguard raced over the final bridge across the Rhine, then it was blown up. After a month of some of the bitterest fighting the Canadians had seen, the campaign for the Rhineland was finally over. The Canadians on the west bank knew the next weeks of battle must be their last.

For the first time, the Fourth Division began employing German civilians on work details. Rhinelanders were taken under guard to bury dead animals, dig ditches, and to carry rubble to repair the roads. The troops were "heartily in favour of this form of non-fraternization."[27] The troopers also noticed the Rhineland teemed with livestock and its cellars were full of food, a stunning contrast to conditions a short distance west in the Netherlands. They took advantage of the brimming German farms, taking all kinds of food, and there was no shortage of fresh eggs to replace the powdered ones they were served.[28]

Fighting through the Hochwald Gap and Rhineland cities had taken a heavy toll on the Fourth Division. Many infantry companies were reduced to the size of a platoon. Losses of tanks had similarly gutted the strength of the armoured regiments. Reinforcements were slowly trickling in, but were not nearly sufficient to make up for dead and wounded, consisting of some of the first conscripted men the army sent overseas against their will.[29]

After the bitter fighting for the Rhineland, the Division needed a chance to train reinforcements and reequip the regiments. The Fourth returned to the Netherlands with those goals in mind. Their recce parties found billets and harbour areas near their former locations. On March 12, the Headquarters Squadron moved to Boxtel, a few miles south of Vught. Many were housed in the Ursula Klooster, with the vehicle harbour at St. Theresia School. The people of Boxtel took in the Division as old friends, and the Canadians immediately began refitting for the next push into Germany.

As important as it was to reequip and incorporate reinforcements, the troops also were given time to relax. An officer's club was opened in nearby S'Hertogenbosch, a St. Patrick's Day dance was held in Boxtel, film nights were arranged, and names were drawn for a lucky few to proceed to Paris or England on seven-day leaves. One of the officers returning from Paris described it as a place where "everything is done for the soldier's enjoyment whilst on leave."[30]

The Fourth was warned it would return to Germany as soon as the Rhine was breached and there was sufficient room in the bridgehead to allow the armour to operate freely. Operation Plunder began on March 23,[31] crossing the Rhine at the cities of Wesel and Rees. Intense bombing and artillery bombardments preceding the crossings flattened both cities. This early success meant the Fourth had to prepare to move forward at the end of March. Once across the Rhine, the Fourth would hold the far right flank of the Canadian army as it pushed north and east.

Just before joining Operation Plunder, the Headquarters Squadron assembled on parade to be read personal messages from Montgomery and Churchill. Rumour among the Squadron's troops was that German defences were crumbling on the eastern bank of the Rhine, and there might only be a few days left of organized resistance. For months such ideas had circulated, only to see the German defence stiffen. Everyone hoped this time it was true.

Shortly before leaving Boxtel to join the offensive, General Vokes held a conference of all unit commanders. He described the plans for the Fourth's move across the Rhine, and his optimism that German positions on the Canadian's front were precarious added to the feeling the end was close.

The General's optimism may have lessened regrets the troopers felt leaving the relative comfort of Boxtel and Vught for the rigors of living under canvas in the cold and rain with the renewed threats of shelling, mortar bombs, and mines. Moving out on March 30, the Fourth headed east through Nijmegan into Germany. The soldiers spent their first night near Kleve, the Rhine crossing to take place the next day at the city of Rees.

They found the road to the Rhine bridge clogged with Canadian and British vehicles. The Headquarters Squadron joined the line, crawling to the crossing the engineers had named Black Friars Bridge. Twenty boats, each barely bigger than a rowboat, supported each side of the roadbed, lashed together and held in place by lines stretching across the river. On top of this was laid prefabricated metal sections of Bailey Bridge resting on the gunwales. The floating structure was surprisingly strong and buoyant, even taking the weight of the Division's tanks, although they had to cross slowly and stay widely spaced. Driving on the swaying, dipping bridge, floating only a foot above the swirling dark water, was nerve-wracking enough, but it was made worse by the shells from German artillery landing all around the bridge, sending spouts of water high into the air.

After crossing the Rhine, the Fourth swung sharply north. Its path through the meandering border between Holland and Germany crossed back and forth. In Holland, ecstatic but half-starved throngs came out to greet them, unfurling orange sheets and Dutch flags from their windows and cheering the passing troops as liberators. Passing back into Germany sometimes within less than an hour, the Fourth found well-fed civilians hanging white sheets from their houses.

Before they had entered Germany, a concerted campaign was aimed at stopping Allied soldiers from fraternizing with Germans. The orders were strict, those disobeying them were subject to punishment, and were reinforced by warnings that German civilians were dangerous. This was the message in a story published in the Canadian soldiers' newspaper *The Maple Leaf.*

Just in case anyone thinks children are children the world over, he should take a careful look around some of the conquered towns of Germany.

Here is a story confirmed by a battalion medical officer concerning a German boy ... a very young German boy. It happened near Cleve, just beyond the Reichwald amid what used to be the secondary defences of the Siegfried Line.

The boy is said to have approached a soldier with a request for chocolate. The soldier knew the rules against fraternization, but somehow, Canucks are soft with children. He put both hands in his trousers pockets to hunt.

When he did so, the boy drew a pistol and shot him in the abdomen.

Was the story true or hearsay? Might it even have been invented to make Canadian troops think twice about fraternizing? Equally blatant messages were contained in a small booklet titled *Your Future Occupation*,[32] issued to Canadian soldiers. It told the troops "Don't believe there are any good Germans" and "A German is, by nature, a liar." It claimed German women carried concealed knives and were trained to use them on Allied soldiers they seduced. It also said not to give German children candy as they had done in other countries. The idea of preventing contact between Allied soldiers and Germans came from the highest levels of the Allied army. It was meant both to protect Allied soldiers and to punish Germans. It was based on the premise that aloof but professional soldiers would impress Germans who, it was believed, were taught to revere military order. It was also intended to punish the German people for supporting the Nazis, which "brought them complete defeat and … caused the other people of the world to look upon them with distrust."[33] The non-fraternization order also told them to keep official contact to the minimum necessary.[34]

———————◆———————

The situation for the German army in April 1945, as the Fourth worked its way north, was increasingly hopeless. They had no answer to Canadian superiority in firepower, especially in the air and in armour. The war turned again to one of pursuer and pursued, with intermittent small but fierce battles. In early April the Headquarters Squadron constantly pushed forward, sometimes relocating several times a day, liberating numerous Dutch towns as the Fourth chased the fleeing Germans. From Millingen, Germany, on April 2, the Squadron headed north to Westendorp, the Netherlands. On April 3 they moved to Geesteren and the next afternoon reached Wegdam. The frequent moves were slowed by the constant rain, which had made the fields and roads muddy quagmires.

Sometimes the Fourth met strong resistance, but other times they would find the enemy had withdrawn. Inevitably, the fast-moving Canadians bypassed German troops not ready to surrender. This sometimes left pockets of resistance, and dangerous firefights on the flanks and rear of the Headquarters Squadron.

The Fourth advanced rapidly, from Almelo through the towns of Borne and Coevorden. Securing these Dutch towns, they turned straight east, their objective the city of Meppen, six miles inside Germany. By the time forward units of the Fourth arrived, they discovered all the bridges across the Ems River, which splits the town in two, had been blown. The enemy was believed to be waiting on the far bank, but when Canadian troops crossed, they found most German troops had departed.

The poor condition of the roads and the marshy ground made movement slow and largely limited it to a few main routes, which themselves broke down under the heavy armoured traffic. As a result, the Headquarters Squadron waited in Oldenzaal for the Division's main fighting regiments to push ahead. While waiting there, late on the evening of April 8, a lieutenant from the 102nd Battery of the Eighth Canadian Light Anti-Aircraft Regiment arrived at the Headquarters Squadron. Under strong guard he brought two Headquarters soldiers, Private Pollard and Trooper Stepanishen. The lieutenant said they were arrested after a German farmer had come to him for help, complaining two Canadian soldiers were in his farmhouse "abusing the women folk," as well as stealing a pocket watch, two gold rings, and a bottle of liquor.[35]

The two soldiers were transferred under arrest to the Headquarters Squadron, while the officer second in command immediately left for the farmhouse, near Esche, just across the border. With him came Private Strub, who would act as interpreter, and a medical orderly. At the farmhouse the officer took statements from each of the adults, while the orderly conducted a physical examination of the women.[36] The next afternoon, two sergeants from the Provost Corps arrived at the farmhouse to conduct their own investigation.

With the way ahead cleared, the Headquarters Squadron joined other Fourth Division units in Meppen. Soon after arriving, Major Campbell and the Recce Officer proceeded to Sögel, Germany, in search of their next harbour. Only that morning in Sögel, Canadian troops at a field hospital had nearly been overwhelmed by a German counterattack. A heavy fog had reduced visibility, and the Canadians were by then used to frequently hearing their own troops firing captured German weapons. This prevented the attack being detected before it was practically on the Canadians. Only a few were able to put up a defence, some medics obtaining weapons from patients.[37] To one side, about twenty Germans fanned out to take the Canadians from the flank, but a small party of troops took up firing positions behind a brick pile and held them off, despite being sniped at by civilians. The attack on the isolated Canadian unit went on for two hours, ending only when a troop of tanks arrived.

It is perhaps the only time the Headquarters Squadron war diary carries an angry remark, saying there was no doubt civilians in Sögel had "aided and abetted the attack" and stating, "They will no doubt pay a big price for this folly and treachery." Civilians becoming involved in battle made the Canadian soldier's job nearly impossible. There was no urge to shoot civilians caught up in areas where battles were taking place, but the anger could be overwhelming when bypassed civilians took up arms against the Canadians.

Seeing the situation in Sögel was not yet secure and with his primary duty to protect the Fourth's general staff, Major Campbell postponed the Headquarters Squadron's move. When it finally entered Sögel, much of it was found demolished by Canadian bombardments. It was like most Germans towns in which the enemy chose to stay and fight — fortified areas were pounded to pieces by artillery fire and pummelled by mortars and tank cannons. In the aftermath of such battles, many towns had few buildings left unscathed. It was a contrast to the fighting in the Netherlands, where consideration was given to the presence of civilians in the towns when the Germans made a stand.

Over the coming days, civilians filtered back to Sögel, doubtless to retrieve valuables left behind after hurriedly leaving when the Canadian assault began. The returning civilians were chased away by the Canadian troops, while the destruction of the town was complete when, according to the war diary, Sögel was turned into "a heap of rubble. It is being demolished to provide rubble for road building." This would have been the "price" the Squadron's war diarist suggested the civilians in Sögel would pay, the destruction of their homes ordered by General Vokes.[38]

Not all German civilians resisted the Canadian troops. While in Sögel, the local German police handed over to the Headquarters Squadron members of the German underground they had arrested. In nearby Rastdorf, the Burgomaster contacted the Headquarters Squadron to report sixty paratroopers hiding in the area who were proposing to break out to make their way back behind German lines. Two days later the same Burgomaster reported he had seven German soldiers locked up and requested an escort to take them to the POW cage. These soldiers, it can be speculated, wanted to surrender to the Canadians but were unsure how to do so safely. Sergeant Blackwell from the Squadron, with a truck and a few men to help guard the prisoners, obliged the request. There was a constant trickle of surrendering German soldiers who had decided their war was over, and the Sergeant "added two more to the bag" who surrendered to him before he could reach the POW cage.

The Canadian superiority in firepower was offset by casualties and losses of tanks. The Headquarters Squadron manpower shortage was made worse when four of the Shermans were given to the Fourth's armoured regiments to replace their destroyed tanks. The Headquarters tanks were to be replaced by seven Staghounds, requiring additional men be taken from other Squadron duties.

German units were even more badly worn down. Their reinforcements were limited to the young, the old, and the partially infirm. Despite the declining quality of German combat troops, their officers picked where they would make their stands, defending well-chosen positions usually with just enough veterans to stiffen the young and inexperienced soldiers and the civilian "Volksturm" troops used as a last resort. Against such inexperienced soldiers, the Fourth's armoured strength should have proven overwhelming, but in northwestern Germany the marshy ground restricted the tanks to the main roads, neutralizing much of their advantage.

Leaving Sögel, the Fourth continued northeast, where a fierce battle took place against a strong force of paratroopers at Breddenburg. When the path was cleared, the Headquarters Squadron moved to Neuvrees, a town about five miles southwest of Friesoythe. There were frequent reports of roving bands of German troops behind the front line. Whether they had stayed hidden as the line of battle swept past them or had infiltrated the spotty Canadian front line was impossible to tell, but there was a constant need for guards to protect the perimeter of the harbour.

The city of Friesoythe was captured after a sharp exchange with two hundred paratroopers from the Seventh German Parachute Division. German civilians again were believed to have taken part in the battle and this time were blamed for killing the Argylls' commanding officer, Lieutenant-Colonel Fred Wigle.[39] When General Vokes was told civilians were responsible for the death of Wigle, he ordered the town destroyed.[40] "We used the rubble to make traversable roads for our tanks," Vokes would later write.[41] There were also reports Canadian soldiers evicted German civilians before setting their houses and a church on fire in reprisal. [42, 43]

Heading northeast along the main road from Friesoythe, the Fourth came to the Kustin Canal and the village of Barkendorp. The recce units arriving first found the north side of the ninety-foot-wide canal strongly held. Meeting strong resistance at this stage of the war was disappointing. The end of the fighting was clearly imminent, perhaps just days away, and no one wanted to take unnecessary risks. Yet many Germans defended their country as fiercely as ever. There were some exceptions, though, showing evidence of dissatisfaction among German troops. This was demonstrated when several officers arrived together at the Headquarters Squadron POW cage. They told the Canadian officer who questioned them that they had deserted from the Abwher, the German Army intelligence service, "voluntarily surrender(ing) out of genteel disgust at what they term the mismanagement of the Wehrmacht by amateurs."[44]

The nearness of victory did not stop the Fourth attacking across the Kustin Canal. The initial assault was made by the Algonquin Regiment at midnight on April 15. It was clear from the response that the German commander in the area planned to resist with everything at his disposal. German artillery hammered Canadian positions on both sides of the canal, and there were incessant counterattacks and enemy infiltration, threatening the Algonquins who held the north side of the canal. The canal was under such heavy German fire that resupply and reinforcement during daytime was nearly impossible. Carriers and anti-tank guns were ferried across the canal by raft, and in the end, despite the heavy shelling, Canadian engineers completed the bridge, allowing tanks to cross.

When the first tank drove onto the bridge, it came under fire from an 88 hidden on the right flank, shells narrowly whizzing past. The scene was repeated as each tank crossed and, after several narrow misses, the seventh was hit. Fortunately, it did not break down on the bridge or worse, explode there, but instead continued across and only burst into flames two hundred yards up the road.[45] With armoured reinforcements on the north shore of the Kustin Canal, the Germans withdrew further north. The desperation of the German defence was apparent to Headquarters Squadrons troops when they crossed to the north side, seeing for themselves the fields littered with German dead as Major Campbell had reported when returning from looking for their next harbour. In sunshine and warmth in the late afternoon on April 18, the Squadron relocated to a new harbour at Altenoythe. The move was slowed by cratered roads and many large, buried sea mines, which had to be dug out and hauled away before the advance could continue.

On April 22, court martial proceedings against Private Pollard and Trooper Stepanishen took place. The trial was held in the farmhouse near Esche, where the alleged crimes had taken place. The court sat until three a.m. and those taking part returned to the Headquarters Squadron as day was breaking. The verdict would not be released until it was confirmed by senior army staff.

———◆———

There was a surreal contrast between the heavy fighting taking place at the front and activities only a few miles behind the front lines. Perhaps none was as odd as the creation of a schedule of exhibition softball games, the Headquarters Squadron putting three teams together. With heavy combat taking place at the nearby front, the war diarist noted how fortunate one of the softball teams was to have two strong pitchers. The Canadian army's RCA Band put on a concert one evening, and on other nights, movies were set up for the troops.

Major Campbell and the tank troops were among those experiencing this strange incongruity. For the Major, one day he was attending a concert given at the Headquarters and the next the vehicle carrying him came under strong mortar and shell fire while looking for a new harbour near the German towns of Osterscheps and Edewecht. The next day he reported narrowly escaped being shot by a German sniper who was "luckily a poor shot."

The Fourth continued advancing north towards the German town of Bad Zwischenahn. The town sits at the southern end of a small lake, the Zwischenahner Meer, with a large airbase on its western shore. The weather had turned from warm and sunny to windy with heavy rain, and it was again impossible to get warm. The engineers were hopelessly swamped with clearing mines and repairing the roads. Russ was at times put in charge of road-building parties with Headquarters Squadron troops, working with the engineers to make the cratered roads passable.

Even though there were only scattered engagements, German troops frequently harassed the Canadians with shelling, appearing without warning and to devastating effect. On April 27, when the Headquarters Squadron was moving into a new harbour, a German spotter must have radioed the co-ordinates location. Five 10.5-cm shells came screaming down. A piece of shrapnel hit the Squadron's Lieutenant Earl Phillips in the chest while he was guiding vehicles into the entrance of the harbour. The metal shard passed right through him, exiting near his spinal column. Although paralyzed from the waist down, he was conscious the entire time he was being evacuated to the 12 Canadian Light Field Ambulance. The war diarist said, "He will be greatly missed and quite impossible to replace." Shells continued to fall nearby but none landed inside the Headquarters harbour.

Following Major Campbell's close calls at the front, he had the Headquarters troops called together. He dressed down the soldiers for their slackness, particularly the lack of alertness of the guards and the generally poor readiness of the troops to defend themselves. They must constantly bear in mind fighting was going on less than two miles away and the only protection against infiltration or attack was what the Squadron provided for itself.[46]

Though slowed by the poor condition of the roads, the Fourth continued pressing north. The Lincoln & Welland Regiment got on to the high ground at Specken, just a few thousand yards southeast of Bad Zwischenahn, pushing on against heavy mortar fire. On the left flank, the Lake Superior Regiment reached the railway line but could not cross because the road was blocked by boxcars, and any attempt to move them was stopped by shelling.[47]

April 30 was miserable. The winds, which never seemed to stop, were especially strong, pushing cold rain and snow. The bleak day became worse when word was received that Lieutenant Phillips had died that morning at the Canadian field hospital in Friesoythe. He was buried in the hospital grounds with a specially painted cross marking his grave.[48]

The Germans continued to put up strong resistance near Bad Zwischenahn. To the west of the town German opposition was weaker, allowing the Lake Superior Regiment to advance to the town of Rostrup at the base of the meer. A German prisoner of war revealed that troops near there belonged to Battalion Hillibrecht, consisting of First Battalion of the 63 Paratroop Regiment and the 21 Werfer Battalion, and though they had very few Nebelwerfers left, there was a sizable body of infantry troops. The Argyll and Sutherland Highlanders were sent forward with one squadron of tanks from the Canadian Grenadier Guards, passing through the Lake Superior Regiment in Rostrup.[49, 50] Just north of them at the Bad Zwischenahn airport waited Battalion Hillibrecht and a final battle.

TEN

Verlorene Illusionen
Lost Illusions

When Frank was released from hospital in July, 1945, and tried reporting back to his unit, he found the German headquarters in the Finnish town of Nautsi had been dissolved and his unit disbanded. In the past year the tide of war had shifted drastically in favour of the Allies. Canadian, British, and American armies had invaded Sicily and then mainland Italy in 1943, where they were slowly pushing north. Berlin and every other large German city were being heavily bombed. Soviet troops had forced Germany's Army Group North to retreat to Estonia and Latvia, as well as pushing German armies back across the Ukraine and Crimea, by late summer entering Poland. On June 6, the D-Day landings had opened a third front in France.

Instead of being sent to one of these fronts, Frank was assigned in July, 1944, to an officer's training course at a military academy in Valdahon, France. A greater contrast to northern Finland was hardly imaginable. He went from living close to nature's extremes north of the Arctic Circle to the rich farmland and pastoral villages of eastern France. Another difference was that German troops had been invited into Finland and were treated as allies and friends. In France, Frank was, for the first time, stationed in a country held by military force against the wishes of its people. Nevertheless, though he spoke not a word of French, he found the people friendly. They were also welcoming in what he thought might be a uniquely French way. When he checked into the hotel in Valdahon, the desk clerk asked if he preferred his room with or without mademoiselle.

Valdahon is a small town not far from France's eastern border with Switzerland and Germany. In the summer of 1944, it was restless with activity by the French Underground. The Fallschirmjäger unit to which Frank was assigned as an officer cadet was occasionally sent in search of French partisans.

On one occasion, as they approached a village, the bells in the church began ringing. It was a signal that Germans were coming. The Germans told the villagers to leave their houses and put them under guard in the village's small square, near the church. Soldiers went from house to house, searching for weapons, radios, or other signs of the partisans. Suspecting an ambush, the officer in charge pulled women, girls, boys, and the pastor from those assembled in the square and told them to stand with the soldiers. They left the town together, each soldier accompanied by a civilian. Either because the civilian hostages shielded them, or because there were no partisans waiting, there was no ambush. In all the search operations Frank participated in, not once was a partisan found, and the search missions seemed to him little more than shows rather than serious military operations.

In July, an assassination attempt on Hitler was planned by senior German army officers and carried out by Colonel Claus von Stauffenberg. Operation Valkyrie, the failed conspiracy, created tension within the German armed forces as suspicion spread about who was loyal. The allegiance of professional officers in particular was questioned, and for a while there was concern an internal revolt against the Nazis was imminent. One of the short-term results was that German units were restricted to their barracks, and ordinary soldiers were required to greet one other using the raised right-arm salute, something not previously required.

Officer training school at Valdahon was abruptly cancelled in the wake of the breakout by Allied forces in Normandy in late August. All available soldiers were being sent to the western front, at this point pushed back into the Netherlands, and Frank and his fellow cadets were ordered to reinforce Fallschirmjäger units fighting there. However, travel from Valdahon was slowed by partisans, who repeatedly stopped the trains by loosening spikes on the rails or rolling boulders onto the tracks. The train's progress was even slower along the Doubs River, where the rail line ran along a steep cliff. If the partisans sabotaged the rail line there, a fast-moving train would plunge into the river below. The train moved at a snail's pace until it left the steep-sided valley, and the expected partisan attack or sabotaged rails never materialized.

Since the Allied breakout in Normandy, German troops had withdrawn north and east, yielding territory in order to gain time to move reserve units forward and strengthen defensive positions. Frank joined the newly formed First Fallschirmjäger Army in the Netherlands, commanded by Colonel General Kurt Student. Student was instructed to gather all available Fallschirmjäger units and to position them in front of the Albert Canal.[1] Fallschirmjäger from across Germany and the occupied countries were ordered to join units on this part of the front. Frank arrived in early September, his new unit located along the Maas-Scheldt Canal in southern Holland.[2]

The First Fallschirmjäger Army was composed of seven regiments, totalling twenty thousand paratroopers. They were a mix of veteran Fallschirmjäger like Frank, Flak troops, mail clerks and office workers, and new recruits, some as young as fifteen. One unit was sent to the front while in the middle of basic training, receiving uniforms and weapons only after arriving in the Netherlands. Their training was so incomplete that only at this point were they taught how to use their weapons. There was even a Fallschirmjäger penal battalion, sent to the front wearing uniforms designed for troops in the tropics.[3] Not only some of the foot soldiers lacked battle experience. The majority of the battalion and company commanders were similarly inexperienced.

The relative quiet on the front allowed the Fallschirmjäger units to consolidate their defences. But the calm was broken on September 17, when the Allies launched the largest airborne assault ever seen. It coincided with a strong armoured push north into the Netherlands. It was the beginning of Operation Market Garden.

The airdrop deposited Allied paratroopers at several drop zones behind Student's First Fallschirmjäger Army. This was the "Market" part of Operation Market Garden. "Garden," which began at the same time, was a thrust north by British armoured forces to link up with the paratroopers. Market Garden was one of the first direct encounters between Allied paratroopers and Germany's Fallschirmjäger. To accomplish its objective, the British armoured force would have to push from northern Belgium into Holland, passing through the First Fallschirmjäger Army and keeping the corridor behind them open. The First Fallschirmjäger Army would seek to blunt the thrust and to collapse the corridor in on itself.

The British armoured attack had three prongs — a central force towards the first objective, Eindhoven, with additional forces to the east and west protecting the centre. The Fallschirmjäger regiments to the east of Eindhoven retreated slowly to the northeast, fighting rearguard actions as they withdrew. Reaching the Deurne Canal between Wessem and Nederweert and the Zuid Willems Canal, they established a more solid line of defense.

On the morning of September 19, a Panzer brigade with a Fallschirmjäger battalion counterattacked west from the Dutch city of Venlo, attacking the British flank through the town of Helmond, their objective the town of Son on the highway just north of Eindhoven. This force was stopped by heavy Allied artillery and tank fire within sight of its objective, the bridge over the Wilhelmina Canal. Slowly, the German force was forced to retreat. Heading for the city of Helmond, they withdrew to the east side of the Zuid Willems

Canal bisecting the city, fighting street to street. In an attempt to cut off the German force in Helmond, the British attacked at a crossing point several miles south of the city. But the small bridgehead was heavily contested. Slowly the British pushed forward, the swampy ground hindering the use of tanks, putting the onus on the infantry.

The Allied airborne thrust was over within a week of starting. It had created a salient into the German lines as far as the city of Nijmegen, but to the east of the salient the First Fallschirmjäger Army held a strip of Holland to the west of the Maas River. Somewhere in this pocket was Frank's unit.

On September 27, orders were issued to Dutch civilians to evacuate Overloon and villages to its east. The civilians had to leave behind any possession they could not carry and make their way east towards the German rear lines. This was a dilemma for the civilians for several reasons. First, possessions left behind might be looted. Second, Dutchmen between sixteen and sixty were being sought by the Grüne Polizei, members of the German Gestapo who were sending men from occupied countries back to Germany as forced labour. Those who ignored the evacuation order and stayed behind hid themselves. The evacuated civilians walked east in the pouring rain, not knowing when they could return or what would be there when they did.

In late September, an American division replaced the British on the front along much of the Maas salient. They would lead an attack, which, if successful, would push the First Fallschirmjäger Army and Frank across the Maas River. But when the American assault began on September 30, it was quickly turned back by strong fire from mortars, 88s, and machine guns. The attack resumed the following day, but once more bogged down under strong fire from the German lines. Over the coming week, Fallschirmjäger counterattacks took back some of the mile of ground lost to the Americans.

The front line in the Maas salient was an unwelcoming place for troops of both sides. According to one Fallschirmjäger, life was dangerous, dirty, and unpredictable.[4]

> The (enemy) is only 200 yards away from us and treats us every morning to a loud reveille with half an hour of artillery fire. You get used to it eventually. It is simply a matter of luck whether you're hit or not. Last night my canteen was shot off the parapet of my trench. You really must fight for your life here. Hopefully we'll be back in reserve soon. I have not washed for a week. No, this is not exactly my idea of a good

life: sleeping in a hole, eating whatever grub they can get to us, usually with dirt in it. Yesterday a shell dropped nearby. Promptly our hole caved in and we had to dig another one again.

British troops replaced the Americans massing for a new attack. The morning of October 12 an artillery barrage and air raid preceded the beginning of the assault. British infantry with tank support attacked behind a creeping artillery barrage. They met a German defence consisting of minefields, anti-tank fire, Nebelwerfers, and mortars. In the face of strong resistance from the Fallschirmjäger, the British slowly fought their way into the ruins of the Dutch town of Overloon.

Though lacking the artillery and aerial firepower of the Allies, German defenders fought ferociously. All along the front, German positions were being hammered without mercy by planes and artillery. The Fallschirmjäger response came when the bombardments ended and British infantry and tanks appeared — the main German weapons were the mortar and machine gun against infantry and the Panzerfaust and anti-tank guns against armour. Eventually the outgunned and outmanned Fallschirmjäger had no choice but to withdraw across the Loobeek Canal, their men exhausted, their forces decimated.

The British attacks were relentless as regiment after regiment was thrown into battle against the Germans. At the Loobeek Canal, two fresh divisions were brought forward, while the Germans had no rested divisions to bring into the battle. There were barely any replacements at all for those wounded, killed, or taken prisoner.

On the morning of October 16, Allied armoured divisions began another advance. They tried breaching the narrow Loobeek using foot-bridges for the infantry and fascines, essentially a large bundle of logs put in place by a special tank to be used by the armoured forces. The footbridges were successful, allowing infantry to slowly cross the canal, but the fascine bridge collapsed under the first tank to try it. The Loobeek was breached at several other points by British and American forces, threatening to cut off Fallschirmjäger at portions of the canal that had held. They had no choice but to retreat. Having no further canals to take defensive positions behind, the Fallschirmjäger retreated to the only defensible places left, the small towns, villages, and woods in front of the Maas River, even occupying and fighting from medieval castles. However, one by one, each town, village, and wood was liberated, usually after a fierce battle.

The Fallschirmjäger defended their positions so determinedly because their orders were to hold the Maas Salient at all cost, and against over-whelmingly superior forces, they did. At this point, many German soldiers still believed the war could be won. Many of their officers, while perhaps not believing the same, thought the sacrifices they asked of their troops could make for better terms in an armistice.

In places, the British and American troops were now within two or three miles of the Maas River. To the relief of the hard-pressed Fallschirmjäger, the attacks slowed when the Allies decided to divert supplies from the Maas Salient to the area east of Antwerp. The Allies were so short of supplies, it was impossible to carry on more than one operation at a time.

The surprising cessation against the Germans in the Maas Salient gave the battle-weary Fallschirmjäger time to gather themselves. Facing them in the line was a relatively small force of U.S. and Belgian forces. No one on the Allied side believed a strong German attack feasible. They were wrong. German high command planned a surprise attack from the Maas Salient.

Two fresh divisions were brought forward, a combined twenty-six thousand troops of the Ninth Panzer and 15th Panzergrenadier divisions, supported by a large number of artillery pieces. They would pass through the exhausted Fallschirmjäger regiments and assault the slim Allied force facing them. A few Fallschirmjäger troops would join the attack.

The offensive began October 27, taking the Americans by surprise and easily reaching its objectives that first morning. But the success quickly came to a halt when the skies cleared and Allied planes entered the fighting. German tanks and self-propelled guns were restricted to the main roads by the swampy ground, making them easy targets. The offensive had come close to creating a major breakthrough, but by October 29, it was obvious any element of surprise was lost. The German attack stalled, allowing American and British reinforcements to move forward. On November 1, the attack force withdrew behind the Maas River. At about the same time, the Allied high command shifted supplies back to the Maas offensive.

Once again the Allied attacks began against the Fallschirmjäger positions. The British and Americans advanced with tank support, artillery barrages, and fighters and fighter-bombers harassing the Germans. Most of the Allied attacks were held up by a strong response from the Germans. But it was clear the inevitable conclusion would be the elimination of German forces west of the Maas River and the end of the Maas Salient. On November 28, German forces held only three small pockets west of the Maas. By December 4, these had all succumbed to the Allied onslaught.

Pressed by Americans and the British, the Germans had to either retreat or be destroyed. By the end of November, Frank's unit was decimated. The survivors of his unit crossed the Maas River at the city of Roermond, in the southeastern Netherlands, some of them swimming as their retreat turned into a disorganized route. After three months of a living hell in the Maas Salient, and the disorderly retreat across the Maas, Frank was told to report to a reserve unit at Frankfurt an der Oder, in eastern Germany.

◆

Frank's orders instructed him to travel to Frankfurt by train "by the shortest route possible." Train travel by day was impossible due to Allied bombing, so at each stop he would make his way to a train station as evening approached and look for the routes posted there. Train schedules and routes changed constantly, and travel on civilian trains was continually disrupted by those rushing men and supplies to the front. Though needing to travel straight east, Frank found the train routes took him south to the city of Karlsruhe in southwestern Germany. It was one of the cities he had visited when hitch-hiking across Germany as a fifteen-year-old.

What he found there when he arrived was no longer a shock to the now twenty-year-old who had now seen so much destruction, much of it recently in the Dutch towns demolished in the Maas Salient. Karlsruhe, too, was devastated, like every major city he had passed through. Many buildings were nothing more than piles of brick. Others were bombed-out shells, the walls still standing but the roofs and floors collapsed inside in piles of rubble. Seeing the destruction of the Fallschirmjäger regiment he had been with in Holland, the deaths of so many men he fought beside against the Allies, and the ruined cities, it was impossible not to be inured to the suffering and destruction everywhere he looked.

Very slowly Frank made his way across Germany. Finally he reached Aussig, a city in eastern Germany not far from Frankfurt. It was also less than twenty-five kilometres from his home in Leitmeritz. Frank saw two trains sitting on the platform, one scheduled for Frankfurt, the destination he was ordered to report to, the other travelling in the opposite direction, toward his family in Leitmeritz.

The train he boarded soon got underway, and before long its rocking relaxed him and he fell asleep. A touch on his shoulder caused him to come half awake, and he saw standing before him a captain from the military police. Frank froze. The officer held out his hand, asking for Frank's orders.

There was no way to avoid the inevitable as the captain studied the stamps on his marching orders, revealing where Frank had come from and when and where he was to report.

"Why are you traveling to Leitmeritz?" he wanted to know. "There are no trains to Frankfurt an der Oder from there."

Frank did not answer immediately. What could he say? "My parents live there," he finally admitted.

Without saying anything, the captain took Frank's order book. In it he wrote the date, time, and route. He returned the papers.

"I warn you, *Fahnrich*,[5]" he said, "so far you are just a few hours late reporting. If you do not report within twenty-four hours you will be considered a deserter."

Ignoring the warning, Frank continued on to Leitmeritz. He was growing indifferent to the war. Considering all he had experienced and seen, it was perhaps the only sane reaction he could have had. In the past few months he had barely survived being seriously wounded in Finland, seen his unit destroyed in the Maas Salient, and been part of the mad retreat across the Maas River. During his haphazard journey across Germany he had seen the tremendous toll Allied bombing had taken. Finally, this officer on the train, whose job it was to be a sort of school hall monitor, and who may never have been at the front, called Frank a deserter. He now saw things clearly. And with this clarity came the realization of how futile the war had become. Of course, he thought, he still wanted Germany to prevail, and he would still carry out his pledge to serve his country, but he could not see how it was possible to win the war.

Frank arrived at Leitmeritz and found it untouched by bombing. His unannounced arrival at home was a complete surprise to his parents and two little sisters (his youngest sister had been born after he had left for Finland and this was the first time he had seen her). Frank spent three days at home. His mother fussed over him and his father wanted to hear what Frank had seen and experienced. Frank showed them the wounds in his neck, arm, and chest from the grenade shrapnel, the scars still fresh, at which Frank's father unconsciously rubbed the old bullet wounds in his leg.

It was the first time in two years Frank had enjoyed the comfort of home and especially his mother's affection. He had not realized how much he had missed them. Soaking in the bathtub, eating her cooking, and walking the familiar streets, he found things almost as they had been before the war.

One change was in Theresienstadt, a mile south of Leitmeritz. The garrison town was no longer used by the army. Since 1941, the SS had been using it as a concentration camp for Jewish civilians.[6]

After three days at home, he knew he had to leave, to report to Frankfurt an der Oder. He donned the uniform his mother had cleaned, and she and his sisters gathered, trying not to cry as they said goodbye. Whether they would ever see each other again, none could foretell.

Frank reported to his new unit at Frankfurt an der Oder. On his arrival the local commander called Frank to his office. He informed Frank that because of the notation on his travel papers, he was charging the young soldier with desertion. The officer said he would have to answer the charge before a court-martial, and if found guilty, a death sentence was possible. He advised Frank to find himself a good lawyer.

"Desertion?" Frank replied. "But I am here!" The officer's shoulders twitched, but he said nothing. Frank carried on as though the charge did not exist.

In Frankfurt, he learned he was to rejoin officer's training at the War Academy at Schloss Werneck, near Schweinfurt. Frank was not arrested, but neither was the charge dismissed. With it hanging over his head, he reported to the War Academy. There things still operated as if it was peacetime. He attended lectures, was taught the difference between bravery and courage, and learned about strategy and tactics. The food was wonderful, and he slept in a bed with sheets. Remembering the constant cold and wet in the Maas Salient, he felt he had found an oasis in a country at war.

Frank in March, 1943, after promotion to the rank of Gefreiter in the Fallschirmjäger, designated by the two wings on the collar of his jacket.

———————◆———————

The respite at Schloss Werneck was an impossible promise of good times that could not last. It came to an abrupt end in March, 1945, when Frank was ordered back to the Western front. He was told the desertion charge was dropped and he was promoted to Meldegänger (lance corporal). He was assigned to the Seventh Fallschirmjäger Division, recently transferred north from Alsace to the area of the German–Dutch border near the cities of Venlo and Kleve. The Seventh Fallschirmjäger was part of the First Fallschirmjäger Army, the same army group he had been with in the Maas Salient.

When he joined the Seventh Division in March, the western front was under assault by the Allies over most of its thousand-kilometre length. The Canadians and British had breached the Westwall (called the Siegfried Line by the Allies) in the north, and in the south the Americans were enlarging a bridgehead across the Rhine.

Frank reported to the northern sector of the Seventh Division's part of the front, near the city of Wesel. But Wesel came under massive artillery fire almost immediately. The artillery barrage that began the offensive destroyed Wesel, paving the way for the breach of the Rhine.

The pressure from Canadian and British forces flooding across the Rhine was intense, forcing the First Fallschirmjäger Army, and with it the Seventh Division, to withdraw or be destroyed. Frank fell back with his regiment. Fighting a rearguard action, they retreated northeast, constantly pressured from behind and from the air.

The First Fallschirmjäger Army was now commanded by General Günther Blumentritt. He realized the end of the war was close and the situation hopeless.[7] There were significant gaps in his army's front, and no reserves to stop an Allied breakthrough. German artillery support was weakening, and the Allies had total domination of the skies, the Luftwaffe long since focusing all its attention on the streams of Allied bombers attacking German cities. The few German tanks available were in perpetual danger of attack from the air, and if the tanks did engage the Allies, they were hopelessly outnumbered.

Frank was an exception as a reinforcement, a trained veteran soldier. Most reinforcements Blumentritt had were either too young or too old, and all were virtually untrained. So unsuitable were they that sending them to the front invited their slaughter. Still, most of these boys and old men reported when called, willing to give their lives for their country. Though the situation was clearly hopeless, the Germans defended fiercely.

Blumentritt's plan for withdrawal was aimed at getting as many of his troops as possible to relative safety beyond the Küsten Canal. Once there the Fallschirmjäger could turn to face their relentless pursuers, forcing the Canadians and British to fight while they built new bridges across the canal.

But to reach the Küsten Canal, Frank's unit was in near constant retreat, travelling at night and sleeping in slit trenches during the day to avoid Allied air attacks. The pressure from the Allied troops on the ground and from the air was unending, and staying alive was a matter of endurance and luck. In the next few weeks the cycle of marching, digging trenches, sleeping, and marching again was all Frank knew. His unit barely stayed ahead of the Allied forces that pursued them on all sides. By April 8 they had reached Fürstenau, and on April 12 had retreated a further twenty-five miles to Gross Roscharden.

The fatigue was overpowering, with little food or sleep, constant retreat, and no way to escape exposure to the foulest cold winds and incessant rain. Frank must have let his nerves show to the sergeant in his platoon.

"Stay with me, Benjamin," he said, calling Frank by the friendly name his comrades used because he was the youngest in the platoon. "Do that and you will not be killed." Frank hoped the sergeant was right, but he wondered how much longer any of them could go on.

But he had no time to dwell on when the misery would end. These days were if anything worse than those in the Maas Salient. It was all he could do to hang on and hope to survive another day. Supply was a huge problem on the front line, since motorized vehicles had long been targeted by Allied pilots. Trucks were scarce and fuel often impossible to find. The troops had requisitioned anything with wheels, even using baby carriages to carry ammunition. What artillery remained was pulled by horses taken from the Netherlands, and when the horses gave out, the soldiers pulled the guns by hand.

With great difficulty they reached the Edewechter Damm, the road leading to the village of Barkendorp and the relative safety of the Küsten Canal. Though the futility of the situation was clear to everyone, the Fallschirmjäger continued to fight on. Behind them came the relentless Canadians, in front of them a small resort town called Bad Zwischenahn.

ELEVEN

The Last Battle – Das letzte Gefecht

By early May 1945, months of unrelenting retreat from the advancing Allied armies had brought Frank's unit to the airfield near the town of Bad Zwischenahn. The town lay nestled on the southern shore of a small lake where, in peaceful times, German families had once come to sail and enjoy the quiet countryside. These days, Canadian soldiers swarmed around this once favoured vacation spot.

A smile briefly crossed Frank's face as he recalled his visit to the airfield at Oschatz shortly before enlisting, where he had photographed airplanes taking off and landing. He had thought he could use the pictures to impress the Luftwaffe recruiter. How long ago that now seemed, and how naïve he had been! And how ironic that as the war neared its conclusion, once again he was at an airfield. No planes flew now at Bad Zwischenahn. Once it was one of the Luftwaffe's largest military airfields, now the airport was deserted, its three asphalt runways pockmarked by craters from bombs, with hardly an unmarked stretch of tarmac.

Frank's unit was dug in northeast of the airfield, facing the Canadians at the far end of the runway. They had arrived only recently, having fought Canadians in a series of running battles in which there were many casualties. Replacements coming forward were boys, sixteen and seventeen years old, maybe younger. They looked up to Frank as one of the few veterans in the unit, although he was barely twenty.

The one hundred and fifty soldiers in Frank's unit had dug their trenches among bushes, outside the trees lining the airfield. It offered little cover. The soil was saturated from days of rain, and their trenches were half-filled with water. But since his boots and socks and almost every other part of Frank were already soaked, having to sit half-submerged would make little difference.

There were no plans to attack the Canadians at the other end of the runway, and the Canadians had up to now stayed to their end of the airport, where there was a large airplane hangar and a concrete tower. Frank and his unit were content to stay where they were. Everyone knew the war would end any day, and no one wanted to die meaninglessly.

However, on the Fourth of May, the Canadians launched an assault. The Canadian advance seemed reckless as it came forward, totally exposed to Frank's unit in a straight line down the half-mile long runway. The new recruits watched anxiously as the Canadians advanced towards them, waiting for the order to open fire. The assault was led by tanks, behind which followed infantry on foot. The rain had made the soil too soft for the tanks to advance anywhere except down the runway. The narrow path of the Canadian attack took away the tanks' ability to manoeuvre, and they had to advance at a walking pace so they would not outdistance the infantry. It made an easy target for the waiting Germans.

As the Canadian tanks advanced up the runway, they opened fire on the German positions with their 75-mm guns. The shells exploded behind and in front of the line of trenches where Frank's unit waited, while the Germans replied with their mortars. When the Canadians got within about four hundred metres, German machine guns opened fire. Closer yet, and the rest of the German soldiers opened rifle fire. They were answered by the cannons and machine guns of the Canadian tanks. The Canadian infantry did not fire back but walked forward into the storm of bullets. The Canadians who were struck by German bullets or shrapnel from the mortars fell forward like sheaves of wheat cut down by scythes. Despite the fierce fire they faced, the Canadian infantry just kept coming.

What courage they show, Frank thought.

When the Canadian tanks got within a hundred metres of Frank's unit, rockets began lashing out at them from the German trenches. Each rocket produced a cloud of smoke, revealing the location of the firing team. The smoke attracted fire from the Canadians tanks, but in their trenches the firing teams were protected and able to fire rocket after rocket.

Jets of orange flame suddenly erupted from the front of several of the Canadian tanks. It was the first time Frank had seen a flame-throwing tank. The oily flame flared towards the entrenched Germans. When it came in contact with someone, it stuck to their clothing, setting them on fire, igniting the fat in the victim's body and causing a horrible death in which the body seemed to shrink almost instantly to the size of a child, leaving a charred corpse, frozen in agony.

The Germans fought back desperately. The noise of the guns was deafening, and the exploding shells from the oncoming tanks jarred the ground and sent showers of mud and shrapnel into the air. The advancing Canadian infantry was thinning under the fire of the German small arms and machine guns. When the oncoming tanks were no more than fifty metres away, there was a blast and a cloud of white smoke from the German line, followed in the next instant by an explosion on one of the Canadian tanks. It was a Panzerfaust. Immediately a half-score more Panzerfausts fired.

At that moment the Canadian attack ground to a halt. So many of the Canadian infantry were lost that they could no longer do their job of protecting the tanks. The infantry began pulling back, and Frank watched the tanks stop then reverse, firing on the German positions as they withdrew.

A terrible price was paid by both sides in the battle. Frank could not understand why the slaughter at the airfield of Bad Zwischenahn was necessary. Everyone knew the war was on the verge of ending, and the attack, even if it was successful, meant absolutely nothing.

Late in the evening, there was shouting and smalls arms firing from the southern end of the airport where the Canadians were located. Frank's unit came to alert, thinking a night attack was being launched. But no Canadians came back down the runway, while the sounds of shouting and gunfire continued. No one said anything, but most suspected what the sounds signified.

That evening Frank's unit received word that at 0800 hours the next morning their war was over. They were told to surrender to the Canadians. As word spread, there was apprehension they were to surrender that to the unit they had just fought. They did not know if the Canadians could be trusted not to take revenge. The Canadians had a reputation for reprisals against surrendering Germans, outdone only by the Poles among the Allied forces. There was much discussion that night about whether they should surrender or leave. A few slipped away in the darkness.

Frank woke to a sodden and grim morning. As the hour of surrender approached, the commanding officer instructed the troops to clean their uniforms as best they could and put on their medals and decorations. Some of those who had pistols threw them in the nearby lake, thinking they might recover them later. Others kept their pistols, so that if the Canadians began taking retribution, they would at least not die without defending themselves.

Shortly before 0800 hours, the German troops assembled on the runway. They stood lined up in their ranks and waited for the Canadians. They would surrender proudly and with dignity. All eyes watched as at the appointed hour a jeep drove forward from the Canadian lines. It came down the runway, coming to a stop in front of the German commanding officer, with Frank standing nearby. The Fallschirmjäger stood at attention.

The jeep contained only two men, an officer and his driver. The Canadian officer walked towards Frank's commanding officer, who stood waiting in front of his assembled troops. A few words determined that the German officer spoke only German and the Canadian lieutenant only English. Frank, who was the only man in the unit who spoke English, stepped forward and interpreted for them.

———————————•———————————

The fighting around the lake at Bad Zwischenahn is very severe.
— War Diary entry for the Headquarters Squadron,
Fourth Canadian Armoured Division. May 1, 1945

Russ had heard that fighting at the airport had been fierce. The Germans from slit trenches at the north end of the runway had put up a tremendous fight against the attack by the Fourth's armour and infantry. When the order for the attack had been issued, no one questioned aloud the need for it. But no one wanted to be injured or killed so close to the end of the war. The meaningless attack went ahead as ordered.

That night after the attack, at 2135 hours, the Canadians at the airport received word by radio that all German armies in Northwest Europe would surrender unconditionally at 0800 hours the next morning.

The war was over! The Germans had surrendered!

Word spread quickly among the troops, and celebrations began soon afterward. The commanding officer ordered the men be issued a double ration of rum, and bottles of spirits were issued to the officers. This was supplemented by bottles of alcohol taken from civilians. Celebrations went on into the early morning marked by shouts of joy and firing into the air.

During the celebrations, Russ was summoned to Major Campbell's tent. He was told he was to accept the surrender of the German soldiers defending the airport, the ones who had fought so ferociously.

The morning dawned with the weather as foul as it possibly could be. The rain pelted down, driven by a harsh, cold wind. In his tent Russ shaved and brushed the mud off his uniform as best as he could. It was an odd feeling to be receiving the surrender of men they had been fighting only hours before. He reported to Major Campbell for last-minute instructions, saluted, and left the major's tent, climbing into the waiting jeep. He and his driver left the Canadian lines and drove toward the waiting Germans.

Word had spread among the Canadian troops the Germans at the airfield were surrendering that morning. Many gathered at the edge of the runway to watch the two lone Canadians crossing the airfield. In the distance they saw the German soldiers standing at the end of the runway. Many of the Canadians pulled out their binoculars to watch. They wondered whether the Germans soldiers who had fought so hard the day before would surrender peacefully. Canadian tanks on the edge of the runway trained their cannons on the Germans. But if it came to needing the tanks, it would be of no consequence to Russ, who carried only his pistol.

As the jeep slowly drove down the runway, it passed a Canadian tank disabled in the previous day's fighting. Russ understood why only two Canadian soldiers were sent to take the surrender. Sending troops in force might cause the Germans to believe they were being attacked and try to defend themselves. He also knew, should the Germans decide not to surrender, he would not return.

Russ instructed the driver to stop the jeep in front of the waiting Germans. The paratroopers were lined up on the runway, standing at attention in the pelting rain. He could see the medals pinned to their uniforms. He surveyed the waiting Germans, noting the two men standing in front of the assembled German troops, one of them, an officer, was presumably this unit's commander, the other, a young man, stood one step behind and to his right.

———————•———————

The Canadian lieutenant walked along the row of German soldiers, looking at the neatly set up Panzerfaust and machine guns in front of them. The German officer and Frank followed behind.

"Where is your artillery?" the Canadian wanted to know.

"We have had none for some time," Frank interpreted.

"Was this unit the one fighting here yesterday?" the Canadian inquired.

Frank's throat tightened. He knew the unit's war diary was complete up to the previous day. It showed exactly where they had been and where they had moved lately. On April 8, 1945 in Fürstenau-Vechtel, on April 12 in Gross Roscharden, on May 2 in Elmendorf. In addition, each day's orders spelled out where each company had been and what fighting had taken place.

"What weapons did you use against the tanks on the airfield?" the Canadian asked.

"We used Panzerfaust and Ofenrohren." Frank came to a halt with the word "*Ofenrohr*." He did not know an English word for it. The name was a play on words and meant furnace pipe. He showed the lieutenant the sheet metal tube, firing rockets that with luck could stop a tank. The Canadian recognized it as a German bazooka.

———◆———

Russ left the German officer and the young interpreter where they stood and walked slowly down the row of soldiers. He saw they had tried to clean themselves up, but they were a ragged and dirty lot. Their hair was matted, their eyes hollow. Some were wounded, with bloody bandages wrapped around an arm, leg, or head. He looked at their faces and felt ill. How young they were! So many of them looked like little lost boys. But by god, he thought, they fought like tigers!

Russ stopped at the end of the line and looked back, the Germans remaining at attention, silent and still. Then he walked alone along the line. He could feel their eyes locked on him. Across the runway, the Canadians looking through their binoculars saw Russ walk to the centre of the line of troops.

———◆———

Frank watched the Canadian lieutenant stop, then turn abruptly away, walking down the German lines, looking at the troops. Then he went back to the front of the assembled Germans, raised his right hand … and saluted them.

———◆———

In the days following the end of the war, Russ and Frank worked together closely. Each day Russ made his way from the nearby tow of Rastede to meet with Frank, who translated the instructions Russ had for the German troops. Russ had to explain the meaning of the word "fraternization." Frank had never heard the word before.

"Canadian soldiers," Russ tried to explain the meaning, "are forbidden from having personal contact with Germans." Generally this order was ignored, and a healthy black market quickly arose.

The men in Frank's unit waded into the lake to retrieve their pistols. The pistols were traded for cigarettes, and though they did not want to barter their medals and decorations, they did so for food and coffee. Most of the German troops had received the Wound Badge and some the Iron Cross First Class. In the last months of the war, many men had earned the Close Combat clip, and many also had Tank Destruction medals, a bar for destroying an Allied tank, worn on the upper sleeve. None of the men in Frank's unit had received the Knight's Cross. Many of the men had done enough to earn one, but their battalion commander had none left to award. The Canadian troops gladly took them all.

When German civilians heard about the bartering, there was no stopping them taking part. This developed into a healthy market trading of Canadian supplies for farmers' goods. Eggs were exchanged for coffee, chickens for chocolate, and just about anything could be had for cigarettes. On all sides a booming business was carried on. In this way the Canadian troops supplemented their military rations with fresh farm produce. Russ employed Frank to trade with the farmers. A blind eye was cast at this fraternizing, and all sides benefited.

When not passing Canadian instructions to the German soldiers, Frank and Russ spent time talking about their plans now that the war was over. Russ told Frank he planned to volunteer for the Pacific force, to fight the Japanese. Frank was focused on finding his family. Russ was very curious about whether Frank and other young Germans would become "Werewolves," as German resistance fighters were known. After Russ's first-hand experience fighting

The flat fields of the airport at Bad Zwischenahn are evident behind the abandoned Messerschmitt Bf109 aircraft being examined by a Canadian soldier on May 4, 1945.
(Canada Dept. of National Defence/Library and Archives Canada/PA-168423.
Photographer Lieutenant Christopher J. Woods)

the young German soldiers, he told Frank, he doubted they wanted peace. Russ seemed convinced they would go underground and continue fighting against the occupation forces and, from what he had heard from Frank, they would particularly want to fight the Russians.

For a week Frank's unit stayed at the airport. Then word came they were to move. When Russ came to say goodbye, he extended his hand. In Russ's hand was a piece of paper. Written on it was an address in Owen Sound.

TWELVE

Coming Home
Wieder daheim

On May 5, 1945, fighting in northwest Germany was over, though the surrender of German troops elsewhere in Germany was still several days away. The Germans had truly held on to the bitter end. Many had fought ferociously long after the outcome of the war was inevitable. Many had paid for their patriotism with their lives, and taken with them the lives of Canadian volunteer soldiers. The Canadians had also pressed home their attacks when they knew doing so was hardly necessary, since in the final days of the war, with the Russians fighting in the streets of Berlin, the end was imminent.

By most reports, the initial response of Canadian troops was a collective sigh. To the Lake Superiors, it was said, "the cease-fire came more as a surprise than as a relaxation. The first reaction was one of incredulity."[1] Among the Algonquins, there was no cheering and no visible sign of emotion.[2]

Perhaps the lack of emotion was a sign of a wall soldiers built to separate themselves from the terrible sights and experiences of war. Dulling their emotions was a form of self-protection. Long before, they had grown sick of seeing friends die, tired of seeing the towns and cities of Europe devastated by shelling and bombing, and seeing too many haunted faces on the endless streams of refugees. The refugees were far too many to offer meaningful help to beyond sharing some food or a couple of cigarettes before moving on. This emotional shield helped them through difficult times, dealing with the fear of death, debilitating injury, and disfiguring wounds. Even though the war was over, it was difficult to express the great happiness they should have felt.

Canada's soldiers in muddy, cold northern Germany on May 5 could think of little beyond the fact that they would get to go home to their families. The celebrations that night were liberally supplemented with alcohol, accompanied by the firing of weapons into the air and, in some cases, the lighting of large bonfires that may have symbolized the end of long years of training and fighting.[3]

The Headquarters Squadron had moved to Rastede, a town east of the Zwischenahn Meer on the opposite side of the lake from the airport where

Russ had accepted the surrender of Frank's unit. The weather continued cold, and the rain turned the fields to mud where the Squadron set up their harbour. But it was only intended to be temporary accommodation, as Major Campbell ordered Russ to evict German civilians in Rastede from their homes. The Germans were to be given a short time to take what belongings they could carry and leave. The Canadian troops would move from their tents and use the homes that night.

Instead of leaving to carry out the order, Russ waited in front of Major Campbell, who sensed the lieutenant had something to say.

"Is there a question, Colombo?" Campbell asked.

"Yes, sir. It's cold, the wind is whipping the rain, and it will be dark soon. Frankly, sir, all there are in this town are old men, women, and children. It isn't right to put them out of their homes," Russ said.

"You have your orders, Lieutenant," Campbell said, waiting for the most junior officer in his command to leave and do as told. Russ didn't move.

"I can't do that, sir," Russ said.

"Are you refusing a direct order?" An edge entered the Major's voice.

"Stopping this sort of thing is why we've been fighting this war, Major," said Russ.

Campbell had heard enough. He directed a tirade at Russ, who continued standing at attention, eyes straight ahead as he took Campbell's dressing down without responding. But as the Major continued, Russ's own anger grew. When Campbell finally paused in his outburst, Russ met the Major's eyes with an icy stare. Campbell called his adjutant and told him to have a provost escort Russ to his tent, where he was to stay until a court martial was convened.

Russ saluted, turned sharply, and left the tent.

With Russ refusing to carry out the eviction order, Campbell himself started the job, moving the Squadron's officers messes into houses "requisitioned by the Military Government," then busied himself "trying to locate suitable buildings for the other ranks mess."[4]

Russ waited for Campbell to call his court martial. But it never came. On May 8, VE day was announced, signalling that fighting on other fronts was over. Shortly after, Russ was ordered to resume his duties.

While the threat of court martial was never formally removed, days passed with none coming. Had it been called, Russ would have admitted his "guilt" and the court would have had no choice but to pass judgement on him for refusing to follow an order, even if it had sympathized. Being court martialled would have cost Russ his officer's rank and resulted in his being Discharged with Ignominy and potentially a jail term.

With the end of hostilities, the troopers began relaxing. The Squadron's tanks were taken away. Major Campbell addressed the Squadron troops, explaining in detail the War Gratuities Act, telling them when they could expect to receive leave, and the level of conduct expected of them in Germany now that the war was over. As if to emphasize his point, the next day he tried four cases of Squadron soldiers on duty "not being able to contain themselves and (carrying) their celebrating a little too far."[5]

It was clear the troops would have to be kept busy. There were tens of thousands of young Canadian men with little to do now the fighting was over. If they were left idle while waiting for repatriation, trouble was sure to follow. Some Headquarters troops were given the job of fixing Rastede's swimming pool for the troops to use. Others began smoothing off an area for a softball diamond. General Vokes convened a meeting attended by Campbell at which a training policy for the Division was laid out, which would emphasize "cleaning up, smartening up and as much in the way of sports as possible."[6]

On May 13, a Thanksgiving Church parade was held. General Vokes took the salute by the troops, and after the service had the troopers gather around him, thanking everyone in the Headquarters Squadron for their loyalty and support. He also cautioned them to think seriously about their return to "civvy street." After the march-past, the Headquarters Squadron's officers assembled in the small theatre in Rastede, where the General addressed them. He thanked and praised the officers for their loyalty and job well done, encouraging them to do everything possible in providing advice and guidance for the troops.

The troopers were mainly concerned about when they would be going home. It was decided not to send Canadian units home en masse, but on a man-by-man basis according to a points system that took into account length of service, time in Europe, and the period they were in combat. The morale of those expecting an early return was high, while those with low point scores realized they would be fortunate to return before 1946.

On May 15, word was received that the sentence of Private Pollard was approved by senior command, and as soon as it arrived at the Headquarters Squadron it was "promulgated on parade" by Major Campbell. Pollard was sentenced to "penal servitude for five years." The war diary provides no explanation of what became of the charges against Trooper Stepanishen, the other man charged. He presumably had been cleared at the trial. Soon after Private Pollard was taken to jail, Captain Beatty travelled back to Esche, Germany, and personally returned the gold watch and two gold rings Pollard had taken from the family.

It should come as no surprise that some Canadian soldiers were guilty of serious offences. Donning a uniform does not make a person a hero, no matter how much they might look the part. These were just men like any others. Most were good men. Some became heroes. But all who volunteered had come from civilian lives and been put into the middle of a war. There, they experienced previously unimaginable situations in settings where social restrictions moderating personal behaviour were absent. The most extreme example of this dichotomy is also the most basic: they were trained to kill other men and told it was their duty to do so, an act at any other time society teaches is the most abhorrent behaviour imaginable. Under these circumstances it is not surprising many soldiers found themselves doing things that in normal circumstances they would never have considered. But as in any large group of people, the army contained some who lacked much in the way of moral self-restraint. Such people are part of any society, though fortunately a minority. At its core war is an amoral and antisocial activity, making it easier for the minority who are naturally amoral and antisocial to express themselves.

Although the war in Europe was over, the war in the Pacific still ground on. Men in Canada's Active Force in Europe were being encouraged to sign up to fight in the Pacific Theatre, but few were doing so. It was going to be difficult to put together an active Canadian force for the Pacific, since most of the volunteer army wanted to go home and get out of the army as quickly as possible.

Russ was one of the few who volunteered for the war against Japan. On May 18, he signed a form declaring:

> I, Donald Russel Colombo, now a member of that part of the Canadian Army placed on Active Service, do hereby volunteer and engage to serve in the Pacific Theatre of War for the term of my engagement as set out in my officer's declaration paper.

The declaration was witnessed and signed by Major Campbell. Jim had signed on for the Pacific force three days earlier. The war diary reported "some very valuable members of the HQ will no doubt soon be leaving for home due to their volunteering for service in the Far East."

Privilege leaves, sports events, and sightseeing tours of the submarine pens at Wilhelmshaven could do only so much to keep the Canadian troops occupied. Enforcing the non-fraternization order to keep Canadian soldiers and German women apart was increasingly difficult, both for the troopers and the officers who were ordered to enforce the regulation. According to the war diary, the non-fraternization order, though backed up by threat of hefty penalty, was "carried out faithfully during the day, however at night — well you can't say because you can't see very well at night. The German girls (you've never seen a blonde until you go to Germany) generally speaking did everything they could to aggravate the situation." And, "it is becoming increasingly obvious that the non-fraternization policy is imposing a con- siderable strain on (the soldiers). To date they have accepted, with reasoned judgement fortified with the possibility of severe disciplinary action, the necessity of obeying this order implicitly but the order doesn't change human nature. The local frauleins, raised on a philosophy of 'strength through joy' and finding their former companions in our POW cages, are very reluctant to accept this official jilting. They are becoming bolder each day."

———————◆———————

In the middle of May, Russ was told he was to travel to the Netherlands to take part in a "Victory Parade," General Crerar's idea for the First Canadian Army. It would be held in The Hague, and Russ was delegated as a Headquarters Squadron representative. The parade was a massive display, with twelve thousand troops taking part. Tanks from the Three Rivers Regiment lined the roadway[7] and long columns of Canadian and British infantry, sailors, and marines marched the parade route in a drenching rain, accompanied by sixteen pipe and five brass bands. The thousands who lined the parade route and rooftops cheered the Allied troops but reserved their loudest cheers for the one thousand men and women in the parade who had been part of the Dutch underground.[8] An artillery salute was fired by the 1st Canadian Infantry Division while planes from the Royal Canadian Air Force flew past.[9]

The procession wound its way through The Hague to the reviewing stands, where Prince Bernhard of the Netherlands took the salutes of the troops as they marched past. The stands were flanked by twelve Long Tom guns, and in front stood fourteen Sherman tanks from the Calgary Regiment. When the pipe bands reached the reviewing stands, they wheeled alongside four massed bands, playing the columns along in their march.

Joining Prince Bernhard in the review stand were Canadian Generals Crerar and Simonds, with Canadian division commanders, chiefs-of-staff, and members of the Netherlands Military Government. Russ marched towards the prestigious review party with other members of the Fourth Canadian Armoured Division. As one, the marching troops' heads snapped to the right and their hands rose in unison to salute Prince Bernhard. But Russ's eyes were immediately drawn not to the prince, but to one of the honour guards in front of the review stand. He remembered another day when the rain had also been beating down. There in the prince's honour guard was a face he had not seen for nearly a year but would never forget. It was the jeep driver, the man who had run away when the two German prisoners had attacked Russ in the woods in Normandy.

———◆———

Russ returned to the Headquarters Squadron in Rastede, but it was only to get ready to leave Germany permanently. On May 26, the Squadron moved to the Netherlands, arriving near the city of Nijverdal. Most of the men were accommodated in billets with Dutch families and "all ranks seem quite pleased to be back in a friendly country."[10] The Dutch indeed appreciated having the Canadians nearby, as the civilians swarmed through the harbour and provided an audience for the cooks in the Squadron kitchens. This friendly trespassing unfortunately provided some civilians with more temptation than they could bear, leading to a few incidents of theft of cigarettes, food, and in one case a pistol. The pistol was too important to ignore and it led to the decision to ban civilians from the camp.[11] However, the Squadron's stay in Nijverdal was short-lived. Within days they moved to the town of Almelo. The officers were housed in a castle called Huize Almelo, in the centre of the city.

Daily drill practice was ordered by Major Campbell to keep the troopers occupied, but the sessions were clearly unpopular with both the NCOs running them and the troops. Russ had the dubious honour of bringing the NCOs up to speed on some of the finer aspects of drill. Most were only concerned with getting home as soon as possible. They had received some indications they might be home sooner than later, but when an interview with the prime minister quoted him as saying an early return was not possible, the troops were caught off guard. It was looking as though many would be in Europe into the New Year.

An article in the *Globe and Mail* reported,

> Mr. King said provisional arrangements have been made for the return to Canada during the next six months of all Canadian service personnel who have been overseas more than four years, except those who will serve with the army of occupation and certain key personnel.

However, priority on the available shipping space went in order to operational forces heading for the Pacific, casualties who could be moved and liberated prisoners of war. Mr. King's statement added: "… it is expected that all personnel in these categories will be in Canada by autumn."[12]

One soldier who was not worried about an early return home was Jim Derij. After volunteering to go to the Pacific, Jim had been ordered to stay in Germany for the time being. He left the Squadron on June 2 to take the job of Camp Commandant of the 3rd Canadian Division Occupation Force. He was outfitting his new command with vehicles and personnel from the Headquarters Squadron. General Vokes also left to command the Canadian Occupational Force in Germany. On June 9, Major Campbell gave a farewell speech to the Headquarters Squadron, announcing he was joining Canada's War Crimes Commission. He was to work on the legal team prosecuting among other cases that of Generalmajor Kurt Meyer, for the crime of having overseen the killing of Canadians who had surrendered to the 12th SS in Normandy. Then, on June 21, Russ left the Netherlands for England. Like others who had signed on to join Canada's forces in the Pacific war, he was given priority to return to Canada. After several weeks in England, space on a ship was assigned.

———◆———

Russ arrived in Canada on July 24 with little fanfare as the ship eased into the dock. The arrival of his train in Toronto likewise lacked ceremony. He made his way to Toronto's Army District Depot Number 2. He stayed only long enough to be given landing leave, a thirty-day hiatus from the army. For the first time in four years he headed home.

After the tumult of war and the enforced uniformity of military life, the transition to small-town Ontario, even though temporary, must have seemed like a dream, familiar yet unreal. There were no bombed-out buildings, no refugees waiting for resettlement, and no bombs exploding and shots being fired. It was a tremendous feeling to be back in Canada, but in some ways, it may have felt emptier than he had thought it would.

Unlike those who planned to leave the army, Russ was not overly concerned about what awaited him at home. He did not have to worry about finding a job in Owen Sound, which he was glad of, since prospects of a career for him were in doubt. When he had left Owen Sound with the Foresters, he was twenty-five. Now as he returned, Russ was almost thirty.

Up until joining the army, he had only been able to find temporary work as a labourer, requiring broad shoulders but little from his brimming mind. It would have been hard to go back to his former way of life. The past five years in the army was the longest he had been in one job, and he was an officer with combat experience and a good service record. The fact he had signed on to fight in the Pacific might indicate Russ hoped to stay in the army and make it a career. As his train neared Owen Sound, he realized he would have to break the news to his mother that he had volunteered to go back to war.

There was no homecoming parade for Russ, or for any of the other Foresters who arrived back in Owen Sound one at a time. How long ago it seemed and so much had happened since they had departed for Camp Borden. Russ realized now how little he had known. The train slowed as it entered Owen Sound, stopping at the station directly in front of Kennedy's foundry. The war had made the foundry prosperous again, most of those hired during the war healthy young men who had chosen not to volunteer for active service.

As a volunteer for the Pacific, Russ was one of the first active service soldiers to return to Owen Sound. Few gave more than a passing glance to the black-bereted soldier walking along 14th Street West. They were used to seeing uniformed men in town, although few of the original volunteer Foresters had returned in over three years. Everything Russ saw was reassuringly as it had been when he had left. Reaching the intersection where he had stood with his father when Charles was unable to breathe, Russ caught sight of the big maple tree outside his home. When the front porch came into view, it seemed so long ago since he had sat with his friends and Blanche had embarrassed him so badly, calling him Sweet in front of them.

The front door was open. He called to his mother, "Can a soldier get a cup of coffee here?"

There was a cry from the kitchen. Blanche rushed to the hallway where Russ stood framed in the doorway. She cried as she hugged him.

His brother Jack joined them in the reunion, and Russ asked them to sit at the kitchen table as he opened his bag. From it he drew gifts brought from London, Amsterdam, and Paris. Then he took out the souvenirs he had smuggled home — a naval officer's short sword with an eagle perched atop the ivory handle, and a paratrooper's knife and a German officer's pistol, both obtained while he was at Bad Zwischenahn. The pistol felt uncomfortably out of place here, and Blanche didn't touch it, or any of the other military items. When Jack finished hefting the pistol, Russ returned it to his bag.

Over the next few days of his landing leave, there was time to enjoy the other luxuries of home. Dinners prepared by his mother, leisurely soaking in the big clawfoot bathtub, sleeping in his own bed. At times it felt like a dream. But he knew it was real, if temporary. Following this leave he would report to Toronto and await orders taking him to the Pacific.

The army planned to send just one division to the Pacific, but finding enough volunteers was proving difficult. Russ was classed among the "most select group," classed in the highest medical category, between nineteen and thirty-three, and single. He would first be ordered to a Canadian base for training to become familiar with the American equipment they would use. Then he would travel to Camp Breckinridge, Kentucky, for final training.[13]

But on August 7, while on leave in Owen Sound, news was released that the United States had dropped a new type of bomb on Japan, a bomb so powerful it alone destroyed the entire city of Hiroshima. Two days later, a second atomic bomb was dropped, annihilating Nagasaki and those within it. After Nagasaki, speculation was that Japan must surely surrender without need of invasion. On August 14, newspapers and radio carried the news everyone hoped for — after five and a half years, the war was over. Spontaneous celebrations erupted throughout Owen Sound and other cities across Canada. Church bells rang, cars drove through town with horns bleating, and people came out to share the moment. Russ celebrated with everyone else, but he could not help wondering about his immediate future.

It seemed unlikely to Russ that he would be going to the Pacific, but despite Japan's surrender, he still had to report to the army at the end of this leave.

———————————•———————————

Travelling by train to Toronto in late August, he began thinking about what he would do if the army no longer wanted him. In a matter of days, in almost miraculous fashion with the dropping of the atomic bombs, the world had forever changed, and with it Russ faced an uncertain future.

There was nothing for Russ and the other soldiers to do at the army barracks in Toronto beyond wait for official word about what awaited those who had signed on to go to the Pacific. There was little doubt among those in the barracks that the army would go back to its prewar state, and practically everyone would be released from service. Talk naturally turned to their plans now that there was to be peace. Russ had little to say, since no job waited his return.

About a week after arriving at the barracks, Russ fell ill. It hit him with no warning. On September 7, he went to see the camp doctor, who wrote, "This officer was feeling well until after the noon meal when he developed a dull aching pain beneath the right lower ribs, which was aggravated by deep breathing." The doctor noted, "He has felt nauseated but has not vomited. At 1230 hrs, he reported to (the infirmary) at which time he felt faint. He has been drowsy and sleeping since. At 1400 hrs it was rather difficult to arouse him…. He seemed dazed and speech was stammering in character."

While Russ felt physically sick, he had no signs of an infection or injury. The doctor noted his "temperature was 98.0, pulse 70, respiration 20." Russ was admitted to hospital for observation. "Observations: Low voice, slight stammering. Pupils, cranial nerves, reflexes OK. Straight leg raise OK. Chest, heart, abdomen not remarkable. Impression: Functional or organic nervous illness?" Russ was suffering from what today is recognized as Post-Traumatic Stress Disorder.

How many of Canada's returning veterans displayed similar symptoms is impossible to say, although it seems likely many had some of the signs, ranging from feelings of impending doom striking from nowhere, waking in the middle of the night in a cold sweat, uncontrollable shaking, or signs of physical illness like headaches, shortness of breath, or chest pains reminiscent of a heart attack. Panic attacks could be triggered by everyday events, like a car backfiring, boarding a crowded bus, or any number of seemingly innocuous things. The sorts of feelings the veterans experienced were in some ways worse than the experiences they had faced during the war. At least during the war, the massive jolts of adrenalin would focus the mind and body until a particular threat was over. Some had not been able to take the stress of war while it was happening, and those men had been sent from the front lines to recuperate. Some were able to return to their units after a few days of rest. Others were never able to get over the mental trauma. For soldiers trying to hold themselves together at the front lines, dealing with men who had "lost their nerve" made the situation extremely difficult.

Back in Canada, some men who had been able to hold themselves together through intolerable conditions now began displaying signs of nerves. Others, like Russ, were seeing the stress they had been under come out in the form of physical illness. Regardless of what the soldiers told themselves to conquer their symptoms, their bodies and minds were behaving involuntarily. They were like springs wound too tight for too long. Now that they were unwinding, they often did so in uncontrollable ways.

Russ's symptoms lessened, and within a week he was released as "fit for duty." He stayed at the army's Depot Number 2 in Toronto, finding time to travel to Hamilton to visit Gerry and Marge Johnson. They had moved back to Hamilton in December, 1941, where Gerry was employed at the elevator manufacturer, Otis Fensom, who became the largest anti-aircraft manufacturing plant in the British Empire, producing the Bofors anti-air-craft gun. Russ seemed to them unchanged by the war, the same quiet and serious person he was before he had left.[14]

While Russ appeared to have returned the same as when he had left for the war, for many returning veterans there was a need for patience while they sorted out the incongruities between the past five years and the lives they were expected to resume. Civilians in general had little of patience for returning veterans, who were supposed to settle down and settle in. Everyone wanted to get on with their lives. But there would be break-ups in family relations and unpleasant incidents involving some veterans. What was needed was patience and tolerance of their behaviour.[15] Veterans of the First World War could understand what this new batch of soldiers were going through, but most civilians had no understanding of the mental turmoil the war caused.

On October 11, the army prepared to release Russ. They no longer had need of his services. There was a medical check-up, which found him in excellent shape. Then there was an interview with an army counsellor, whose notes assess Russ's plans for the immediate future. They state:

> Colombo is a tall, well-built officer of 29. Neat in appearance and with a quiet, friendly manner, he gives the impression of being a reliable and conscientious worker.
>
> Leaving high school with a Jr. Matric, Colombo was unable to secure steady employment due to the economic conditions of the 1930s. Employment of a temporary nature in the unskilled field was taken anywhere opportunity presented itself.
>
> Enlisting in the Army as a private, his initiative and leadership qualities enabled him to reach commissioned rank.
>
> Colombo plans to return to his former employment with the CNR. His status with the company is not clear at this time, according to his statement, due to the temporary nature of his work prior to enlistment. He appears suited for a position calling for much greater skill and responsibility

than this job did. Unfortunately, he feels he is too old for training and could not afford the financial strain.

On October 13, 1945, Russ's service in the Canadian Active Force ended. He signed on to be a reserve officer in the Canadian Militia, perhaps in the faint hope it would lead to an opportunity in the permanent forces. Or maybe it was his way of keeping in touch with a way of life he had grown accustomed to.

Now he was free to do whatever he chose. But what was he to do now that he was out of the army? Unskilled labouring jobs held little appeal, but they were all he had done outside the army since he was sixteen. He had not finished high school and couldn't imagine doing so now.

At least the uncertainty about finding a job was going to be eased by the savings he had accumulated in the army. One-fifth of Russ's pay was waiting for him, a monthly cheque for that amount sent to his mother over the past five years.[16] His savings would have amounted to more than a thousand dollars, a small fortune to him but little enough for five years taken from the prime of life. It would give him a start, some time to find work, and to settle back into civilian life.

After arriving in Owen Sound, it wasn't long before he raised the subject of his army savings. Blanche had received Russ's monthly cheque, as well as her own allowance from the government as a soldier's widowed dependent mother. When he asked his mother to write him a cheque to transfer his savings, Russ was shocked by her answer.

Blanche had given his army savings to his brother, Verdun. He couldn't believe what she had said. Verdun had come to her from Philadelphia for money to finance what he described as a once-in-a-lifetime opportunity. All he needed was help purchasing the material for a manufacturing venture. His plan, he had told her, was sure to be a big success. With two young sons, Paul and Don, it would be a chance for him to give his family some financial security.

For the moment, all the money Russ had was what was in his wallet. His experience was one shared by a number of servicemen returning from over-seas. It was a regulation that the army deducted part of their pay and send it to a parent or wife in Canada. However, it was entirely up to the person receiving it whether to save it on the serviceman's behalf. They were free to spend it if needed. Some soldiers returned to find every penny accounted for. Others found it had all been spent.

Russ would at some point receive mustering-out pay, monthly payments from the federal government given at his army pay rate. It would last about a year. But when it would begin arriving, he had no way to tell. While Russ's anger was directed at Verdun, Blanche, who had control of the money, had made the decision to help Verdun and her two grandchildren.

Despite the disappointment, Russ wanted to do something for his mother. For this he used what was called his reestablishment credit. Returning servicemen were eligible for a one-time federal grant. It could be used for a wide variety of goods and services, from buying or renovating a home to purchasing household goods. Russ used his grant to buy Blanche a new fridge and stove, replacing the antiques that were almost twenty years old, as well as a modern clothes washer and dryer, making her one of the first to have these in Owen Sound.

In the next few days, Blanche received a letter from the Canadian government. Inside the official-looking envelope was a letter bearing an official seal.

> Dear Madam. It is with much pleasure that I write … to congratulate you … on the honour and distinction which has come to your son … through his being Mentioned in Despatches in recognition of gallant and distinguished services. The KING'S Certificate in connection with this award will be forwarded in due course.

Few received the honour of being Mentioned in Despatches. The award is a single bronze oak leaf, awarded for gallantry in battle or for actions on and off the battlefield. Of the nearly half million Canadian soldiers who served overseas in World War II, just over 6,400 received the award.[17]

With none of his savings to fall back on, finding work became Russ's priority. When he had enlisted, he had been a temporary worker for the CNR. Government policy was supposed to ensure those enlisting received their former jobs back. But no one really knew how employers would treat these regulations. Russ's was a tenuous case, since he had not been a permanent employee. Would they tell him the rule didn't apply to him? Or offer him the part-time work he'd been doing before the war? The CNR, though, was a government-owned railway. When he went to ask about his old job, not only did they give Russ his former job, but instead of bringing him back as a temporary worker, they hired him permanently.

Working at the CNR, life as a civilian settled into a comfortable pattern. His job took him around the district, staying in towns across southern Ontario, riding the trains on track maintenance detail. Throughout the year, friends from the Foresters Active Force volunteer regiment arrived back from overseas. The Foresters had been disbanded in England during the war, and the men dispersed as reinforcements across the army. Most meetings with other Forester were happy occasions, catching up on news about where each had served during the war.

To all appearances, Russ had made a seamless transition to life in Owen Sound. The truth was different, as he told no one about the fear eating at him. The nightmares were terrifying. Waking suddenly, yelling, jumping out of bed, unable to breathe, sweating even on the coldest nights, shaking. Often, he relived that night in the woods and the rain with the two German prisoners, remembering the blood and hair matted on his boots when he'd woken the next morning. It was a dream repeated over and over. During the day, he would recall his decision to let the prisoners out of the jeep to give them rain gear, and cursed his bad judgement. He was not hesitant to tell people about killing the two German prisoners, and it must have given some form of relief to tell the story.

He might go days or weeks without a recurrence of the nightmare, then for no apparent reason, it would strike for nights on end. At times, the thought of going to sleep almost caused him to feel sick. Some veterans in his situation turned to alcohol to dull the senses, but Russ was not one of them. A year passed, then two, and through that time, Russ suffered through it alone, telling no one his secret terror.

THIRTEEN

Kein Zuhause für einen jungen Soldaten
No Home for a Young Soldier

Frank's unit was told to prepare to leave Bad Zwischenahn. They were going to leave the airport and walk to an internment area somewhere to the north. The Fallschirmjäger formed into their platoons and companies, the remaining horses were harnessed one last time to wagons carrying their supplies, and the column of soldiers marched north. They were dirty and dishevelled and were not only watched over by their former enemies but were reliant on them for all their needs. Frank looked at their sorry state and wondered at the sad condition of the "glorious German army." Despite being defeated, he felt no dishonour — they had fought bravely for their country, they had survived, and now they had only themselves to be concerned with. Their thoughts were turning to what lay ahead.

What would happen to them was unclear. They were not prisoners but nor were they free to go home. The war was over, but they remained under the authority of the German army, even though Germany's government had ceased to exist and there was no one for the army to be accountable to. Their country was occupied by their former enemies, the Communists controlled Berlin, and no one could say what was to happen to them.

Though his future was unclear, Frank shared the youthful hope many of the teenage soldiers displayed as they talked while marching north. Most in Frank's unit had not graduated from high school. Only rarely did anyone know where their family was, or what had happened to their parents, brothers, or sisters. None had a job to go to and the small amount of money any of them once had was already gone for food. While wanting their discharge papers, no one knew if they would be allowed to travel to where their homes had been, or what they might find once they arrived there. For a German from the Sudetenland, such as Frank, the uncertainty about home and family was even greater.

The remnants of the Seventh Fallschirmjäger Division marched thirty-five miles north from Bad Zwischenahn to the city of Jever. They were among the more than one hundred thousand German soldiers brought there to be interned on a peninsula bordered on three sides by the North Sea. On the southern flank, the canal between the rivers Ems and Jade formed a barrier keeping the soldiers in place. They were ordered by their officers not to attempt to leave. They were confined until the Allies decided their fate.

They were still guarded by Canadian soldiers, although since Frank was no longer responsible for liaison with them, he had little contact with the Canadian troops who were now their guards. The Canadians' main task was to prevent unauthorized Germans leaving. Most of the interned German soldiers lived on farms in the area, helping with fieldwork.

As the weeks passed, Frank saw soldiers being discharged. Those whose homes were in the British sector were discharged first. Receiving the necessary papers, they happily packed their few belongings in their knapsacks and simply walked away. Discharge came easiest to those from farming families, so some pretended that was their case. Next, those whose homes were in the American sector were discharged. The Russians were not yet allowing German soldiers to return to their sector, while those whose homes were in the French sector were hesitant to return there, since rumour had it former German soldiers were being sent to work in French coal mines. For Frank, whose home was in Czechoslovakia, there was no word.

One day Frank noticed a group of officers whose uniforms he did not recognize touring the internment area. His spirits rose when he heard them speaking Czech. He approached them and spoke to them in their language, asking them to arrange his discharge and travel documents so he could return to Leitmeritz.

Their response was brief and curt. "Certainly not, you Germans were defeated and are not coming back." Frank's response was angry and searing. He was shocked at the implication of what they were telling him.

The Czechs had been there looking for non-German Czechs who had served with the German army. They did not want Sudeten German soldiers released from internment. What Frank did not know was in Czechoslovakia, ethnic Germans were being rounded up and placed in internment camps. Their homes and possessions were being expropriated by the Czechs and claimed as war reparations. The Allied powers had agreed the Czechs could expel ethnic Germans to Germany, even though German cities were in ruins from heavy bombing and an influx of millions more refugees would add to the crisis conditions.

Knowing none of this but seeing he would get no help from the Czechs, Frank realized escape was the only way he would get out any time soon. He walked the few miles from the farm where he was staying to the canal, to see what his chances were of escaping across one of the bridges out of the internment area. During the day he saw the bridges guarded by Canadian soldiers. They allowed civilians with travel permits to cross, but only solders holding discharge papers were able to leave. At night Frank saw that the crossings were unguarded. The bridges, which could be swung aside to allow ships to come up the canal, were at night swung from the far bank, leaving a gap perhaps small enough to jump across. He returned to the farm and made plans for his escape.

The next evening he made his way to the bridge. He had left his few personal possessions behind, so if someone came looking for him, they would think he was returning to the farm. As night approached, the Canadians prepared to leave, as they had done before, swinging the bridge from the far bank but leaving the small gap. As the Canadians guards drove off, Frank remained hidden, scanning the far shore for any lights or noise.

Satisfied there were no guards on the far bank, he made his way onto the bridge, crouching to remain hidden as he made his way across. All was silent, the slow-moving water beneath him making no sound. Nearing the far side of the bridge, Frank stood and began running. Reaching the end of the bridge he leapt, propelled with all his strength. He was suspended there momentarily, not knowing if he'd make it across the gap. He came down and felt firm ground under his feet. Without losing a step, he ran into the darkness, his heart pounding, liberated not only from the Allies but for the first time in years from the German army.

Frank's plan was to head to the American military zone near Bremen. Rumour had it the Americans were more lenient than the British in issuing discharge documents. He would need those papers if he were to carry out the plan for what he must do now that he was free. However, to get to Bremen he had to avoid military patrols, which were everywhere. In his Fallschirmjäger uniform, he was at risk of being stopped, and if stopped without discharge papers, he would surely be arrested. As he walked the hundred kilometres to Bremen, he avoided checkpoints on the main roads and cities and hid from approaching army vehicles.

In Bremen he found an American army camp. Now he would have to be brazen, as he would have nothing to show if he was asked to present his papers. He boldly approached the camp sentry and asked to be directed to the officer dealing with discharges. As Frank had hoped, the sentry assumed only a properly discharged German soldier would dare to come to an American base. He pointed to one of the buildings.

Presenting himself to the American soldier in the office, Frank did not hesitate. He asked to be given discharge papers. The American sergeant asked a few questions. What was his rank? What military unit did he belong to?

Where had he come from? And where did he intend to go if discharged? Frank told him he was travelling to Leitmeritz in Czechoslovakia to look for his family. To Frank's relief, the sergeant began typing the information into a form. He was issuing the discharge papers!

Helping him with the spelling of Leitmeritz, Frank noticed the American, after signing his name to the document, had written "Major" underneath. Despite having the discharge and travel documents almost in his hands, Frank could not stop himself asking the sergeant how he was entitled to sign as a major. The sergeant handed Frank his papers and told him to "piss off." Frank's affection for the Americans, this one at least, was growing.

Frank was now "officially" a civilian, free to leave and travel. Well, he was at least as free as was possible in occupied Germany. With no money to travel or eat, he needed to find work before he could try to reach Leitmeritz. Travelling from town to town, he found a pharmacist in the town of Ovelgönne who was in need of an assistant. He took the job.

Frank realized his discharge papers would let him freely cross the bridge at the canal where he had been interned. After a few weeks he decided to return to the farm where he had been interned to retrieve his backpack and his few possessions. Feeling safe, he retraced his route north. His arrival back at the farm created a big stir. The farmer with whom he had worked and lived had reported Frank missing to the battalion commander, and a search had been underway. With his discharge papers in hand, Frank reported to the captain in charge of his unit to settle the matter. The officer was relieved to see him.

Frank told his captain the entire story of his escape, travelling to Bremen, and of the discharge issued by the Americans. The captain asked to see the discharge papers. Frank took out the document and handed it to him. He watched with pleasure at the look of amazement on the officer's face. Thoughtfully, the captain carefully folded the document. But instead of handing it back to Frank, he placed it in his desk drawer.

"You are under arrest," he said quietly. The Canadians had told the German officers if any of their men left the internment area illegally, the officers would be held responsible, and it could affect when the officers received their own discharge papers. Despite Frank's protests that he had been discharged by the Americans, he was taken back to the farmhouse and locked in a room.

Two days later he was taken under guard to the commander of the battalion. He told Frank that based on the evidence the captain had presented, he was to be court martialled for desertion. When Frank argued the war was over and military tribunals were no longer valid, he was told what he had done was against the law.

"What law?" Frank asked. "There are no longer courts or judges in Germany."

"It is the law of the victors," the battalion commander said sternly. To retain discipline among the thousands of German soldiers, the Allies allowed German officers to continue to function in their command roles.

Since Frank had left the area illegally, the battalion commander told him, his discharge papers were not valid. The charge was desertion. Court martial for desertion was previously punishable by the death sentence. Some Germans who had deserted during the war were executed even after the war was over. In the Netherlands, two deserters who had turned themselves in to Canadian troops were handed over to German soldiers, who sentenced the deserters to death, even though the war had been over more than a week. The Germans received trucks to travel to the execution site, along with Canadian rifles and bullets to carry out the execution. With a Canadian officer accompanying them, the Germans executed the men.[1]

Frank's punishment would either be removing land mines under the control of British troops in Wilhelmshaven, or working as forced labour in coal mines under the French. Either punishment was almost certain to be a death sentence.

After his trial, Frank was taken back to the captain who had arrested him. The captain felt some remorse at the severity of the punishment — Frank was being punished for doing what all the soldiers wanted to do, including the officers — to go home to their families.

He said, "Promise me you will not try to escape. Give me your word of honour you will not try, and at least you will not have to be confined to quarters." Frank refused.

He was taken under guard back to the farmhouse, where he was again locked in a room. That night, when everyone in the house had gone to bed and the house was silent, he put straw under his blanket in the shape of a body and easily broke out of the room. Picking some vegetables from the farmer's field and putting them in his knapsack, he ran through the night. Reaching the canal by morning, he hid.

Waiting for night and the Canadian soldiers to again pull back the bridge and leave, he once more escaped by jumping the gap to the far shore. Needing new discharge papers, he retraced his steps back to the American camp at Bremen. There Frank found the same American sergeant he had dealt with previously. The man recognized him and asked why he had come back. Frank explained he had lost his discharge papers and asked for new ones to be issued. This time he did not question the sergeant signing the papers as a major. He was also given a travel permit and a railway ticket to the Czech border near Leitmeritz. Frank's opinion of Americans could not have been higher.

In the internment camp, Frank had found many of the German soldiers apathetic now the war was over. However, travelling through Germany, he felt the general population was anything but despondent. Far from it, the country was in an uproar! Everybody seemed to be on the move, and people were travelling in all directions. Despite the destruction everywhere, and despite the country being occupied by foreign armies, everyone was busy and seemed to want to bring things back to normal as quickly as possible.

When Frank reached the train station in Bremen, he found the trains jammed full of thousands of people, some carrying backpacks and suitcases, those without luggage clinging to the outside and some to the roofs of the cars as they travelled from one crowded station to another. The rain of sparks from the coal burning steam engines burned holes in the clothes of those riding on the outside. Frank happily mixed in among this mass of people. With the travel pass in his pocket, he had no trouble passing through the occupation zones. Somehow, something positive shone through in his mind as he travelled through the broken German cities — it was the memory of his travel across Germany as a boy in 1939. Only he was twenty-one now, not fifteen. The German Reich no longer existed, and Germany was smaller. Despite what he and other Germans had been through, he felt a sense of renewed optimism and energy in the country.

When his train passed from the American into the British Occupation Zone, British soldiers ordered everyone who looked like a former German soldier to leave the train. Discharge documents were examined and luggage searched. From Frank's time in Lapland, he owned a flashlight charged using a hand crank. The British soldier examining Frank's possessions played with the flashlight like a fascinated child. He put it in his pocket without saying a word and motioned Frank to move on.

At Göttingen the train entered the Soviet Occupation Zone. From there Frank and others travelling east had to disembark and walk several miles to a town where the next train east was to be found. Some had paid guides to take them past Soviet patrols. Frank, who was going in the same direction, was told to either pay forty marks to join them, or to leave. Instead, he followed some distance behind the group, composed mainly of women and old men, as they all headed east. As they neared a village, the guide started to walk away from the group, over their protests, leaving them to go on alone.

As they neared the village they were stopped by an armed patrol of Germans, wearing uniforms Frank did not recognize. They claimed to be working on behalf of the Russians. The patrol's leader asked each person how much money they carried. When it came Frank's turn, the head of the patrol addressed Frank as "Comrade" and explained they were "not interested in people like him — they were looking for profiteers." According to the size and number of pieces of luggage, a "toll" was fixed. Usually the toll was paid by giving up one or two pieces of luggage.

A young woman in the group was one Frank had seen saying farewell to a young man in Bremen. Frank had talked to her on the train and learned the young man was her fiancé, and she was travelling back to Leipzig, where she lived. When the border patrol asked her for money, she showed them her ring and pointed to Frank, telling them he was her fiancé. Without hesitation Frank embraced the attractive young woman, kissing her on the lips. It was easy for him to make it look real; she was beautiful. The patrol left her alone, and she went with Frank to the train station in the village.

The woman left the train at Leipzig. She gave Frank a hug, although he had hoped she would kiss him again. He watched as she descended and walked away down the station platform. Travelling east, Frank arrived in Dresden where he heard that Sudeten Germans were being expelled from Czechoslovakia, that there had been retribution by the Czechs against Germans near Leitmeritz, and some Germans hanged from trees. He also heard that Germans from Leitmeritz were being deported by ship down the Elbe River. Lists of those already sent were said to be available in the German city of Riesa.

At Riesa, Frank found the passenger lists he had heard about. Searching through the pages, he saw many familiar names, but no trace of his parents or sisters. When he met people he knew from Leitmeritz, he learned his family was still alive and being held there in an internment camp, and were to be deported to Bavaria. Frank thought he could reach them at the camp and bring them out of Czechoslovakia himself. He travelled to Zinnwald, where he boarded a train to the Czech border. Sitting in front of Frank in the half-full train sat a pregnant teenage girl, quietly crying. At the border they both disembarked. With tears in her eyes, she whispered in Frank's ear, "Do not go on. They will kill you."

Frank did not understand the girl's warning and walked up to the border crossing. He saw armed Czech guards on the other side of the border; it did not look promising. He went to the stationmaster and asked if he thought his travel documents and discharge papers would allow him to travel to Leitmeritz.

"Are you crazy?" was all the surprised stationmaster would say.

Going to the border crossing again, Frank saw a woman approaching from the Czech side, a long scarf draped around her body. The guard ordered her to remove the scarf, and in doing so she revealed underneath several layers of clothing and a bag. Without warning, the Czech border guard began to beat the woman with the butt of his gun, knocking her to the ground. Frank was less than five metres away. He walked away in disgust, angry both at the guards and his inability to help the woman.

When he told this story to the stationmaster, Frank was told Germans owned houses on the other side of the street, but these were in Czechoslovakia. Sometimes the owners tried to bring their belongings into Germany. Some were unfortunately discovered by the border guards. There was nothing they could do to help.

Frank reluctantly accepted he had no choice but to abandon his plan to travel to Leitmeritz. It was a wise decision. He had heard stories of violence against Germans, but he did not realize the extent of the mistreatment. German soldiers, even those with discharge papers, if found by the Czechs, were often beaten or killed. Those surviving were thrown in camps where conditions were often inhumane and the guards cruel. Now Frank understood what the girl from the train was trying to warn him about. He decided his only option was to wait for his parents and sisters to be released. He also accepted that returning to Leitmeritz was out of the question — his home there no longer existed. But where was home now? At that moment, the word "home" had no meaning to him.

The Allies had decided to allow the Czechs to expel Sudeten Germans. In addition to forced resettlement of hundreds of thousands of ethnic Germans, Czech anger towards Germans led to numerous instances of brutality. Frank's family was fortunate to have avoided events such as the Ústí massacre and the Brno death march. The worst that had happened to Frank's family was being interned and having to wear white armbands, while his seventeen-year-old sister was forced to do menial labour at a bakery in Leitmeritz.

With travel into Czechoslovakia impossible, Frank returned to Ovelgönne, where he resumed work in the pharmacy. He also began thinking about what he wanted to do with his life. His first goal, he decided, was to resume his education.

The war, which in his teenage mind had seemed exciting in 1941, now could be seen for what it actually was. He could not believe how blind he and so many Germans had been, that they could have believed the world would sit by and watch while Germany claimed by force a nation of Germanic peoples stretching across central Europe. Now Germany had lost the right to express itself nationally. It was an occupied country whose independence and future government were far from clear.

Central Europe was in tremendous flux, and Germans could do no more than watch as their country's borders were redrawn. Massive changes were made to the eastern border. Poland was allowed to absorb more than a hundred thousand square miles. Frank's former home in Leitmeritz in the Sudetenland was given to a reconstituted Czechoslovakia. The movement of Germany's borders was agreed to by the Allied powers and recognized by a nascent East German government in the Soviet Zone, although hardly independent of Josef Stalin and the Soviet Union.

Frank and his family were among the close to eleven million ethnic Germans from Czechoslovakia, Poland, and Hungary expelled from their homes and deported to Germany. German cities were in ruins, and the refugees made the housing and food shortages even worse. So many ethnic Germans were shipped west from Poland and Czechoslovakia that rural Bavaria's population increased by thirty percent, despite wartime casualties. Upon arriving in Germany, displaced ethnic Germans were viewed by some native Germans with disdain. They were treated as outsiders, often ostracized and discriminated against. Though Frank and his family had survived the war, they had lost their home and possessions, and had to settle in a country openly resentful of their arrival.

FOURTEEN

An Unexpected Life
Ein unerwartetes neues Leben

In January, 1947, a letter arrived for Russ in Owen Sound. The return address was in Germany. Russ at first thought it might be from Jim, who he believed was still with the Canadian Occupation Force in Germany. But when he saw the name written above the return address, Russ knew immediately who it was from. It brought back a flood of memories. He read the following:[1]

> January 1, 1947
>
> Dear Mr. Colombo!
>
> I don't know if you can remember the days in May 1945, when you had stayed at Rastede. In this time I was a standard bearer by the German parachute troops and found myself in a farm near Rastede. Can you now remember the hours we have spoken together about many things? — Some days before I found in my pocket-book a peace of paper with your address and now, as you can see, I am very interested what had happened with you since that time. Would you be so kind and answer if it should be possible? I remember that you had told me you would go to Japan. Happened it?
>
> And now I will tell you something about my fate since that time. The next day after I have seen you last times, we marched into the internation area northern the Ems-Jade canal. I stayed there till Oktober. Then I had been discharged and began to seek my parents who had lived till the capitulation in Czechoslovakia. I must expect, that they had been turned out and began to seek from town to town, from one refugee camp to the other. I sought in the whole British zone, crossed at times the Russian border and sought there, crossed two times the Polish border; nothing was to

be found. I am speaking fluently Czech. I tried to come into the Czechoslovakian republic god sake, it didn't succeed. But I was lucky and could send a letter to my parents who lived still in the same town. Then I returned back into the English zone and became an assistant in a chemists shop. I had to gain money.

In May 1946 I could begin my studying on the university in Hamburg. But I got no lodging and had to go by train from Schleswig Holstein every day. It was not easy but I put up with it. Add to this, the eating was not enough. In May 1946 my parents had been turned out and went to Swabia in the south Germany, American zone. In August the term was finished and I went to Dillingen (Danube) and continued my studying here. In the next term I will study at Heidelberg and make my examination as an interpreter in Russian, Polish, Czech and English Language. Now I will finish. It would become a novel. I cannot write all to you what had happened and what I have seen, but remember that it is not all gold what is shining. And now I wish you supplementary a happy new year and please answer if you won't have anything to do.

Your
Frank Sikora

Russ and Frank exchanged several letters in the years following the end of the war. With what would be his last letter to Frank, Russ arranged to have a CARE package delivered. Frank replied with the following:[2]

Munich, March 1st

Dear Russel!

Shall I tell you how lucky I was when I received your letter!? It is nearly a year now since I wrote you last times. Sometimes I thought why you are not writing. I found various reasons. I looked for the fault on my side, but I didn't come to any end. And now, nearly a year later I can read that you are in the best of health. I don't know what I have to think. You write that you are just naturally lazy. Maybe, but idleness can not be anything in connection with it.

Please Russel, excuse these lines, but all these thoughts oppressed me during a long time. I repented my last letter. I regretted the tenor. You will ask me why. Maybe my reasons are ridiculous. But not for me. You wrote so hearty, so full of feeling. Please be sure, I didn't write the first time with the mental reservation to get anything from you. It was painful for me when you offered your help. That was the first reason why I didn't write anymore. The second was, that I feared you could have some unpleasantness through my letters. I thought you fear the censorship because it is an evil of mine not to take my mouth quiet. Now the censorship is lifted up.

This I would tell you, but now let us talk from other things. Your announced parcel did not arrive till now. I beg you, you have much expenditures and will put also my mind into dissension. I thank you very much of course. I thank you in the name of my little sister, but more I cannot do at the moment.

Now, what had happened in the last year!? I am studying in Munich now. My principle subject are Slavic languages. My sideline is English. In two years, so I hope, I will get my doctor. The subject of my dissertation is not yet clear. But I must decide now. It was not easy of course, and it is not easy also today. But I was lucky and I hope I will continue. I earn my money from month to month, sometimes more, sometimes less. Never mind! — Just now it comes into my head! Do you remember the day when you bought eggs?

You gave me 50 Marks. The peasant's wife demanded 2 Marks. You said I should give her all the money. I considered, 20 cents I had in my pocket, she will have money enough, I kept it to myself. This was the money which gave me the start in Hamburg. These 48 Marks were the financial base of my studying.

A late confession. Don't smile, you see, you had helped me more than one time and more than you know.

And what are you doing now? Are you still alone? What about your work? I hope our correspondence will become better in the future. Enclosed I send you a picture of me and of our little one. I have not more and no others for now, for we have lost all our pictures in Czechoslovakia. If we will get some more new ones, I will send them later. My picture is from the time when I was by the parachuters, the second from 2 years (later) ago. Could you also spare a picture of yourself?

But now I will finish my letter. I hope to hear soon from you and remain

Yours,
Frank

In the late 1940s, Russ's life had settled into a comfortable pattern. He lived in his boyhood home with his brother Jack and his mother, worked at the CNR, refereed lacrosse games, and trained with the Foresters Militia. He dated several women but none became a serious relationship. In the spring of 1949, at the age of thirty-three, Russ seemed a confirmed bachelor.

He had remained friends with Gerry Johnson and his wife Marge. Russ regularly visited when he had a weekend off. At times he would ask if he could bring a friend to Hamilton. One weekend that spring, Russ called with a request to bring a friend, and Gerry figured the friend was one of the men from work, as had been the case previously. When Gerry opened the door on Friday evening, there stood Russ, beside him an attractive woman, with green eyes and wearing bright red lipstick and her long, dark hair pulled back in a ponytail. Gerry was tongue-tied.

Hearing Russ's voice, Marge came to greet him as Gerry ushered Russ and the young woman into their home. Russ introduced her as Betty Olmsted, an Owen Sound girl he had met working in Palmerston. Betty was nine years younger than Russ, and her fun-loving, outgoing personality complemented Russ's quiet manner. Their visits to the Johnsons in Hamilton became a regular event.

Gerry and Marge were surprised when, after only a few months, the man they believed was a confirmed bachelor announced that he and Betty planned to marry. Their surprise changed to bewilderment when Russ revealed privately to Gerry that Betty was expecting a baby, and that it was not his. Russ explained he had learned the news when he and Betty were driving to Owen Sound. Betty had fallen silent as they drove, and when Russ looked at her, he saw she was crying. Confused, he asked what was wrong, and she at first refused to tell him. But when he insisted, she finally told him she was in trouble and didn't know what to do. She said she was pregnant, that she had slept with a previous boyfriend just once and now was caught. The father of the baby refused to accept responsibility. Betty told Russ her parents would disown her and her baby. She was alone and had no idea what she was going to do.

It is hard today to understand how difficult it was in the 1940s for an unmarried woman who became pregnant. Straying from the accepted moral code, overnight Betty turned from a "good girl" into a "bad girl." Bad girls "went all the way," good girls did not (or at least did not get caught). Men were excused for their role, while women were held to account by a society that placed shame on them. Betty realized when it became known she was pregnant and unmarried, she would be considered tarnished, someone no "respectable" man would ever want to marry

It was normal for a man in Russ's position simply to fade away. He reacted in precisely the opposite way. Before they reached Owen Sound, he proposed marriage. It wasn't what she had been seeking; she had merely needed to tell someone. He told her he was proposing because he was in love with her. But just as important must have been his instinct to be on the side of someone needing help. She accepted his proposal. Though she was honest to say her feelings did not match his, she hoped that would change as she accepted his offer out of her hopeless dilemma. But there was a condition to Russ's proposal. He said she should give up the baby for adoption. After that, they would start their lives together.

The condition was not unusual. Adoption of fatherless children was the standard way unwed mothers and their babies were dealt with. There were as many as twenty homes for unwed mothers across Ontario at the time, where unwed expectant women were expected to go until their babies were born.

To avoid the gossip that would surely be directed at them, it was decided that Betty should go away until the baby was born. With Russ's encouragement, Gerry and Marge invited Betty to live with them in Hamilton. No one knew her there. However, the attempt to shield Betty's reputation by hiding her (and by extension, shield Russ) only reinforced to Betty that she had done something disgraceful.

She found a job in the restaurant of Hamilton's posh Connaught Hotel, until carrying the heavy trays of food up the stairs from the kitchen became too much for her. Several weeks before the baby was due to be born, Russ took Betty to a home for unwed mothers in Toronto.[3] Here, the shame of being an unwed mother turned nightmarish.

Expectant mothers were confined to the home, allowed out only under escort. Betty's only contact with the world outside was through a pay phone and Russ's visits. The women were continually told they had disgraced themselves and their families. They were there to give up their babies, they were reminded, the only decent thing to do in light of the "loose" behaviour that had gotten them to this place. The staff worked hard to extinguish any hope that the women might keep their babies, telling them the best thing they could do for themselves and their baby was not to even see it after it was born.[4]

Despite the attempts by staff at brainwashing her, when Russ visited on weekends Betty tried to convince him they should keep the baby. But Russ refused to hear it. Already word had slipped out in Owen Sound that she was having a baby, and he argued it would be better for the child not to grow up with the stigma that would surely be attached to it.

A rumour circulated among the expectant mothers that women were being coerced to sign their children over for private adoption. One of the women whispered to Betty that the director of the facility had come to her when she was in labour, demanding papers be signed handing over the baby to her. Speculation was the babies were being sold by the director through private adoptions. The young woman was despondent at having given in to the pressure, her baby having been immediately taken away without her having the chance to hold it or give it a single kiss.

When Betty went into labour, just as she had been warned, the director of the home came to her. At first, the woman was pleasant as she explained how they could find a nice home for the baby. She placed the consent forms and a pen on the table. But when Betty refused, the pretence of pleasantness disappeared and the director began threatening. Alone, in pain from her labour, verbally assaulted, and frightened, she refused to sign. The baby was born in early August, a girl she named Nancy.

Betty and Nancy stayed together in the mothers' home for about a week. Her attachment to her baby grew stronger, and she couldn't imagine not keeping her. But Russ was insistent they should continue as planned. As hard as Betty tried to convince him, he refused. With no place to go and no one to turn to, Betty felt she had no choice but to agree to the adoption, and she gave Nancy to the provincial agency looking after public adoptions.

Russ and Betty married in Hamilton in September, 1949, in a small civil wedding attended only by Marge and Gerry. Nobody from Betty's family came. Neither did Blanche, his brother Jack, or any of their friends. She went to live in the Colombo house Russ had grown up in. It was an extremely difficult time for her. She privately grieved for her lost baby, with no one she could tell who would want to hear about her feelings. Ongoing public humiliation also came her way. Some in town went so far as to throw public insults at her, and even at her brothers and sisters.[5] When Russ and Betty attended a dance for the Foresters militia and sat with the officers and their wives, the table sat in total silence until they left to join the NCOs and their wives, who provided a friendlier reception.

Russ continued working with the railroad maintenance crew in Palmerston, returning on weekends. Otherwise Betty was alone with Blanche and Jack. Despite having lost a baby in heartbreaking fashion, and being the one thing Betty most wanted, Russ would not agree to another one. He was adamant he did not want children, and despite her pleas, he refused. But late in 1951, Betty finally gave Russ an ultimatum: either they would have a child or she was leaving. Their first child was born later that year. They named him Charles Gerald. They moved out of the home they shared with Blanche and Jack. Two years later, another son, Stephen, was born. In 1958, they had a daughter, Catherine Blanche. Nearly ten years after giving her baby daughter away, Betty finally had a daughter.

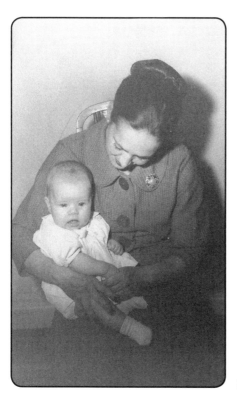

Betty Colombo and daughter Cathy.

Betty and Russ in the late 1950s.

Russ with sons Stephen (left) and Gerry (right).

All seemed well, but it was not destined to stay that way. In 1959, Russ at forty-three was still physically very strong, so when an anvil needed moving in the CNR workshop, rather than asking for help, he decided to move it himself. He lifted it from the workbench, but when he turned to carry it across the workshop, something gave in his lower back. It seemed to make an audible sound, like someone popping a thumb out of their mouth. He finished carrying the anvil but knew he had hurt himself. At first there was numbness in his legs, but within days a shooting pain began pulsing down his right leg, all the way to his foot. When he consulted a doctor, the numbness was so complete that he could not feel a needle pricked anywhere along his leg from hip to foot. The doctor told Russ he had herniated a disc in his lower back. Sometimes this injury recovers by itself, the doctor explained, but if it did not, Russ would require surgery to repair the ruptured disk.

As weeks slipped by, the pain worsened, becoming almost intolerable. There was no relief, not by sitting, standing, or lying down. He could not work and was eventually laid off. It seemed unlikely he would be able to return to the physical job he had held at the CNR.

Painful surgery to repair the herniated disc was finally performed. While recuperating, Russ looked for work. With no formal training to fall back on and no income to support his wife and three young children, their financial situation was quickly becoming critical. In desperation he turned to a good friend who sought help from the mayor of Owen Sound. The mayor, Eddie Sargent, contacted an acquaintance in the Conservative Party of Ontario, and through them a job was arranged for Russ in the Ontario Civil Service. The job was in Toronto, and with no other options, Russ and Betty moved their young family from Owen Sound.

Russ's job was with Ontario's small Citizenship Division. Immigrants were considered the responsibility of the federal government, since it was Ottawa that granted newcomers the right to enter the country. The result was that little money was put into immigration services by either the federal or provincial levels of government, and the wave of European immigrants seeking a better life in Canada after the war received little support upon arriving.

Russ entered the Citizenship Division as an outsider, a recipient of a position based on charity rather than qualifications. He had no formal knowledge about the job, while his co-workers had specialized university degrees. Russ had not even completed high school, and other than the army, his work experience was that of a hand on the railroad and before that a lumberjack. It is hard to appreciate how unpromising and humbling the situation was. Few would have expected any advancement for the "lucky" recipient of the position. Stepping into this post was far from easy for Russ. Were it not for his responsibility to his family, he would never have accepted charity. But he possessed one thing his co-workers may not have had: a first-hand appreciation of the suffering experienced by many European immigrants during the war.

That knowledge could have been what sparked his wonderful blossoming. In addition to his understanding of the hardships of immigrants, Russ possessed a bright mind, and if he decided to do something, nothing would stop him.[6] No one at the Citizenship Division realized this former railway worker could have been, had his path taken him that way, an intellectual of the highest degree.[7] While he wasn't the type to stand up and draw attention to himself, it soon was clear he was capable of taking on bigger challenges. A remarkable rise followed, from proverbial pencil-sharpener to the division's leading problem-solver.

Russ's arrival in the early 1960s coincided with the beginning of a shift in attitude within Ontario's Cabinet towards immigrants. There was a realization that helping newcomers adapt made them more productive citizens. Another more political factor likely shifted government attitudes. The growing immigrant communities in Ontario, especially those in Toronto, tended to congregate in the same neighbourhoods and vote along similar lines, making them potential swing voting blocs in some ridings. A government seen supporting immigrant communities stood a chance of gaining the new immigrants as committed voters.

The shift happened as Russ was developing into a rising talent in the Citizenship Division. His ideas gained influence. He also became a trusted advisor to the Minister of Citizenship, John Yaremko. Yaremko, who was Provincial Secretary as well, was the second most powerful member of the Conservative government in Ontario, behind only Premier John Robarts. Yaremko benefited from Russ's innovative ideas for improving immigrant services, and Russ's increasingly sought-after talent for speech writing. By the mid-1960s he was writing speeches for the premier and was a leading figure in the division when Bob Welch replaced Yaremko as Citizenship Minister and Provincial Secretary.

Russ had overcome nearly insurmountable obstacles to become successful. It may be that his work with immigrants filled deeper needs. He was still haunted by the effects of post-traumatic stress, and the near-total focus on his work provided a means of release. For Russ, the ability to spend nearly all his energy on a challenging career in which he excelled allowed him to tire himself mentally. It also gave him an area to focus on outside of his young family.

Russ gave every appearance of strength and normalcy to the outside world, and there were good times. During occasional holidays the family grew closer and nightly discussions around the dinner table on current affairs during the late 1960s engaged everyone in stimulating debate. But like many war veterans, he found it difficult to develop a closeness with his family.

As his son Gerry entered his teenage years, Russ increasingly found fault over minor issues, while the rebellious attitude Gerry shared with Russ

Russ greets new Minister of Citizenship Robert Welch.

fanned their friction. As their alienation grew, it not only pushed Gerry away, but also further alienated Betty. While Russ sniped at Gerry, Betty after nearly twenty years still vainly sought to learn from Ontario Children's Aid what had become of Nancy after her adoption. Russ was estranged from Betty and Gerry and distanced himself from his other two children through his long hours at work. Helping immigrants may have made Russ feel he was doing something he could not do during the war, but it could not bring him a sense of peace with his family. Through all this, he continued suffering recurring nightmares of the two German prisoners he had killed in Normandy.

When a new director of the Citizenship Division was needed, Russ was selected. It was a bold appointment rewarding ability and accomplishments ahead of university degrees. In only seven years, Russ had become leader of a vibrant division of the Ontario civil service. He was largely responsible for the development of Ontario's English as a Second Language (ESL) program, which galvanized teachers in the province in an exciting new enterprise. He was highly respected in Ontario's immigrant communities, and his talents were noted as far as the office of the premier. He was at the centre of planning to streamline Ontario's departments into what at the time were called "Super Ministries." His speech-writing skills were widely recognized and at one point he was asked to prepare a speech for Prime Minister Pierre Trudeau. It was a request he debated turning down, as Trudeau's anti-war, pro-"Zombie" attitudes were well-known. It was a group Russ still despised.

The high esteem for Russ was such that, in the run-up to the Ontario provincial election of 1971, he was asked to stand as a candidate for Parliament on behalf of the Progressive Conservative Party. It was an exciting opportunity, and the possibilities for the future seemed practically endless.

FIFTEEN

Als Deutscher unterwegs
A German on His Way

A year after the end of the war, Germany existed like some character in a Kafka novel. The country was in effect held prisoner, scarcely allowed to move, this once conquering nation now run by its conquerors. Once it pushed its borders outward, now they were collapsed inward. It was divided into four Occupation Zones, one each for the British, Americans, and French in the West and the Soviets in the east. Berlin, deep inside the Soviet zone, was itself divided into four Occupation Zones. There was no German government, and all administrative aspects of the country were run by the Occupying Powers, with no stated plan for the future. Millions were unemployed and all were reliant on rations for food.

Despite Germany's physical ruin and the difficult living conditions, some signs of normality were emerging. In 1946, German universities were reopening. It was a sign of hope for young Germans. Frank applied to the University of Hamburg and towards the end of winter learned he was accepted, with studies to begin the summer of 1946. Hamburg, like most German cities, was largely in ruins and housing was in short supply. The nearest town with lodging was Neumuenster, several hours' travel by train to and from Hamburg each day. The university had few books or study materials, and instead of studying, the students spent considerable time helping rebuild the university, much of which was destroyed by Allied bombing. Frank refused to help with the rebuilding. He told the school authorities he had served five years during the war and that contribution was far more than most of the students now enrolled. The school considered the matter and in the end agreed with him.

Frank lived day-to-day, spending more effort trying to survive than studying. Food was in very short supply, especially in the large German cities. Each month, like other Germans, Frank received a food ration card. In addition to food, it also entitled him to a few packages of cigarettes, which when sold on the black market provided just enough money for his rent and train travel to the university.

From the time he had joined the Luftwaffe in Leitmeritz, to his escape from incarceration near Jever after the war, Frank's personal life had barely existed. He'd had to put his own wishes on hold for years, but now he undertook one of the most personal activities possible — he wanted to learn. While the buildings at the university were gradually reconstructed, brick by brick, Frank devoted himself to Socrates, Tolstoy, Gustav Freytag, and Martin Luther, whose writings lost nothing if read while sitting on a crumbled wall instead of in a classroom.

What did make it difficult to focus on learning was the incessant hunger and, except in summer, the constant cold, since coal was expensive and in short supply. So when he received a CARE package, Frank was ecstatic. In those difficult days, CARE packages were like treasure chests. The Allies had only recently lifted the restriction preventing CARE packages being sent to Germany.

In a letter Russ had warned Frank to expect the package, but when word came of its arrival it still was tremendously exciting. The contents of the box were wonderful, including two pounds each of coffee, sugar, and margarine, and a pound each of honey, lard, jam, raisin, and chocolate, plus five tins of meat. In all, the CARE package weighed more than twenty-five pounds. The contents were far too valuable for Frank to keep. Their sale gave him enough money to live on for several months and still help his parents and sisters. He was quick to send a letter of thanks.

Frank's parents had arrived late in 1946 from Czechoslovakia. They had been in an internment camp near Leitmeritz for more than a year and were being resettled in the small village of Schabringen, in Bavaria. Frank's father found work as a clerk in a factory. To be nearer them, Frank decided to seek a transfer from university in Hamburg to one in Munich, which was less than sixty miles from Schabringen. However, when he investigated enrolling at the university in Munich, he learned the American authorities, in whose Occupation Zone the city was located, would not allow those who had been Nazi party members to register as university students.

Frank in his apartment in the late 1940s during his studies at the University of Hamburg.

Frank's parents were also concerned it would cause them problems if they were identified as party members. The father of Karl Habel, Frank's friend from Leitmeritz, had been the highest-ranking party member in Leitmeritz and the man who had briefly made Frank a Pimpfe leader in Leitmeritz. He had been executed after the war. Frank worried he might not be allowed to enrol in university at Munich because, when he was seventeen, his mother had enrolled him in the Nazi party. He realized his name would be recorded in the party registers, which were now held by the Americans. Going to the American authorities, Frank appealed for approval to enrol at university in Munich. To his relief, the Americans permitted it. The fact that he was seventeen and it had been his mother who signed his registration with the party, and records showed Frank had never paid party dues, saved him from further problems. In the fall of 1947, he was accepted at the Ludwig–Maximilians-University in Munich to study for his doctoral degree in Slavic languages.

Partway through Frank's studies for his doctoral degree, he transferred to study in Switzerland, where for six months he attended the University of Zurich. In late February, 1948, came the news that the Communist Party

A view in the late 1940s of the main staircase leading from the atrium of the Ludwig-Maximilians-University in Munich, showing damage to the interior and missing windows. In 1943 in this atrium, Sophie and Hans Scholl, members of the White Rose anti-Nazi group, were arrested for distributing leaflets calling for the overthrow of the Nazis.[1]

in Czechoslovakia had taken control of the government in a coup. This prompted a stream of Czechs to leave the country. Czech students attending the university in Zurich began raising funds to help the refugees, and Frank stopped to speak with them. In flawless Czech, Frank spoke with a young Czech woman. She assumed Frank had fled from the Communists and asked if he needed assistance.

"That would be very helpful," Frank told her. "My family became refugees from Czechoslovakia because we are Sudeten Germans." From the expression on the young woman's face, it was as if Frank had told her he had the plague.

Frank asked her, "Why does the fact we are Sudeten Germans matter? Czechoslovakia was always my family's home before we were forced to leave."

"We are only helping those who fled the Communists," she said coldly.

"I understand. But my family did not leave by choice, we were forced out," Frank replied. "Don't you feel any sympathy for us, as well as those who left Czechoslovakia by choice?" He knew the answer without hearing her reply.

Several weeks later he had a few days break and decided to travel to Geneva. His conversation with the young Czech girl had made him curious and given him an idea. At Geneva, he made his way to the International Red Cross building. This was world headquarters of the benevolent global institution whose main mission was to help those suffering in the aftermath of the war.

Frank was at first overwhelmed by the building. It was like a massive manor house, with pillars, portals, marble staircases, and ornately decorated halls. He asked to be directed to the office responsible for Czechoslovakia. His purpose, he told the receptionist, was to register for assistance as a refugee. He was shuttled from room to room, given a piece of paper stamped to indicate why he was there, and sent to still more offices in the elaborately decorated building. Finally he arrived at an office, staffed by a Czech, where his refugee claim was to be processed.

"And where did you come from in Czechoslovakia?" Frank was asked in Czech.

"Leitmeritz, in the Sudetenland." Frank looked unwaveringly at the official sitting behind his desk.

"Is this your idea of a joke?" The reply was indignant. "The International Red Cross does not deal with Germans."

"I suspected as much," Frank replied, "but I wanted to hear it for myself. I find it sad that even the Red Cross distinguishes people in need based on whether they are Czech or German. This is why problems happened there in the first place." He turned and left without waiting for a reply from the clerk, who was at a loss for words. Frank was not shocked. It confirmed what he already knew: there was no sympathy for Germans.

Frank returned to Munich and in 1951 completed his doctorate, earning the distinction of graduating *cum laude*. Shortly afterwards he received word his application had been accepted to become a Fulbright Scholar at Georgetown University in Washington, D.C. His course in East European Studies was supported by a scholarship of $150 a month. The foreign students in the program all had graduate degrees and were mixed with American students. Frank's studies were part of a program for students from the former Axis countries of Germany, Japan, and Italy. The goal of the program was to educate future leaders from those once totalitarian countries about freedom and democracy. During the course, Frank asked how the American "re-education" programme was viewed by a student from Japan.

"You are in this programme too?" Frank asked after they had introduced themselves.

"Yes," was the reply, "they want to teach me what it is like to live as a free man in a free country."

"Have you learned it?" Frank inquired.

"Well, the Americans are so happy when they think they have taught us something, so why spoil it for them?"

During a break in studies, Frank decided to strike out on his own to learn about America. As he had done years before as a boy in Germany, he now did as a man in America, standing at the side of the road, his thumb extended, hitch-hiking. From Washington he travelled south to Key West, and from Florida took the famous Route 66 to California. In hours talking with Americans, he found most remained friendly after learning he was from Germany. Their conversations often turned to the war, and he would answer questions about his military service in the Luftwaffe, and try to explain the difference between Germans of the Reich and ethnic Germans. He was surprised at how many knew about the Sudetenland and Sudeten Germans.

In the fall of 1952, after successfully completing his studies at Georgetown, Frank returned to Germany. He pondered possible career choices. The professor with whom he studied in Munich tried to convince him to follow an academic career. But he was drawn in a different direction. He applied to the newly formed German Foreign Service, and after meeting with its director, in January, 1953, he was offered a position in the diplomatic department.

Germany had by this time evolved into two distinct countries. The former Soviet Occupation Zone had stayed under Soviet control and become the German Democratic Republic (GDR). In the rest of Germany, the amalgamated Occupation Zones governed by the United States, Britain, and France had been renamed the Federal Republic of Germany. While full sovereignty for West Germany was still nearly two years away, the people had elected a parliament and chosen Konrad Adenauer as the first Chancellor of the Federal Republic.

Frank joined the West German Foreign Service when it was only about eighteen months old, and the Federal Republic had existed fewer than five years. The new German Foreign Service was growing and had the difficult task of representing Germany around the world, including countries they had inflicted grievous harm upon. Frank's first foreign posting was as an attaché in Marseilles, France, followed shortly afterwards by assignment to the German embassy in Athens. Both countries had suffered long and difficult occupations by Germany during the war.

Frank was now in his early thirties and was making plans to marry. His beautiful fiancé, Marianne, came from a wealthy family. However, her mother had ambitious plans for her daughter and was unprepared when she presented her husband-to-be. It was hard for her to accept into her conservative, well-to-do family a future son-in-law who was a refugee, and not quite a real German. When Frank's mother heard of her reaction, she took the criticism of her son as a personal slight. She would not accept being looked down on or patronized. Many among the hundreds of thousands of ethnic Germans who came to Germany penniless from Czechoslovakia, Poland, Lithuania, and other German enclaves to the east faced similar prejudice. Despite the tension, Frank and his fiancé married.

Their first two years as newlyweds were spent in Athens. Frank's next posting was London, where he was the lead staff member at the embassy dealing with Communist issues. He wrote numerous papers analyzing all aspects of the subject. His background in Slavic languages made him one of the few Germans in the Diplomatic Service who could read texts coming out of the Eastern Bloc. Frank's insights won him recognition as a leading authority in this area in the German Foreign Service.

He made important contributions in the debate within the German Foreign Service concerning German-Polish relations. Poland was among the most difficult issues facing Germany. The friction complicated relations for the Americans and British with the Polish government, since support of any kind for the Federal Republic of Germany was contentious to the Poles. The brutal treatment of Poland by Germany during the war made the Poles unwilling to compromise on any matter or to forgive German actions. Among the most difficult issues was the post-war Polish border, which had shifted more than a hundred and fifty kilometres to the west, transferring large parts of territory that had been German to Poland, including much of Prussia. East Germany's government, a puppet of the Soviet Union, had recognized the new Polish border, but the Federal Republic of Germany refused to do so despite being strongly pressed by the Americans and British. Frank was among the first in the German Diplomatic Service to make the case there would be no returning to Germany's pre-war borders, and politicians would do well to accept the new border with Poland.[2]

Having a family and being a member of the German Foreign Service was difficult. In 1957, his son, Frank Michael, was born in London, and in 1959 Frank moved the family to Bonn, where a daughter, Cornelia, was born in 1960. In 1961, the young family moved to Hong Kong, followed by transfer to the German delegation at NATO headquarters in Paris, and then to Brussels in the 1960s. When he was transferred to Brussels, his wife and children remained in Paris, and Frank commuted between the cities on weekends.

Frank's interest in Eastern Europe remained strong. When the German Foreign Service opened an embassy in Yugoslavia, he volunteered to be posted to Belgrade as press secretary. In 1972, shortly after a German embassy was opened in Warsaw, Poland, Frank was one of the first to move there. This time he relocated by himself. His wife chose to stay in Germany rather than move their children. His son was now in high school and his wife was a high school principal.

Frank with his teenage son Frank and daughter Cornelia.

During one of his trips from Germany to Poland, Frank fulfilled a request from his mother to drive there by way of Leitmeritz. It was close to a decade since she was deported, and she insisted on seeing their former home. Leitmeritz had survived the war almost unscathed.[3] Frank parked his car in the centre of Leitmeritz, in the same square where years earlier the Pimpfe had run amok, and watched his elderly mother march off by herself. Two hours passed before he saw her walking back down the street. He asked how it had gone. His mother told him she went to the Czech bakery she had shopped at before they were forced to leave, and where Frank's sister was forced to work during their internment. She said that before coming back she'd thought she could never forgive what the Czechs had done to them. Now, seeing how bad things were for them under the Soviets, she felt they had it worse than they had in 1945. And, his mother added, she did not in the least feel sorry for them.

Posted to Warsaw, separated from his family for long stretches, Frank became romantically involved with a beautiful young secretary at the German embassy. The affair might have gone unnoticed, except the woman, Gerda Schroeder, was a spy for the East Germans. This was unknown to Frank, but known to West Germany's spy agency. His affair with the secretary was recorded without their knowledge, and when she was exposed as a spy, it threatened to implicate him as a conspirator. Weeks of intrigue in Warsaw between the East and West German spy agencies followed, involving armed guards watching the secretary to prevent the East's agents rescuing her, a clandestine car trip to the Warsaw airport, and a last minute inspection by Polish security forces on board the plane that could have seen Frank and the secretary seized and given to the East Germans. In the end, they were flown out of Poland to West Germany.

On the day he returned to Germany, on his way to his wife, who still knew nothing of his affair, Frank passed a newspaper stand. Among the newspapers his eyes were drawn to the front page of *Bildzeitung*. On it was a large picture of the beautiful Gerda Schroeder. He bought a copy of the newspaper and read the story of the incident, which had been leaked to the press. Included in the newspaper article was a description of Frank's romantic tryst.

Frank was eventually exonerated on the charge of espionage, partly due to recordings made of their liaisons at her apartment that proved nothing political was discussed, and partly from testimony by Gerda that her affair with Frank was purely romantic. However, he was forced to retire from the German Foreign Service, not for spying, but on the charge of bringing disrepute to the government.

The affair also put an end to Frank's marriage. Alone, with little income, he moved to Bonn, where he rented a small one-room apartment. He turned his attention to writing, producing a book whose title in English was *Socialist Solidarity and National Interests*, published in 1977. It was a scholarly examination of the relationships among Czechoslovakia, Poland, and East Germany, and reflected his personal experiences and professional understanding of those countries.

Frank was involuntarily retired from the German Foreign Service. He had accepted this punishment without complaint and without appealing the decision, even though colleagues in the Foreign Service and his lawyer felt the penalty was far too severe for the indiscretion he had committed. Four years after his forced retirement and with the encouragement of former colleagues, he applied for reinstatement. To his great pleasure, he was welcomed back.

His first assignment on returning was to Seoul, South Korea, where he was the Permanent Representative of the Ambassador. In 1981 he was assigned to the embassy in Tel Aviv, Israel. Relations between Germany and Israel remained highly strained. Frank was assigned there because he was one of the most senior members of the Foreign Service, and was very well known for the work he had done seeking the reconciliation of Germany with Poland. However, considering his age, most Israelis correctly assumed he had been in the German armed forces during the war. Reaction was usually hostile, even violent, but he found personal acceptance by some Israelis was possible.

Frank, who professes he himself did nothing wrong during the war, faced the reality that as a German he was held personally accountable for wartime atrocities, carrying on his shoulders national guilt. As a seventeen-year-old, he had responded just as thousands of young men in Canada, England, and America, and for the same reason, because he was told his country needed him. Ironically, having been a young man wanting to be responsible and patriotic now stained his reputation. The concept that there was such a thing as a "good" German was impossible for many to accept.

After four years in Israel, Frank wanted to end his career in the Foreign Service at home in Germany. In 1984, he returned to Bonn, and in January, 1985, he retired, this time of his own accord. In 1997, he remarried to Gisela Kaempffe, a member of the German Foreign Service he had met while both were stationed in Tel Aviv. When she was assigned to Tokyo as the head of the Political Section, Frank travelled with her, looking after their household while she worked.

In 2004, Frank's autobiography, *Als Deutscher Unterwegs*, was published by Dr. Bachmaier Verlag, a Bonn publishing house. Frank had long kept a diary of his life, and Gisela had typed his handwritten notes, adding to them Frank's additional reminiscences. Translated, the title is *A German on His Way*, reflecting Frank's lifelong journey to understand what it means to be German.

These days Frank and Gisela split their time between two homes. One is a rustic setting in Bonn, the former capital of West Germany, where Frank and Gisela can sometimes be found walking through the nearby forest, enjoying the peace of nature and small city life. Their other home is in Berlin, not far from the historic street Unter den Linden and the famous Brandenburg Gate. When in Berlin they often dine at an Italian restaurant not more than fifty metres from their Berlin apartment, where the owner entertains his patrons with a badly sung Italian aria as he uncorks a bottle of wine for them.

After dinner, Frank and Gisela take the walk to their apartment slowly, his arm in hers for support, since his breathing these days is increasingly difficult. In the courtyard outside their apartment is a garden, and in the garden is a small manmade pond with a fountain. The water splashing on rocks in the pond is a peaceful sound amid the noise of Berlin and reminds Frank of the rivers near his home in Freistadt long ago.

Frank Sikora and Gisela Kaempff-Sikora in 2009 at their apartment in Berlin.

SIXTEEN

Finding Frank
Auf der Suche nach Frank

MAY 2008

At the height of his career, Russ was struck down by illness. It was 1971, and he was just fifty-six. His illness was the loss of a great friend to Ontario's immigrant community. I was sixteen and lost a large part of my father to the massive stroke that hit him at work that morning. It paralyzed his left side and sentenced him to nearly a year in hospital. Russ fought hard during that year to recover enough to come home, still partially paralyzed but eventually able to walk with a cane. In 1980, declining health forced him into the Veterans' Wing at Sunnybrook Hospital in Toronto. Less than a year later, Betty died without warning. I had travelled from the hospital where she had been to Sunnybrook. Russ sat on the bed in his spartan room, and when I told him of her death, he wept.

He fought on until the age of sixty-seven, once again defying the odds by shrugging off several major illnesses. The fierceness with which he hung on to life seemed by sheer force of will. But nearing the end, he told his son Gerry to bring him the German pistol he had brought home from Bad Zwischenahn, wanting to end life on his own terms. Gerry refused.

As difficult as his fight was against physical illness, the battle he waged to come to terms with what had happened during the war was far harder. Death gave him release from the demons that had tormented him so many years.

———◆———

I knew my father had a letter from someone in Europe, but I had not read it for years. Nevertheless, I knew exactly where to find it, in a worn cardboard box.

I was the willing recipient of the box, for its contents represented all that was left of my family's too-brief time together. I dutifully took that box as I moved from house to house. When it was time for the next change of residence, the box was unearthed, and I would browse what lay inside. I remembered each item exactly, the pictures always evoking strongly bittersweet feelings of a family that was always incomplete. I felt better when the box was returned to its resting place in the back corner of my deepest closet.

I had never paid attention to the letter, and until recently it had carried no significance to me. But I had grown curious to learn more about my father's war experiences. I found it in the box, where I knew it would be. When I began reading, something wonderful happened. It was as though a code was broken, and I could at last understand the meaning of the words. It was a story about my father I had never known, unfolding in amazing texture in a way no letter had ever done.

I read the letter quickly, tripping over some of the words in the expressive but slightly imperfect English used by the writer, who had signed only "Frank." My excitement grew. I went back and read the letter again, this time more slowly.

"Dear Russel!" it said. *"Shall I tell you how lucky I was when I received your letter!?"*

No, I thought. *Can I tell you how lucky I was to receive the letter!* It was as if my father had left it for me to find after sixty years.

———◆———

Even as a young boy, I knew the most difficult and exciting times in my father's life were when he served in the army during the Second World War. I first realized this after my mother told my father to "take the boys and tell them some stories." She had wanted quiet, but she gave us a gift of some of his memories. My brother and I would happily run ahead of him down the hallway to their bedroom. I was perhaps four and so small, I had to grab onto the blankets to pull myself up off the floor and on top of the bed. He piled the soft feather pillows against the headboard and sat with outstretched legs. My brother and I crawled in close, one on either side of the man who seemed to us a giant. With our heads resting on his chest and his arms around our shoulders, he began telling us stories. While he spoke, I stared into a corner of the room, watching the scenes he described running like a movie in my mind.

For years, those were the only times he spoke to us of the war. Some of the stories were funny, some told of bravery, in some he was angry, and some were very violent. When one story ended, we asked to be told another. They are some of my earliest and strongest memories.

In hindsight, only in the past few years have I gained some understanding of why he chose to tell his young sons and several years afterwards, his daughter, these stories. Certainly our mother never realized he was telling us events that were graphically violent. I have no doubt those stories and the war in general were seldom far from his mind. Some of those memories would wake him in the middle of the night in a cold sweat, yelling. In later years, as he sat alone at the dinner table long after we had left it, I would hear him talking quietly to himself, sometimes just the word "No!" I am sure he was remembering events that disturbed him deeply.

We found more reminders of war in our parents' home. It was a young boy's treasure trove. A German officer's sword, with pearl handle and forged eagle sitting atop a wreath-enwrapped swastika. A heavy black German pistol, a paratrooper's knife, and my father's medical kit containing an assortment of sharp metal instruments, some with brown stains on them. It was probably rust, but as a boy I secretly hoped it was, and was not, blood. The war never seemed far away as I grew up.

———◆———

As a boy, I knew several people my age whose fathers were deeply affected by the war. There was a boy who lived alone with his father in a small apartment in our neighbourhood. It was a shock the first time I saw his father, since his skin was bright pink. The boy volunteered that his father had been a sailor during the war and been burned on board ship. There was also Sharon, a friend from high school. Whenever I visited Sharon's home, her father was sitting in the same leather chair in their living room. I don't know if he could speak; he never said a word when I was there. Without my asking, Sharon explained her father had been a Spitfire pilot and suffered a head injury in the war.

I can remember asking my father if he was wounded in the war — I think I asked if he had received a Purple Heart, the American medal for being wounded in battle. My father said no, he had never been wounded. I was young, and his answer disappointed me. Couldn't he have been wounded just a bit? What bad luck it was for me not to be able to say to friends he had been shot or to see where a bullet wound had been stitched! He never corrected my childhood romantification.

Only now when I think back to how the war affected him do I realize he carried deep wounds — not the physical kind, like the man who had been burned, or Sharon's father. My father's wounds were injuries of the mind and spirit. Psychological trauma haunted him and spiritual injury alienated him from religion.

Could his family have helped him deal with the problems? When I was grown, if I had asked him how I might help, I don't believe he would have even answered. Yet how many times had he revisited in his mind the events that caused his psychological trauma, reliving them over and over? He was unable to forgive himself for the unnecessary deaths of those two young German prisoners in that French forest. Was he unable to live with the raw rage he had unleashed from deep within himself when he had killed the second man?

I wonder if it was that trauma that prevented him from forming a close bond with his children. Did he also sabotage his relationship with the woman he loved deeply, by refusing to accept her daughter, leaving her no choice but to give her baby up for adoption? Was his alienation of his oldest son Gerry part of that sabotage? And did he throw himself so completely into his work to be too tired to feel anything? This is too much amateur psychoanalysis, and it may be only a fraction correct. Or it might explain why his behaviour often fell between indifferent and difficult. The war wounded him terribly, but affected us as well.

———————◆———————

Exhuming Frank's letter in 2008, I examined it for clues to the writer's identity. The author gave little to work with. Frank wrote:

> Your announced parcel did not arrive till now. I beg you, you have much expenditures and will put also my mind into dissension. I thank you very much of course. I thank you in the name of my little sister, but more I cannot do at the moment.

The letter was dated March 1, but gave no year, although from conditions in Germany he describes, it was likely written not long after the war ended. As the story in the letter unfolded, I realized the writer had been a German soldier, in fact a paratrooper. I admit to some consternation in learning my father had befriended a German soldier. It puzzled me he could do so, as I equated German soldiers with inhuman acts of monstrous proportions, perpetrated against the Jews and other innocent victims. Against that doubt I pressed on — surely, I thought, if my father considered this person someone worth helping, he understood something I did not.

I looked for clues to the writer's identity, the most important seeming to be his plan to attend university. I developed the habit when referring to the writer to call him to call him by the name he had signed, Frank, and that familiarity gradually gave the feeling he was already an acquaintance, the feeling one acquires of knowing someone from reading about them in a book.

> I am studying in Munich now. My principle subject are Slavic languages. My sideline is English. In two years, so I hope, I will get my doctor. The subject of my dissertation is not yet clear. But I must decide now.

The words on the page were tantalizing clues but maddeningly incomplete. What I wanted to know were the circumstances leading Frank and my father to become friends. Frank's letter was a small insight, like a crack of light through the bottom of a closed door I wanted to pass through.

I knew from the limited information in his letter that the chances of learning his identity were extremely slight. And even if I could discover who he was, would Frank still be alive, and would he remember my father after so many years? If not alive, would he have left a family who would want to share in this letter? With what little information the letter provided, I began searching for Frank.

The most useful piece of information appeared to be his plan to study in Munich. He hoped, his letter said, to study for a doctorate in Slavic languages. I quickly learned of the Ludwig-Maximilians-University of Munich. It had a department of Slavic languages that awarded postgraduate degrees in the postwar years. That must be where he planned to study, I concluded.

My excitement at this quick success was soon blunted when I was unable to find email addresses for professors in the Slavic languages department, while no one in the administrative arm of the university or its alumni organization responded to my emails. Even the university library failed to reply. Perhaps it was because I was writing in English? But when I translated my request into German, it made no difference. Or maybe my inquiries about a past student breached confidentiality — no one replied, so I had no way of knowing. I had hit a roadblock.

I began seeking alternatives. I thought, if I could gain online access to the university's library I might find listings of doctoral theses published in the 1940s. I checked the university's library webpage and found amongst the information on the page a link to the library's holdings. It sounds like such a small thing to find that describing it now cannot possibly explain my excitement. A treasure hunter scouring for ancient relics might understand.

Following the link with excitement, I found a search engine, in which I was able to sift by year, title, and author's name. Did they include dissertations from doctoral candidates? YES, they did! I shouted something signifying my eureka moment to Sonia, wife and patient supporter. These few paragraphs don't nearly do credit to the weeks I spent engrossed in the search.

Never before and never again will I find it so exciting to search a library catalogue, but examining Munich university's catalogue from my desk in Thunder Bay was absolutely thrilling. I copied the title of every dissertation written between 1946 and 1954 by anyone named Frank, Franz, or with the initial F. When printed, the list was a dozen pages long and contained more than a hundred entries. Holding the sheaf of paper, I felt certain it contained the person who had written to my father.

With red pen in hand, I winnowed down the list. Titles whose topics were medical or biological were first to go. Their removal felt like great progress. Next I removed those in social sciences bearing no connection to Slavic languages. The list grew shorter, and the possible candidates fewer. Soon I began hating the "progress" I was making. I began worrying Frank might not be on the list after all. Maybe he did not go to the university in Munich after all, or perhaps he did not graduate? As entry after entry was eliminated, the pages filled with pen strokes and scratched-off names.

In the end just one name was left on those twelve pages. It seemed incredible to me that this lone remaining entry in the list could be the dissertation Frank had mentioned in his letter. Surely it couldn't be? I had only one ticket left in what had become a personal lottery.

The thesis was titled "*Aorist und Imperfektum*," and was written by Franz Sikora. The library catalogue provided the birthdate of the author, telling me this Franz Sikora was born in 1924. He would have been twenty or twenty-one at the end of the war, and would today (in 2008) be eighty-four or eighty-five, if still alive. But was *this* Franz Sikora *my* Frank?

I felt both encouraged and disappointed. The name was Franz, not Frank, but I had been told that Frank could be an Anglicized version of Franz. However, I still had no contact with anyone at the university, and I doubted they would provide personal information about him, even if any were available.

At this point my search stopped. There was no obvious next step, and I admit to a period of frustration. In some, this can elicit surrender. I am not one of them. During this period of reflection, I had the feeling I had overlooked something. But what was it? After several weeks it occurred to me that I had previously searched the library catalogue for authors named

Franz or Frank. Why not, I thought, search for entries under the name Franz Sikora? He might have published more than just his thesis.

So I entered the name and queried the library catalogue for publications since 1945 by anyone named Franz Sikora. Two entries appeared: one was the aforementioned dissertation, the other was a book published in 1977.[1] Had the same Franz Sikora written the book and the dissertation? Checking the birth year of the book's author revealed it too was 1924, hinting the answer might be yes. But the topic of the book was political, not at all what an academician in Slavic languages was likely to write. And once again I was left with a cold trail with no diverging paths to follow, but at least it was something to work with.

It is worth repeating at this point that I had no idea whether Frank, the letter writer, was Franz Sikora of the thesis, or Franz Sikora the book author. I always considered the possibility that I might be dealing with three different people and realized that I might have to look for Frank through other information in the letter. The problem with that was the letter gave practically nothing else to follow.

I tried contacting the publisher of Franz Sikora's book to ask about the author. But these attempts failed. It appeared the publisher no longer existed. My alternative was less direct and probably only occurred to me because of my experience with scientific literature. I began searching for academic papers in which the book by Franz Sikora was cited. Within an academic community it is common for writers to personally know those whose work they cite. I began contacting writers who had cited the book by Franz Sikora, asking if they were familiar with the author.

It is a testament to those scholars that all my inquiries except one were answered, all politely, all quickly, but all negatively. Yes, they remembered the book, but no, they knew nothing of its author. Each reply provoked a moment of hope, but each time the balloon was pricked mercilessly when I read the response.

Several weeks later, when I had taken a break from emailing strangers about Franz Sikora's book, I received a message from Germany. It was from the only scholar who had cited the book and had not replied. He apologized, but he had not seen my email when he was out of the country. He said that he did not know the author, but suggested I contact an older scholar he thought might know him. He provided the man's name and phone number and said I should call him, since he spoke English.

On this advice I called this older scholar in Germany ... and got an answering machine. I hung up. I called again the next day, and this time when the machine picked up, I left a message saying I would try to call again and hoped to speak with him about Franz Sikora. Through the week I called several more times, only to get the answering machine.

One morning I awoke earlier than usual. I decided to try calling the old scholar one last time. I had the phone to my ear but was not really paying attention to it, expecting to once again hear the answering machine, when to my surprise someone picked up and said hello (in German). It was the old scholar, finally!

I briefly explained my story, telling him Franz Sikora was an old friend of my father and I had a letter I wanted to send him. Yes, the man said, he knew Franz Sikora. Only he went by the name Frank, not Franz. Remembering his words still sends a shiver of excitement down my spine.

"Would you like his phone number?" he asked. (He was still alive!) I was in a state of shock at the unexpected news that this Franz was called Frank. Feeling as if the air had been sucked out of my lungs, I said yes.

Was this Frank/Franz, who had written the book, the one named Franz who had written the dissertation? Was he also the same man who had written the letter to my father sixty years earlier? I needed a few minutes to clear my thoughts and to compose in my mind what I wanted to say, and how I wanted to say it.

———————•———————

My heart pounded. I paced as the phone rang repeatedly. Finally, it was answered.

"Hallo?" The voice on the other end of the line was that of an older woman.

"Hello," I said, "is this the home of Dr. Frank Sikora?"

"Hallo? Kann ich Ihnen helfen?"

"Hello, I'm calling from Canada. My name is Steve Colombo. Is Dr. Sikora there?" I imagined the woman hanging up on a stranger speaking gibberish.

Then I heard her say *"Kanada?"* In heavily accented English she said, *"Ja,* just a moment and I'll get my husband. But he is not so well and it will take him some time to come to the telephone. You will wait?"

"Yes, I will wait," I said. My palms were sweating.

Moments passed. I heard the faint sound of footsteps crossing a room and then heard the telephone being picked up.

"You must be the son!" said the man in Bonn.

"Yes, I am," I said after a brief pause, realizing what those words meant.

SEVENTEEN

Berlin

A year after first speaking with Frank I was on a silver and orange jet touching down at Schönefeld Airport, near Berlin. It was March 2009, and the day was cold and grey, the drizzling rain giving everything a dreary appearance.

I boarded a train from the airport to the city's central downtown station. As I sped along, my thoughts turned to wartime Berlin. I looked out on a modern city, but images appeared of swastika flags hung from buildings, ranks of German soldiers marching stiff-legged through the streets, and Russian tanks and troops fighting house-to-house through the ruined city. The mixing of historical and present-day Berlin created surreal visions, like ghosts on an imperfectly tuned television screen.

Before leaving Canada, I had made arrangements to phone when I arrived at my hotel in Berlin. Gisela answered in her now familiar singsong voice. She would, she told me, walk to the street corner near my hotel, just a few blocks from their apartment, then she would bring me to see Frank. Their apartment would be too difficult to find for someone not familiar with it. It felt absolutely clandestine, like I was to be assessed before being brought to a secret safe house.

The streets in the quiet residential neighbourhood are lined with four- and five-storey buildings, most having small shops and restaurants on the ground floors and private residences above. Waiting outside a small coffee shop near the corner of Pariser and Sächsische Strasse, I saw a distinguished-looking woman walking down the street, protected from the lightly falling rain by a black umbrella. I waved. She nodded and crossed.

"How did you know it was me?" she asked with surprise as we shook hands, her voice immediately recognizable.

"I remembered your picture from Frank's book, but even before you came close I just had a feeling you were Gisela."

"Come with me and I will take you to Frank. It is not far," she replied.

We chatted as we walked under leafless trees lining the street, approaching a large gothic church with a tall pointed steeple, surrounded by a heavy black iron fence. Car tires hissed on the wet roads and left a fine mist in the air. As we walked, my anticipation rose.

Eventually, Gisela stopped, unlocked an outer door and ushered me into a short corridor opening into an inner courtyard, shielded from the bustle in the street outside. She unlocked a second door leading into a small glass-walled elevator. We rode in silence to the fifth floor, looking out on the courtyard. As we left the elevator, at the top of a small flight of stairs stood Frank. We started talking in the hallway, only to have Gisela shoo us inside.

Their apartment is fashionable, elegantly northern European, neither extravagant nor austere. Frank and Gisela were instantly gracious hosts. Considering I arrived a virtual stranger, they were exceptionally welcoming. Still, it was not until the second day that they seemed to truly become comfortable with my presence. Or perhaps I was the one who took some time to relax.

I told Frank I wanted to shake his hand and asked Gisela if she would take a picture of it. Sixty-four years before, I said, he and my father shook hands when they parted in Bad Zwischenahn. I told Frank I thought our meeting should begin with another handshake.

Frank was anxious to get down to "work" right away. It was more than a social visit, since I was doing research for what would become this book. We sat across from each other at his dining table. Initially we engaged in small talk, but before long we began discussing questions I had about his life, as described in my translation into English of his memoir, *Als Deutscher Unterwegs*. Frank seemed to relish talking with me and was willing to answer every question. Gisela brought tea and cake, which we ate as Frank went into detail about the early years of his life. We took a break in the afternoon so Frank could rest and he insisted I visit the Holocaust Memorial in Berlin, which I did with Gisela later that day.

Frank and the author at their meeting share a handshake in memory of Russ's final meeting with Frank, sixty-four years earlier.

There was only one point at which Gisela intervened. I should not, she said, portray Frank's time as a German soldier in anything like a positive light. It was not that all German soldiers had done terrible things, she explained, but that the world would not accept a portrayal of them as decent, sometimes heroic people. To emphasize her point, she recalled an incident in New Jersey in the mid-1960s, when she was a diplomatic attaché. It was the first time since the war that German sailors came into a U.S. city wearing their uniforms. She remembered how badly people responded to the sight. "I thought we won the war?" she heard an American angrily say. That was twenty years after the war ended. Now, more than sixty years since the end of the fighting, she felt the idea of a German soldier from the Second World War being a decent person was still something that would not be accepted.

The following day, as the end of my visit neared, Frank asked what my rationale was for telling his story along with that of my father. I replied that I had grown to believe it is a story of two young men, neither able to understand what war would put them through or how it would forever change their lives. It was during this discussion that the subject arose of atrocities German soldiers committed during the war. It was the only time during our meeting I saw Frank express strong emotion. His voice became intense and he said, "I did nothing wrong!" The anguish in his voice carried a mixture of pain and frustration.

Where does personal responsibility begin and end when others who represent you do wrong? What guilt do German soldiers bear for the Holocaust? Does every patriotic German who served in the war share the guilt of the evil regime directing Germany's armies? If every German from that time shares that guilt, were there acts committed by the Allied armies for which there is likewise shared responsibility? I do not believe the answers to such questions are simple. I can only say that in my heart I feel Russ carries no blemish for the deaths of civilians in the bombings of Dresden or Hiroshima, or for the destruction of Friesoythe by the Fourth Armoured Division as retribution against civilians.

These same questions can be asked about any time and place. Today it is easy to be a bystander when there is questionable conduct by people in organizations we belong to, in the places we work, and by governments that represent us. What responsibility does each of us bear to respond to questionable behaviour when we see it? Why do we choose silence rather than speaking out when something outrageous is said or done? Why do we choose not to step forward when action is perpetrated against a person unable to defend themselves? If we won't respond when it is easy to do so, what would we do if speaking out might carry a personal cost or endanger people and things we value more dearly?

———————•———————

I asked myself several questions at the outset of undertaking research for this book. Was I up to the challenge of living through the Great Depression? How would I have handled the physical and mental challenges and the dangers facing Canadian soldiers in World War II? And would I have been able to accept my enemy's friendship only hours after a battle? I am glad to say I have my answers to these questions, though they are not nearly as straightforward as I had originally thought they might be.

To gain a better understanding of those difficult times, I wanted a more personal sense of the smells, the sights, and the sounds of what men like Russ went through, to see how they fared in those events through their eyes. This has helped me better understand my father, myself, and our relationship. Perhaps it will also help me to speak out against injustice or unacceptable behaviour when circumstance puts me in the position to do so.

I was extremely lucky as I pieced together Russ's story. The greatest fortune was finding Frank, who shared with me his story of my father. That good fortune continues in the personal friendship I have with Frank, and his agreement to let me tell his story here. What follows is one more letter from Frank, addressed to me, but I think with lessons for most people, since who has not at some time in their life felt the need for redemption?

———————•———————

A Letter from Frank

July 4, 2009

Dear Steve,

The last time we talked to each other I had the impression it might be helpful to give you more details about the time following the end of the war.

The war was over and the Germans were defeated. Many of the German cities were destroyed. Thousands of German families, like mine, could not return to the places where their ancestors had lived for centuries. The

Germans became outcasts in Europe. Their neighbours refused to talk to them. They were isolated from other nations.

When German soldiers surrendered at the end of the war, they did not expect to be treated with benevolence.

To their surprise and amazement, the Canadian officer who accepted the surrender of my unit saluted them. At that time we did not realize the importance of such a gesture. It was only years later that it dawned on me: we were given a second chance. It might be the beginning of a turn to the better.

A second chance was given to the Germans of my generation by the people who were most badly persecuted by the Germans: the Poles and Jews.

When I was told that I was chosen to open the first Embassy of the Federal Republic of Germany in Warsaw, I was overjoyed. The East Germans were already present in Poland for many years. Now the Poles could choose between the two groups of Germans. But they despised both. It was left to me how to deal with this situation.

It happened that the Polish Foreign Minister was to go for the first time to Bonn. He was not at ease as I could notice at the airfield where I had gone to bid him farewell. When the German and the Polish flags were unfolded for the occasion and I looked at them, I was stunned with horror. The Poles had put up the flag of the East Germans.

I did not flinch. I dismissed the idea that the Poles deliberately wanted to insult us. The Polish Foreign Minister did not seem to have noticed the ridiculous situation. He instead worried about the absence of his undersecretary, Josef Czyrek. When Czyrek finally arrived, there was a sigh of relief which became audible when the Polish foreign minister embraced his undersecretary and said: "Yuzek, you cannot possibly want me to go there all by myself." In Polish, his words sounded even more anxious. It became clear this would be the beginning of our relationship. Later I met the Polish foreign minister several times. He had been told the story of the mixed-up flags and we laughed about it. He treated me later very friendly. It was a sign of the change in attitude that was slowly taking place.

When, in 1980, I was about to be sent to Israel, I refused to go. I said that I had never met an Israeli of my generation. I was fifty-six at that time, too old I felt to face this challenge, and I was quite unhappy about the decision. The deputy head of the Personnel Department at the German Ministry of Foreign Affairs had been my successor in Warsaw. She dismissed my arguments. She said she had seen the good job I had done in Poland and I could do the same in Israel. She did not share my misgivings and decided that I should go.

To my surprise, in Israel I never had to face a situation where I was asked how I could be a Deputy Ambassador for Germany and at the same time have belonged to the generation of Germans who were personally responsible for all that had happened to the Jews. When I left Israel in 1984, I received two letters of appreciation, which I still cherish today. They were addressed to me personally. One was from the Nahum Goldmann Museum of the Jewish Diaspora — Beth Hatefutsoth. The other was from Yad Vashem, the Jewish people's memorial to the Holocaust.

In 2009, Germany is important not only economically, but also as a member of the European and World communities. The Germans are accepted by all peoples, everywhere.

And for me, it all began with a salute by a Canadian officer, your father, to a group of German soldiers in May 1945.

Frank

NOTES

CHAPTER ONE

1. George Kitching, *Mud and Green Fields: The Memoirs of Major-General George Kitching* (Langley: Battleline Books, 1987).

CHAPTER TWO

1. Each ethnic group in Czechoslovakia often used a different name for the same towns. To the Germans the town was Freistadt, to the Czechs Fryštát, and to the Polish population Frysztat. As Frank's story is told from his perspective, I use German names for towns and cities where multiple names exist.

2. English systems of measurements are used in Canadian contexts to match the usage of the day.

3. After the war, historical documents revealed that much of the violence was organized by the Nazi leadership and largely conducted by their militia (the SA and SS) wearing civilian clothing.

4. *www.ushmm.org/wlc/en/article.php?ModuleId=10007506.*

CHAPTER THREE

1. Paul White, *Owen Sound: The Port City* (Toronto: Natural Heritage Books, 2000), 152.

2. Transcript of an address, "The Last Canadian Battle and the Surrender of the German Army," by Lieutenant-General Charles Foulkes to the Empire Club of Canada on October 4, 1945, Toronto. *speeches.empireclub. org/62271/data?n=2.*

3. J.K. Marteinson and Michael McNorgan, *The Royal Canadian Armoured Corps: An Illustrated History* (Kitchener: Robin Brass, 2000), 81.

4. C.P. Stacey, *Six Years of War: The Army in Canada, Britain, and the Pacific* (Ottawa: The Queens Printer, 1955), 16.

5. Ibid., 287-92.

6. C.P. Stacey and B.M. Wilson, *The Half Million: The Canadians in Britain, 1939–1946* (Toronto: University of Toronto Press, 1987), 32.

7. T.J. Rutherford (editor), *An Unofficial History of the Grey and Simcoe Foresters Regiment 1866 to 1973* (Owen Sound, Ontario: Published by The Regiment, 1975), vi.

8. *The Canadian Forces Manual of Drill and Ceremonial* (National Defence Canada, 2001). A-PD-201-000/PT-000. Viewed at *www.army.forces. gc.ca/lf/Downloads/cfp201.pdf* on November 8, 2010.

9. Jack MacLeod, personal communication.

10. Rutherford, 27–28.

11. *Owen Sound Sun Times*, August 2, 1940.

12. Marge Johnson, personal communication.

13. Jaffray Rutherford, personal communication.

CHAPTER FOUR

1. Sebastian Haffner, *Germany: Jekyll and Hyde: A Contemporary Account of Nazi Germany* (London: Abacus Books, 2008), 62–63.

    Germany: Jekyll and Hyde was written during self-imposed exile and published in 1940 in Great Britain under the pseudonym Sebastian Haffner, a name assumed to protect members of the author's family who had remained in Germany. Churchill reportedly ordered every member of his war cabinet to read Haffner's book.

2. After the war, testimony was given at the Nuremburg Trials that the attacks purported to be by Poland were staged by German troops wearing Polish uniforms to justify the attacks. *en.wikipedia.org/wiki/Gleiwitz_incident*.

3. Edited from a translation from the original newspaper *Rheinische Landeszeitung*, Düsseldorf, viewed at *www.bills-bunker.de/69553.html* on April 20, 2009.

CHAPTER FIVE

1. Rutherford, 32–33.

2. Marteinson and McNorgan, 80–86.

3. Stacey, *Six Years of War*, 292.

4. Less than a year after this convoy reached England, both the *Orcades* and another troop ship in the convoy, the *Duchess of Atholl*, were torpedoed and sunk. For a description of the sinking of the *Orcades* see *www.uboat.net/allies/merchants/ships/2258.html*; information on the sinking of the Duchess of Atholl is available at *www.uboat.net/allies/merchants/ship/2257.html*.

5. By war's end, only one convoy would surpass the 14,023 troops carried in the eight troop ships in convoy T.C.15 (Stacey, *Six Years of War*, 93).

6. John Honsberger, personal communication.

7. Stacey and Wilson, 58.

8. Roy Thomas, "A Forgotten Armoured Arsenal: The Montreal Locomotive Works (*Vanguard Magazine*, May/June 2008). *www.vanguardcanada.com/ForgottenArmouredArsenalThomas*.

9. See, for instance, *www.culture24.org.uk/places+to+go/south+east/brighton+%26+hove/art29725* and *www.mybrightonandhove.org.uk/page_id__6963_path__0p116p182p446p.aspx*.

10. Described at *gordiebannerman.com*. See also *www.veterans.gc.ca/remembers/sub.cfm?source=collections/hrp/alpha_results&people_id=466*.

11. Portrayed at the time as a success, in the raid by 5,000 Canadian and 1,000 British soldiers, about 900 Canadians were killed and almost 2,500 wounded or captured. From Winnipeg's Queen's Own Cameron Highlanders, fewer than 100 of the 565 who had embarked returned to England uninjured and more than 80 percent were killed, wounded, or taken prisoner.

CHAPTER SIX

1. *www.oai.dtic.mil/oai/oai?verb=getRecord&metadataPrefix=html&identifier=ADA322750*.

2. A good account in English of the activities of the German Army in this theatre is by E.F. Zeimke, *The German Northern Theater of Operations 1940-1945*, U.S. Department of the Army Pamphlet 20-271 *(www.ibiblio.org/hyperwar/USA/DAP-Northern/index.html)*. See also B. Mueiler-Hillebrand, H. Reinhardt, and others, *Small Unit Actions During the German Campaign in Russia*, U.S. Department of the Army, Pamphlet no. 20-269, "Small Unit Actions during the German Campaign in Russia" (Washington, D.C.: U.S.

Government Printing Office, July 1953), Chapter 4. *(www.allworldwars. com/Small-Unit-Actions-During-German-Campaign-in-Russia.html.)*

3. J.F. Gebhardt, *The Petsamo-Kirkenese Operation: Soviet Breakthrough and Pursuit in the Arctic, October 1944* (Fort Leavenworth, KS: Combat Studies Institute, U.S Army Command and General Staff College, 1989), Leavenworth Papers No. 17. ISSN 0195 3451.

CHAPTER SEVEN

1. Most likely this is decorated and highly respected Australian war correspondent Alan Moorehead.

2. G.L. Cassidy, *Warpath: The Story of the Algonquin Regiment, 1939–1945* (Cobalt: Highway Book Shop 1990), 50.

3. *www.oldgaffer.com/ww2/blitz.*

4. Cassidy, 68.

5. Matthew Halton, CBC Television Archive, Original broadcast date September 2, 1956. *archives.cbc.ca/war_conflict/second_world_war/ topics/636.*

6. Cassidy, 70.

7. *The Globe and Mail*, December 22, 1945, page 1.

8. *www.rots.fr/news/index.php?val2=90_10.*

9. Stacey and Wilson, *The Half Million*, 36.

10. Based on the recollections of Major General R. P. Rothschild, Major General C. Bethel Ware, and Brigadier-General D. Whitaker from *everitas.rmcclub. ca/?p=11535*, http://everitas.rmcclub.ca/?p=11184, and *everitas.rmcclub. ca/?p=6732*, originally published with permission of J.L. Granatstein in *eVeritas*, the newsletter of the RMC Club of Canada.

11. J.L. Granatstein, *The Generals: The Canadian Army's Senior Commanders in the Second World War* (Calgary: University of Calgary Press, 2005), 162.

12. "... Although the Boche is a very good soldier he is no match for the Canadian soldier. Our troops have been brought up with a different mentality, are individualists and imaginative." From address by Lieutenant-General G. Simonds to officers of the 3rd Canadian Infantry Division and 2nd Canadian Armoured Brigade on July 16, 1944. In: *General Simonds Speaks: Canadian Battle Doctrine in Normandy. Canadian*

Military History, Volume 8, Number 2, Spring 1999, p. 69–80. Viewed online at *www.wlu.ca/lcmsds/cmh/back%20issues/v8n2contents.html*.

13. Based on the recollections of Major General Norman Elliot Rodger from *everitas.rmcclub.ca/?p=7276*, originally published with permission of J.L. Granatstein in *eVeritas*, the newsletter of the RMC Club of Canada.

14. B. McAndrew, D.E. Graves, and M. Whitby, *Normandy 1944: The Canadian Summer* (Montreal: Editions Art Global Inc. Publisher, 1994), 134.

15. Dominick Graham, *The Price of Command: A Biography of General Guy Simonds* (Toronto: Stoddart Publishing, 1994), 151.

16. D.R. O'Keefe, "Double-edged Sword Part I: Ultra and Totalize Normandy, August 8, 1944," (*Canadian Army Journal*, 2010), 12(3): 85–93.

17. Transcription of an interview of Kurt Meyer, part of the Bruce J. S. Macdonald Fonds in the Municipal Archives, Windsor Public Library.

18. Kitching.

19. Graham, 153–154.

20. Kitching, *Mud and Green Fields*.

21. Marteinson and McNorgan, 282.

22. A photograph of General Harry Foster is available at *www.lextec.com/Major%20General%20Harry%20Wickwire%20Foster.html*.

23. H.C. Chadderton, *D-DAY: The Story of the Canadian Assault Troops*, *www.waramps.ca//uploadedFiles/English_Site/Military_Heritage/Media/PDF/dday.pdf* viewed September 27, 2010.

CHAPTER EIGHT

1. Rank equivalent to sergeant.

CHAPTER NINE

1. Cassidy, 130.

2. Mark Zuehlke, *Terrible Victory: First Canadian Army and the Scheldt Estuary Campaign: September 13–November 6, 1944* (Vancouver: Douglas & McIntyre, 2007), 266.

3. Zuehlke, 269.

4. Headquarters Squadron war diary. The actions of Headquarters Squadron tanks in the action to cross the Leopold Canada are inferred. We know from the war diary that the tanks took part in the battle. Unfortunately, in this case and in others, the war diary for the Headquarters Squadron documents only the most general combat details, where they are mentioned at all.

5. John M. Carter. D46319. Died October 25, 1944. Trooper, Royal Canadian Armoured Corps, attached to Headquarters, Fourth Canadian Armoured Division. Son of Alexina Carter Walsh of Point St. Charles, Quebec. Buried Bergen-Op-Zoom Canadian War Cemetery, 8.C.10. From Commonwealth War Graves Commission, *www.cwgc.org/default.asp*.

6. The Headquarters Squadron war diary for October 27, 1944, states "At 1100 hrs one trp of tnks with Lt DR Colombo in charge was despatched in support of two companies of the Lincoln & Welland Regt at Wowsche Plantage (MR 6725). At 1600 hrs the remainder of the tank troop with Lt J Derij in charge joined and the two companies of the Lincoln and Welland went on ahead."

7. In Quebec, opposition to the Canadian Armed Forces goes back to at least World War I. Then, part of the reason for Quebeckers choosing not to volunteer can be attributed to the lack of sufficient French-speaking regiments in the Canadian Army, the reported poor treatment of Quebeckers in English-speaking units, and the use of English as the command language in French-speaking units from Quebec. Against this background, during World War II, it might not be surprising to find many French Canadians viewing "Zombies" as patriotic.

8. Farley Mowat, *My Father's Son* (Toronto: Key Porter, 1992), 88.

9. *The Globe and Mail*, July 20, 1944.

10. Based on the recollections of Major General James Desmond Blaise Smith from *everitas.rmcclub.ca/?p=13149*, originally published with permission of J.L. Granatstein in *eVeritas*, the newsletter of the RMC Club of Canada.

11. United States Memorial Holocaust Museum, *www.ushmm.org/research/library/faq/details.php?lang=en&topic=02#01*.

12. *www.nmkampvught.nl/index.php?id=219*.

13. *www.jewishgen.org/ForgottenCamps/Camps/VughtEngl.html*.

14. *www.shoaheducation.com/camps/vught.html.*

15. *www.jewishgen.org/ForgottenCamps/Camps/VughtEngl.html.*

16. Stacey and Wilson, 48–49.

17. Lance Goddard, *Canada and the Liberation of the Netherlands, May 1945* (Toronto: Dundurn Press, 2005), 146.

18. Kristen Den Hartog and Tracy Kasaboski, *The Occupied Garden: A Family Memoir of War-Torn Holland* (Toronto: McClelland and Stewart 2008), 201.

19. M.O. Rollefson (editor), *Green Route Up: 4 Canadian Armoured Division* (The Hague: Mouton, 1945), 62.

Green Route Up was written by the engineers serving in Fourth Canadian Armoured Division during the campaign in northwest Europe. In its own words:

> Green Route Up was the name of the main axis of advance of the 4th Canadian Armoured Division (4 Cdn Armd Div or 4 Div). It stretches from Caen in Normandy to Wilhelmshaven in Germany. Practically every inch was wrestled from the fanatical enemy by our gallant comrades of the Infantry and Armoured Corps, with the direct support of the Artillery, and all made the greatest sacrifices and paid a heavy toll. The road was littered with the mangled bodies of men and animals, often in a state of advanced putrefaction, and smashed and burnt out vehicles of every description. Thousands of mines were concealed in its surface as well as the enemy's most ingenious death traps. It crossed the greatest water obstacles in EUROPE over which all bridges had been destroyed. Hundreds of huge craters dotted its winding course. But that is not all. The enemy almost invariably stayed and defended these obstacles to the last, showering the sappers with bombs, shells, rockets, mortars and machine gun bullets.

Green Route Up was republished in 2006 and is available online at www.army.forces.gc.ca/41CER/docs/green_route_up.pdf.

20. Better known today as the Battle of the Bulge.

21. Headquarters Squadron war diary.

22. Headquarters Squadron war diary.

23. Headquarters Squadron war diary

24. Medical report in personnel file.

25. Headquarters Squadron war diary for March 6, 1945, "A very unfortunate accident occurred at rear div at approx. 1800 hrs today when S/Sjt WA Shore, ARCO staff stepped on an enemy shoe mine and lost his left foot. A few minutes later another rank from rear div signals corp stepped on another and he too lost a foot. Upon placing the signals other rank on a stretcher Trooper Hancock of ARCO staff stepped on another, blasting his complete right leg off and fracturing the other leg of the signals OR. From this blast Pte Litchfield of ADMS staff was slightly injured as was Fus Cleveland ADJA staff. All were evacuated to medical installations."

26. Russ described carrying three men to safety from a minefield. This Headquarters Squadron war diary entry of three men injured in a minefield in Germany matches details he gave.

27. Headquarters Squadron war diary.

28. Rollefson, 73.

29. Cassidy, 275.

30. Headquarters Squadron war diary.

31. *www.en.wikipedia.org/wiki/Operation_Plunder.*

32. John Raycroft, *A Signal War: A Canadian Soldier's Memoir of the Liberation of the Netherlands* (Prescott, Ontario: Babblefish, 2002).

33, 34. *www.gutenberg-e.org/pfau/chapter3.html.* Citing source document "Policy on Relations between Allied Occupying Forces and Inhabitants of Germany" (September 12, 1944), enclosure in J. L. Tarr to Commanding Generals Re: Policy on Relations between Allied Occupying Forces and Inhabitants of Germany (September 27, 1944), File: 250.1–2, Box 12, G1 Decimal File 1944–1945, Allied Operational and Occupation Headquarters, RG 331 (SHAEF), NACP.

35, 36. Headquarters Squadron war diary.

37. *www.en.wikipedia.org/wiki/12_(Vancouver)_Field_Ambulance.*

38. C. Vokes, J.P. Maclean, *My Story* (Stittsville, Ontario: Gallery Publishing, 1985), 195.

39. Lieutenant Colonel Frederick Ernest Wigle. DSO. Age 31. Argyll And Sutherland Highlanders of Canada (Princess Louise's), RCIC. Grave/ Memorial Reference: IX.A.B. Holten Canadian War Cemetery, The Netherlands. Son of Gerald William and Mary Olga Wigle, husband of Margarei Wilmot Wigle of Waterdown, Ontario. From Commonwealth War Graves Commission, *www.cwgc.org/default.asp.*

40. J.L. Granatstein, "The End of Darkness," *Legion Magazine.* May 1, 2005, at *www.legionmagazine.com/en/index.php/2005/05/the-end-of-darkness.*

41. C. Vokes, J.P. Maclean, 195.

42. *www.en.wikipedia.org/wiki/Friesoythe.*

43. C.P. Stacey, *A Date With History; Memoirs of a Canadian Historian* (Ottawa: Deneau Publishers, 1983) 163–64. Cited in *en.wikipedia.org/ wiki/Argyll_and_Sutherland_Highlanders_of_Canada* (original not seen).

44. Headquarters Squadron war diary.

45. Rollefson, 95.

46. Headquarters Squadron war diary.

47. General Staff war diary, Headquarters Fourth Canadian Armoured Division.

48. Earle Gordon Phillips. Age 26. Died on April 29, 1945. He was the son of Everett Oliver Phillips and Alma Bessie Phillips of Oshawa, Ontario. From Commonwealth War Graves Commission, *www.cwgc.org/default.asp.*

   He was reburied after the war at the Holten Canadian War Cemetery in the Netherlands. Canadian General Harry Crerar ordered all Canadian soldiers buried in Germany, close to 1,500 in total, be brought to the Netherlands for permanent internment at war cemeteries in either Groesbeek or Holten. (*www.legionmagazine.com/en/index.php/2010/05/ the-roads-to-victory*).

49. General Staff war diary, Headquarters Fourth Canadian Armoured Division.

50. "In the West, the Argylls were Busy Seizing the Airfield," F.G. Stanley, *In the Face of Danger* (Thunder Bay, Ontario: Lake Superior Scottish Regiment, 2006), 299.

CHAPTER TEN

1. *www.en.wikipedia.org/wiki/Operation_Market_Garden.*

2. Where and to which unit he joined Frank is no longer certain, so I present the major events involving the First Fallschirmjäger Army in the Netherlands from September to December, 1944, while Frank was posted there, based mainly on A. Korthals Altes and N.K.C.A In't Veld, *The Forgotten Battle: Overloon and the Maas Salient, 1944–1945* (Edison, NJ: Castle Books, 2001).

3. Altes and In't Veld, 18–19.

4. *Ibid.,* 77

5. Rank roughly equivalent to corporal.

6. Theresienstadt became infamous as a show camp for the international community. Nazi propaganda described it as a place for elderly Jews to "retire." The camp was an overcrowded ghetto with internal Jewish administration. In June 1944, it was the site of an elaborate hoax designed to fool the International Red Cross into believing Jewish "residents" were well looked after (*www.ushmm.org/wlc/en/article.php?ModuleId=10007463*). In truth, the camp served as a transit camp for Jews to be moved on to Auschwitz-Birkenau and other camps, where they were murdered. Overcrowded conditions, lack of food and medical supplies, and exhaustion from forced labour caused the deaths of more than 33,000. Of the more than 88,000 who passed through Theresientstadt before being transferred to other camps, it is estimated only 3,500 survived (*www. ushmm.org/wlc/en/article.php?ModuleId=10007507*).

7. *www.en.wikipedia.org/wiki/Operation_Plunder.*

CHAPTER TWELVE

1. Stanley, 304.

2. Cassidy, 328.

3. Sean Longden, *To the Victor the Spoils* (Gloucester: Arris Books, 2004), 333.

4. Headquarters Squadron war diary.

5. Headquarters Squadron war diary.

6. Headquarters Squadron war diary.

7. *www.12rbc.ca/PDF/Anglais.pdf.*

8. *www.paperspast.natlib.govt.nz/cgi-bin/paperspast?a=d&d=EP19450522.2.65.*

9. C.P. Stacey, *Official History of the Canadian Army in the Second World War, Volume III, The Victory Campaign: The Operations in North-West Europe 1944–1945* (Ottawa: Queen's Printer, 1960), 615. Available online at *www.cmp-cpm.forces.gc.ca/dhh-dhp/his/docs/Victory_e.pdf.*

10. Headquarters Squadron war diary.

11. Headquarters Squadron war diary.

12. *Globe and Mail*, May 30, 1945.

13. Stacey, *Six Years of War*, 517.

14. Marge Johnson, personal communication.

15. "The Last Canadian Battle and the Surrender of the German Army." Transcript of an address by Lieutenant-General Charles Foulkes to the Empire Club on October 4, 1945, *www.empireclubfoundation.com/ details.asp?SpeechID=2466&FT=yes.*

16. As a private and trooper, in every month of army service, Russ sent $20 of his pay home, which increased to $25 after receiving his lieutenant's commission.

17. *www.cmp-cpm.forces.gc.ca/dhr-ddhr/chc-tdh/chart-tableau-eng. asp?ref=MiD.*

CHAPTER THIRTEEN

1. C. Madsen, "Victims of Circumstance: The Execution of German Deserters by Surrendered German Troops Under Canadian Control in Amsterdam, May 1945," *Canadian Military History*, 2 (1): 93-113, 1993.

CHAPTER FOURTEEN

1. This is the first letter from Frank to Russ, though it was the second rediscovered. This one was found in 2010 by one of the author's sisters.

2. None of the letters sent by Russ to Frank have been found, while only these two of Frank's were discovered.

3. Most likely Betty was taken to the Victor Home for Girls, which exists today in its original location as the Massey Centre on Broadview Avenue in Toronto.

4. There are many heartbreaking stories of women who endured what was too often the trauma of homes for unwed mothers. A good starting place for those interested in learning more is Origins Canada (*www. originscanada.org*).

5. Personal communication, Ron Olmsted.

6. Personal communication, Marge Johnson.

7. *Ibid.*

CHAPTER FIFTEEN

1. Relatively unknown outside Germany, the White Rose (*die Weisse Rose* in German) was an important anti-Nazi movement within Germany during the war that is well worth studying. The text in English of the six leaflets distributed by the White Rose group is available at *www.whiterosesociety. org/WRS_pamphlets_home.html* or *www.holocaustresearchproject.org/ revolt/wrleaflets.html*. In the White Rose group's third leaflet, published in 1943, passive resistance was seen as the only effective strategy against the Nazis:

> Many, perhaps most, of the readers of these leaflets do not see clearly how they can practice an effective opposition. They do not see any avenues open to them. We want to try to show them that everyone is in a position to contribute to the overthrow of this system. It is not possible through solitary withdrawal, in the manner of embittered hermits, to prepare the ground for the overturn of this "government" or bring about the revolution at the earliest possible moment. No, it can be done only by the cooperation of many convinced, energetic people — people who are agreed as to the means they must use to attain their goal. We have no great number of choices as to these means. The only one available is passive resistance.

The fourth leaflet addresses the matter of German guilt for crimes committed under the Nazis:

> Though we know that National Socialist power must be broken by military means, we are trying to achieve a renewal from within of the severely wounded German spirit. This rebirth must be preceded, however, by the clear recognition of all the guilt with which the German people

have burdened themselves, and by an uncompromising battle against Hitler and his all too many minions, party members, Quislings, and the like. With total brutality the chasm that separates the better portion of the nation from everything that is opened wide. For Hitler and his followers there is no punishment on this Earth commensurate with their crimes.

Sophie Scholl and her brother Hans Scholl, members of the White Rose, as well as Alexander Schmorell, Willi Graf, Christoph Probst, all students at the Ludwig-Maximilians-University in Munich, Hans Leipelt a student at the University of Hamburg, and Kurt Huber, a professor at the Ludwig-Maximilians-University, were executed by guillotine for their involvement in the movement.

2. It would not be until 1990 that Germany officially accepted the loss of 20 percent of its territory to Poland, as Frank had foreseen in the 1950s. Millions of German civilians expelled from former parts of Germany left their homes for East or West Germany. *en.wikipedia.org/wiki/Flight_and_expulsion_of_Germans_(1944%E2%80%931950).*

3. *www.de.wikipedia.org/wiki/Leitmeritz.*

CHAPTER SIXTEEN

1. Franz Sikora, *Sozialistische Solidarität und nationale Interessen: Polen, Tschechoslowakei, DDR* (Köln: Verlag Wissenschaft und Politik, 1977).

AFTERWORD AND ACKNOWLEDGEMENTS

Confessiones Auctoris

I had no idea I would ever write this book. How could I have known? At the heart of this story is a mystery involving my father which I had no idea existed.

Since 2005 I had been researching the period in my father's life when he was a member of the Canadian army. I had obtained his army personnel file and was melding its sterile story with those he had told us decades earlier. I thought I should document his experiences so that his grandchildren could learn about him. But I never imagined this becoming a book for others to read. It would certainly never have happened without Frank's letter to my father.

That letter led to the remarkable discovery of Frank himself in 2008. I realized soon after speaking with him and reading his autobiography, in which my father plays an important part, that there were two stories to tell. One Canadian. One German. As I learned, in some ways they are the same story, two sides of a single coin. It was a story I felt I should share with a larger audience.

Accurately representing events I had no part in, sixty or more years later, was a major challenge in writing these biographies. Ironically, it proved easier writing Frank's story, despite the fact that my father is the other subject of the other story. Frank's autobiography helped immensely. Although I had the challenge of translating Frank's book into English, I also had the luxury of having Frank to check its correctness and his willingness to discuss his life. Russ left no autobiography, nor could I interview him, as he passed away in 1986 when I was thirty-one. His story had to be pieced together from scraps of oral history he shared during his lifetime, interviews with his few remaining contemporaries, and from research of historical documents. While telling Frank's story required hard work, telling Russ's required in some cases exceptional luck.

Almost all events involving Russ and Frank in this book are as told to me or as gleaned from historical documents. In a few exceptions to advance the story I have introduced minor fictional elements into what are otherwise historical memoirs. For those preferring to stick to the facts as they are known, I believe the careful reader can identify these additions. I will describe what I consider the most important here to avoid confusion.

One is the description of Russ searching for two missing tanks from his unit. Historically, two Headquarters Squadron tanks went missing in Normandy, around the time of the battle known famously as the Falaise Gap, described in the autobiography of General George Kitching. Though the nature of their disappearance and the eventual outcome are historically accurate, there is no historical record of Russ searching for the missing tanks. I use the story of the missing tanks to introduce the reader to Russ and two authentic people who figure in this book, Lieutenant Jim Derij and Major Clarence Campbell.

Jim Derij and Russ Colombo had a string of surprising confluences, from Camp Borden, to the Third Canadian Armoured Corps Reinforcement Unit, and then to the Headquarters Squadron. Without certain knowledge, I cast Jim and Russ not just as comrades in arms but as friends. In a few instances I speculate how they might have reacted in certain situations, such as on entering battle in Canada's Operation Totalize in Normandy. Jim, like Russ, received the distinction of being Mentioned in Despatches.

Jim's postwar experiences were tragic. Shortly after leaving the Headquarters Squadron to become Camp Commandant of 3 Canadian Division, Canadian Occupation Force, he was hospitalized with a back injury. For months he was in and out of hospital and never recovered sufficiently to return to active service. The army returned him to Canada and mustered him out. For years afterwards Jim tried to prove his back had been injured while serving in the army. His injury originated when he was thrown from his army horse, Margorie, in the 1930s, and likely was weakened by the years he was thrown about in the turrets of tanks and by the rigors of war. Proving the cause was of course near impossible, and the bureaucrats who opposed him had nothing but time and well-paid positions from which to deny him a full disability pension. Jim had made the army his life, and his back injury disabled him so badly he had difficulty working after leaving the army. Jim died in 1951 of a heart attack. He was only thirty-seven years old.

The Clarence Campbell who appears in this book is the same person who later gained fame as president of the National Hockey League. Before becoming the person we know from hockey, Clarence Campbell commanded the approximately two hundred troopers of the Headquarters Squadron of the Fourth Canadian Armoured Division. There is sufficient historical evidence to conclude Clarence Campbell was held in high regard by many of the people who knew him as an officer in the Canadian army. Lieutenant Colonel Harry Quarton (ret.), in 1944 a lieutenant in the Fourth's Headquarters Squadron, told me Clarence Campbell was one of the finest officers he ever served with, someone who would "support you to the hilt if you did your job." Russ in contrast had an intense dislike of him that lasted the rest of his life.

In the first chapter of Frank's story, I paint a picture of how his father might have celebrated Frank's birth. The gist of the story is true — Frank's father, a wounded veteran of the First World War, named his son in the Austro-Hungarian tradition years after the last emperor's abdication, and worked in the court office of the town of Freistadt in what was then Czechoslovakia, where his son's birth most likely was registered. The description of how Frank's father felt when naming his son Franz, years after Austria-Hungary and the monarchy ceased to exist, is I believe close to the way it must have been. It was a useful way to explain the way Germans in general and Frank's parents in particular felt in the newly formulated country of Czechoslovakia after World War I.

In presenting this story I am indebted to the unnamed authors of Canadian War Diaries. For anyone interested in hearing the authentic voices of Canadian soldiers from World War II, there is nothing quite like these first-hand accounts. Diana Gibson of Library and Archives Canada helped me navigate through the records held by that fabulous institution. Similarly helpful people from the Owen Sound Marine & Rail Museum and the Grey Roots Museum in Owen Sound provided valuable assistance. Professor Mark Kuehlberg of Laurentian University gave direction to sources of infor-mation on logging operations in Blind River in the 1930s. Dr. Jeff Noakes, Second World War Historian at the Canadian War Museum, on several occa-sions pointed me to important sources of information. Michael Benjamin De Groot of Stanford University's Spatial History Project on "Building the New Order: 1938–1945" (*www.stanford.edu/group/spatialhistory/cgi-bin/site/pub. php?id=51&project_id=*), assisted me in obtaining shape files and permission to reproduce maps of 1940s-era Europe used in this book. Professor Veronika Ambros, Department of Slavic Languages and Literatures at the University of Toronto, very generously responded to the queries of a stranger, explaining that Frank and Franz were interchangeable names and agreed that Frank's dissertation title was the only one from a long list that looked like a study in Slavic languages.

I was extremely fortunate to speak with two of Russ's contemporaries. Jack MacLeod, who passed away in 2011 in his nineties in Owen Sound, after seventy years, still recounted events as though they had just occurred. Jack's stories included the first part of the story of the lacrosse sweater and another of the time he was present on the porch of the Colombo house when Blanche called Russ by the nickname she called him, Sweet. My thanks are extended to Jack's son, Bob MacLeod, who obtained a copy of the 1940 Owen Sound Georgians' team championship photograph that appears in this book. Another first-hand source was Marge Johnson, a close family friend, who provided numerous insights about Russ and told me the ending to the story of Jack MacLeod's lacrosse sweater.

I benefited from the generosity of several World War II veterans. One is the aforementioned Lieutenant Colonel Harry Quarton (ret.), a lieutenant with the Headquarters Squadron during the war. While Lieutenant-Colonel Quarton had only a vague remembrance of Russ, his descriptions of the Headquarters Squadron and Clarence Campbell were helpful. Colonel Danny MacLeod (ret.) described for me what it was like to be a Canadian attending Sandhurst Military Academy, where he won coveted prizes sought by envious officer candidates from the British army. Mr. Paul Paolini, who enlisted with the Foresters in Sault Ste. Marie in 1940, generously spoke with me about training at Camp Borden. Mr. Gordon Bannerman, a veteran of the Canadian artillery in Italy and Northwest Europe in World War II, deciphered military photographs and provided helpful comments on the manuscript. Mr. Bannerman read an earlier version of this book. When asked if it captured an authentic feeling of what those times were like he made my day by saying, "It was as if you were there."

I was fortunate to contact James Derry, a nephew of Jim Derij. James generously shared pictures of his Uncle Jim and talked about the three Derij brothers who all were active service volunteers in World War II. James founded the Dominion History Project, a program in Courtenay, B.C., to honour Canadian veterans.

Photographer Professor Werner Kunz (*world.werner-kunz.com*) generously travelled to the Ludwig-Maximilians-University Munich expressly to obtain a modern photograph of the Lichthof.

I also owe my appreciation to a number of friends and family members who read parts of this book at various stages of its preparation. Michael Ter-Mikaelian, my cousin Paul Colombo and his wife Mary, Abby Obenchain, and Steve Grossnickle commented on various parts of the book.

John Robert Colombo, cousin and author known as "Canada's Master Gatherer," brought this book to the attention of Beth Bruder of Dundurn Press. John, a second cousin to Russ, edited the book for style. His belief that this was a story worth publishing was instrumental in making that a reality. Beth Bruder was a champion for this book within Dundurn, and her calm support and encouragement is greatly appreciated. Dundurn Press is a fantastic team to work with. I thank Jesse Hooper for his inspired cover design, Sheila Douglas for patiently waiting for the resolution of contract details in Germany, and Allister Thompson for a wonderful job of copy-editing. I am grateful to Dundurn President Kirk Howard for including this title among the many fine works on Canadian history Dundurn has published.

My sister Cathy and brother Gerry helped unravel our father's story. Nancy, the baby Betty was forced to give up for adoption in 1949, was reunited with us in 1986, though sadly this was five years after Betty passed away. My wish is that Russ and Betty's grandchildren will understand themselves better by learning about their grandparents.

It was an unexpected joy to meet Frank and Gisela. Their generosity in welcoming a stranger to their home and willingness to answer numerous questions and provide whatever assistance I required is deeply appreciated. My hope is that Frank will enjoy reading this book as much as I enjoyed working with him to help create it.

Sonia, my wife and friend, showed great patience with the time I put into researching and writing. Her encouragement and comments through multiple versions of the manuscript helped hone the final product. A devoted and compassionate partner, she understood my need to complete this story.